INSTITUTE OF PACIFIC RELATIONS
INQUIRY SERIES

BRITISH RELATIONS WITH CHINA:
1931-1939

BRITISH RELATIONS WITH CHINA:
1931-1939

By
IRVING S. FRIEDMAN

OCTAGON BOOKS

A DIVISION OF FARRAR, STRAUS AND GIROUX

New York   1974

Copyright 1940 by The Secretariat, Institute of Pacific Relations

Reprinted 1974
by special arrangement with The Publications Center,
The University of British Columbia

OCTAGON BOOKS
A DIVISION OF FARRAR, STRAUS & GIROUX, INC.
19 Union Square West
New York, N. Y. 10003

Library of Congress Cataloging in Publication Data

Friedman, Irving Sigmund, 1915-
   British relations with China: 1931-1939.

   Reprint of the ed. published by International Secretariat, Institute of Pacific Relations, in series: I. P. R. inquiry series.
   Originally presented as the author's thesis, Columbia University.

   Bibliography: p.
   1. Great Britain—Foreign relations—China. 2. China—Foreign relations—Great Britain. I. Title. II. Series: Institute of Pacific Relations. I. P. R. inquiry series.

DS740.5.G5F7   1974   327.42'051   74-6337
ISBN 0-374-92931-9

Printed in USA by
Thomson-Shore, Inc.
Dexter, Michigan

TO MY WIFE

FOREWORD

This study forms part of the documentation of an Inquiry organized by the Institute of Pacific Relations into the problems arising from the conflict in the Far East.

It has been prepared by Dr. Irving S. Friedman, research associate of the International Secretariat, Institute of Pacific Relations.

The Study has been submitted in draft to a number of authorities including the following, many of whom made suggestions and criticisms which were of great value in the process of revision: Professor J. Bartlett Brebner, Mr. G. E. Hubbard, Professor Nathaniel Peffer and Professor Philip C. Jessup.

Though many of the comments received have been incorporated in the final text, the above authorities do not of course accept responsibility for the study. The statements of fact or of opinion appearing herein do not represent the views of the Institute of Pacific Relations or of the Pacific Council or of any of the National Councils. Such statements are made on the sole responsibility of the author. The Japanese Council has not found it possible to participate in the Inquiry, and assumes, therefore, no responsibility either for its results or for its organization.

During 1938 the Inquiry was carried on under the general direction of Dr. J. W. Dafoe as Chairman of the Pacific Council and in 1939 under his successor, Dr. Philip C. Jessup. Every member of the International Secretariat has contributed to the research and editorial work in connection with the Inquiry, but special mention should be made of Mr. W. L. Holland, Miss Kate Mitchell and Miss Hilda Austern, who have carried the major share of this responsibility.

In the general conduct of this Inquiry into the problems arising from the conflict in the Far East the Institute has benefited by the Counsel of the following Advisers:

Professor H. F. Angus of the University of British Columbia
Dr. J. B. Condliffe of the University of California
M. Etienne Dennery of the Ecole des Sciences Politiques.

These Advisers have co-operated with the Chairman and the Secretary-General in an effort to insure that the publications issued in connection with the Inquiry conform to a proper standard of sound and impartial scholarship. Each manuscript has been submitted to at least two of the Advisers and although they do not necessarily subscribe to the statements or views in this or any of the studies, they consider this study to be a useful contribution to the subject of the Inquiry.

The purpose of this Inquiry is to relate unofficial scholarship to the problems arising from the present situation in the Far East. Its purpose is to provide members of the Institute in all countries and the members of I.P.R. Conferences with an impartial and constructive analysis of the situation in the Far East with a view to indicating the major issues which must be considered in any future adjustment of international relations in that area. To this end, the analysis will include an account of the economic and political conditions which produced the situation existing in July 1937, with respect to China, to Japan and to the other foreign Powers concerned; an evaluation of developments during the war period which appear to indicate important trends in the policies and programs of all the Powers in relation to the Far Eastern situation; and finally, an estimate of the principal political, economic and social conditions which may be expected in a post-war period, the possible forms of adjustment which might be applied under these conditions, and the effects of such adjustments upon the countries concerned.

The Inquiry does not propose to "document" a specific plan for dealing with the Far Eastern situation. Its aim is to focus available information on the present crisis in forms which will be useful to those who lack either the time or the expert knowledge to study the vast amount of material now appearing or already published in a number of languages. Attention may also be drawn to a series of studies on topics bearing on the Far Eastern situation which is being prepared by the Japanese Council. That series is being undertaken entirely independently of this Inquiry, and for its organization and publication the Japanese Council alone is responsible.

The present study, "British Relations With China: 1931-1939," falls within the framework of the first of the four general groups of studies which it is proposed to make as follows:

I. The political and economic conditions which have contributed to the present course of the policies of Western Powers in the Far East; their territorial and economic interests; the effects on their Far Eastern policies of internal economic and political development and of developments in their foreign policies vis-à-vis other parts of the world; the probable effects of the present conflict on their positions in the Far East; their changing attitudes and policies with respect to their future relations in that area.

II. The political and economic conditions which have contributed to the present course of Japanese foreign policy and possible important future developments; the extent to which Japan's policy toward China has been influenced by Japan's geographic conditions and material resources, by special features in the political and economic organization of Japan which directly or indirectly affect the formulation of her present foreign policy, by economic and political developments in China, by the external policies of other Powers affecting Japan; the principal political, economic and social factors which may be expected in a post-war Japan; possible and probable adjustments on the part of other nations which could aid in the solution of Japan's fundamental problems.

III. The political and economic conditions which have contributed to the present course of Chinese foreign policy and possible important future developments; Chinese unification and reconstruction, 1931-37, and steps leading toward the policy of united national resistance to Japan; the present degree of political cohesion and economic strength; effects of resistance and current developments on the position of foreign interests in China and changes in China's relations with foreign Powers; the principal political, economic and social factors which may be expected in a post-war China; possible and probable adjustments on the part of other nations which could aid in the solution of China's fundamental problems.

IV. Possible methods for the adjustment of specific problems, in the light of information and suggestions presented in the three studies outlined above; analysis of previous attempts at bilateral or multilateral adjustments of political and economic relations in the Pacific and causes of their success or failure; types of administrative procedures and controls already tried out and their relative effectiveness; the major issues likely to require international adjustment in a post-war period and the most hopeful methods which might be devised to meet them; necessary adjustments by the Powers concerned; the basic requirements of a practical system of international organization which could promote the security and peaceful development of the countries of the Pacific area.

EDWARD C. CARTER
Secretary-General

New York,
April 15, 1940

EDITORIAL NOTE

Special attention of readers is called to the two following studies of the Royal Institute of International Affairs:

G. E. Hubbard, *British Far Eastern Policy,* Information Papers No. 24, Royal Institute of International Affairs, London, 1939.

F. C. Jones, *Shanghai and Tientsin.* Oxford University Press, Oxford and American Council, Institute of Pacific Relations, New York, 1940.

AUTHOR'S PREFACE

A study of British relations with China since 1931 presents certain peculiar problems. Legally China is an independent, sovereign state, enjoying the rights and duties flowing from this status; but actually during the period under review China was still in some respects in a quasi-colonial relation to the Western Powers. Furthermore, China was in constant danger of losing her independence because of Japanese aggression. Great Britain's attempt to maintain her position in China during this period, in which Japanese aggression threatened Chinese independence and British interests in China, forms the main thread of this story.

Throughout the period from the "Mukden Incident" to the outbreak of the present war in Europe, the Conservative Party was in control of the British Government. Britain's China policy was the policy of the Conservative Party, and the opposition had little influence upon it. Accordingly, little space has been given to opposition opinion, but considerable attention has been paid to conflicting attitudes within Conservative circles. Special emphasis has been placed on the opinions and attitudes of the British commercial groups in China which have the most immediate and deepest interest in the affairs of China. The safeguarding of their interests is the primary purpose of British policy in China, although always subject to the larger problems of imperial defense and world politics.

British relations with China from 1931 to 1939 have been the subject of much comment and discussion, but not of serious and scholarly work. The story had to be written from very diverse and, at times, controversial materials, without the benefit of any previous compilation of sources. Because of the contemporary nature of the subject, care had to be taken in the evaluation and treatment of the great amount of available materials. The pitfalls which await those dealing with contemporary topics such as the temptation to use sensational but unsubstantiated reports, have been borne in mind with the hope that they might thus be avoided. However, until certain sources especially the diplomatic papers in the British Foreign Office are available, no discussion of British relations with China can be considered definitive.

The author wishes to express his gratitude to Professors Philip C. Jessup and Nathaniel Peffer, under whose supervision this study was written, for their invaluable assistance. Particular thanks are due to Professor J. Bartlett Brebner for his constant inspiration and encouragement. The author also wishes to acknowledge the helpful suggestions and criticisms of Professors James T. Shotwell, Charles Cheney Hyde, Cyrus H. Peake, Livingston Schuyler and James W. Angell and is deeply indebted to his colleagues in the Institute of Pacific Relations for their help. Special mention should be made of Mr. Nagaharu Yasuo, who supplied valuable material from Japanese sources, and to Dr. Kurt Bloch, who assisted greatly in the preparation of the section on silver.

I. S. F.

New York
April 15, 1940

CONTENTS

Foreword		ix
Author's Preface		xiii
I.	Introduction	3
II.	The Manchurian Crisis 1931-1933	18
III.	From 1933 to the Leith-Ross Mission	43
IV.	From the Leith-Ross Mission to Lukouchiao	64
V.	From Lukouchiao to the Brussels Conference	92
VI.	From Shanghai to Nanking	107
VII.	From Nanking to the Invasion of South China—I	118
VIII.	From Nanking to the Invasion of South China—II	133
IX.	From Canton to the November Notes	157
X.	From the November Notes to the European War	177
XI.	Recapitulation and Conclusion	217
	Appendices	229
	Selected Bibliography	238

BRITISH RELATIONS WITH CHINA:
1931-1939

CHAPTER I

INTRODUCTION

In 1931 on the eve of the new era of war and invasion in China's history, Great Britain was the foreign power which had the most important economic stake in China south of the Great Wall, which divides China proper from Manchuria and Mongolia.

The foundation upon which the trade and investment of Great Britain, as well as of other foreign powers, had developed was an intricate system of legal and vested rights, built up over a long period of time. These were the privilege of extraterritoriality; the opening of "treaty ports" to foreign trade, and in some cases the establishment of "settlements" and "concessions" at these ports; the privilege of leasing certain areas; the right to navigate the coastal and inland waters of China with merchant ships and to police them with foreign men-of-war; the right to maintain military garrisons; and the right to engage in missionary activity. Each of these had its particular significance.

Extraterritoriality is the keystone of the treaty structure in China. It is upon this right of one state to exercise its own civil and penal jurisdiction over its own subjects and citizens within the territorial limits of another state, from whose jurisdiction they are exempt, that most of the other rights in China are based. Thus, the foreigner is immune from ordinary Chinese laws and jurisdiction; he is free from Chinese rates and taxes; and his house and properties cannot be searched or entered by Chinese authorities. Chinese soldiers cannot board ships belonging to foreigners, and Chinese in the employ of foreigners cannot be interfered with or arrested without the consent of the foreigners' own consular authorities.

Extraterritoriality has been of especial importance because of the existence of treaty ports. Indeed, the very establishment of the open port system was largely a result of extraterritoriality, since China insisted that as long as foreigners enjoyed immunity from Chinese jurisdiction, they should be grouped together in specific areas. A "treaty port" in China is one opened to foreign residence and trade by agreement between the Chinese and a foreign government. There are also a number of other open ports, some opened by mutual arrangement and others by China herself. Among the more important treaty ports, along the coast from south to north, are Canton, Swatow, Amoy, Foochow, Ningpo, Shanghai, Tsingtao, Chefoo, Tientsin and Newchwang; and, up the Yangtze valley, Chinkiang, Nanking, Wuhu, Kiukiang, Hankow, Changsha, Ichang and Chungking. At each small port could be found in 1931 the agents of the chief British firms, the Commissioner of Customs and perhaps the consular representatives of the leading foreign powers.

In all these treaty ports the British in 1931 enjoyed extraterritorial rights, but in some these had been elaborated and extended to form settlements and concessions. A "settlement" is an area at a treaty port set aside by the Chinese Government in which foreigners may reside and acquire land. A "concession" is an area at a treaty port which has been leased in perpetuity to a foreign government for occupation by its nationals. In the case of both settlements and concession areas the foreign power or powers exercise administrative authority either by grant or prescriptive right. The Chinese within these areas remain under Chinese jurisdiction and Chinese offenders are dealt with by Chinese courts. In the case of a concession the land is leased in lots to the occupants by the foreign government concerned. In the case of a settlement the foreign property owners acquire their land by purchase from the Chinese owners and hold it under perpetual titles issued by the Chinese land authorities.

In 1931 the British had concessions at Tientsin and Canton and participated in the international settlements at Shanghai and on Kulangsu, an island off Amoy. Although the concession at Tientsin is under British rule, it is the International Settlement at Shanghai which is of most importance to the British. Shanghai in 1931 was the greatest port in Asia and the commercial, industrial and financial metropolis of China.

The International Settlement in Shanghai is governed by a Municipal Council. In 1931 this Council had fourteen members, including five British, five Chinese, two Japanese and two Americans. The Chairman of the Council was British. The Shanghai Municipal Council derives its authority from the Consular Body whose powers stem from the "Land Regulations" of 1869, to which the Treaty Powers have claimed that China was a party but which the nationalist Chinese have refused to recognize.[1]

The leased territory of Kowloon has a peculiar status. Although this territory is held by the British in the form of a lease, China has relinquished all sovereign powers over it. Britain exercises full and unrestricted jurisdiction over everyone within its boundaries, whether Chinese, Japanese or European, and administers this region of 350 square miles as part of its colonial possession, Hongkong.

Extraterritoriality permits the establishment of British courts in China. These are the Supreme Court and the consular Courts known as Provincial Courts. The Supreme Court, which ordinarily sits at Shanghai, but which may sit anywhere else in China, has exclusive original jurisdiction, civil as well as criminal, for the district of the consulate of Shanghai, and concurrent jurisdiction, civil and criminal, with the Provincial Courts in other parts of China. It has also exclusive jurisdiction in all cases of divorce and of trials for murder. The Provincial Courts sit in each of the British Consular districts in China, and are presided over by the consular officials in charge of such districts.

Extraterritoriality has also increased the importance of the right of foreigners to navigate the coasts and inland waterways of China. Foreign vessels, in practice mainly British, starting from a treaty port could, in 1931, visit any locality in the interior which was recognized as a place of trade and which was visited by Chinese vessels under steam. The foreigners, protected by extraterritoriality and other special rights and privileges, penetrated into the remote interior of China. The right to maintain this privilege by force, if necessary, also existed. British men-of-war were permitted to patrol these waters. Besides larger war vessels, which cruised along the coast and up and down the Yangtze river as far as sea-going vessels might proceed, Britain, along with Japan, America and France, maintained a fleet of river gunboats which patroled the Canton and Yangtze rivers, the latter for fifteen hundred miles from Shanghai to Chungking.

In addition to these rights of naval patrol the British in 1931 also had the right to maintain foreign garrisons on Chinese soil. Not only was a legation guard allowed permanently in Peking,

---

[1] These regulations were issued by the consular authorities in Shanghai. For a fuller description see W. W. Willoughby, *Foreign Rights and Interests in China*, Vol. I, pp. 516-19.

but military forces could be landed for the protection of the settlements and concessions.

These rights were the most important of those exercised by the British in 1931, but in addition mention must be made of the privileges granted to missionaries. Missionaries not only have the right to reside in the treaty ports, but may acquire land and reside anywhere in China. Their converts, however, do not, as is sometimes supposed, enjoy extraterritorial rights.

No statement of the legal position of Britain in China in 1931 would actually be complete without including the special position enjoyed by Britain in the Customs Administration. Although the Chinese Customs Administration in 1931 was a branch department of the Chinese Ministry of Finance, the Inspector-General always was British, and he was by far the most important officer. Although the nationality of this official in no way implies that he will be partial to his native country, he is selected with the approval of the British Government.[2]

These rights and special privileges which the British possessed in 1931 were all part of that elaborate structure which the Chinese have often called the "unequal treaties." The significance of these rights, however, was mainly due to their close relation to Britain's economic interests in China, for these special privileges safeguarded Britain's commercial, industrial and financial position in China.

British interests in China in 1931 consisted largely of trade, shipping and investments.[3] The direct trade of the United Kingdom with China (excluding Hongkong) amounted to about £18 million in 1930 or about 7.8 per cent of China's total foreign trade. Imports from the United Kingdom amounted to £8,573,-923 or about 8.3 per cent of China's total imports, while exports to the United Kingdom totaled £9,888,819 or about 7 per cent of China's total exports.[4]

---

[2] In 1898 and again in 1908 China assured Great Britain that as long as British trade should predominate in China a British subject would be appointed to the Inspectorate General. By 1931 British trade no longer predominated in China. However, the Anglo-German Loan of 1898 provided that the administration of the Customs should not be changed during the currency of the loan and in 1931 the loan was still unpaid.

[3] In addition, there were 13,000 British citizens resident in China, an important factor in British policy.

[4] Professor Remer has calculated the total trade for China in 1930, including Hongkong. The total was Haikwan Taels 2,320.1 million ($1,067.25 million) and the British share, Haikwan Taels 216.3 million ($995 million) or 9.3 per cent.

The position of British trade in 1930 contrasted sharply with the predominant position which it had enjoyed in the 19th century, but in shipping Britain still remained paramount. The British percentage of the total tonnage, both Chinese and foreign, in the foreign trade of China and in the trade between the open ports, was about 37 per cent, a larger percentage of the modern shipping in the whole of China's trade than that enjoyed by any other nation. The Japanese percentage was 29.3. In the coast trade, i.e., trade between the open ports, the British flag accounted for 38 per cent of the total tonnage and carried 42 per cent of the value of the total cargoes. If the Chinese tonnage is excluded, the British share of the foreign shipping in the coast trade was 50 per cent.

In addition there was the shipping "under inland steam navigation rules." This was usually referred to as river shipping and included all vessels engaged in trade between the open ports and places which were not open. In this type of shipping, foreign shipping tonnage accounted for only 11.7 per cent, and, of this, the British share was 15.8 per cent.

These figures indicate that at the end of 1930 about one-fifth of the steam shipping in the domestic trade was British and that two-fifths of the foreign shipping was British. The two British shipping firms of Butterfield & Swire and Jardine, Matheson & Company handled most of this shipping.

Of at least equal importance with trade and shipping were British investments in China. These included British holdings of government obligations of all sorts and equally diverse business investments. British holdings of government obligations in 1931 included loans for the general purposes of the Chinese Government, Chinese Government railways, communications other than railways, unsecured loans, and obligations of foreign municipalities in China. The British share of the loans for the general purposes of the Chinese Government amounted to about $79,575,090 at the end of 1930.[5] The British share of the obligations of the Chinese Government railways amounted to

---

(HK. Tl. = Ch$1.50 = HK$1.36 = U. S. $0.46.) (*Foreign Investments in China,* pp. 371-2.)

[5] The loans involved and the total outstanding on December 31, 1930, were:

5% Crisp Loan of 1896.........................U. S. $	8,749,724
4½% Gold Loan of 1898...........................	39,304,885
5% Gold Loan of 1912 (Crisp Loan).................	22,308,800
5% Reorganization Loan of 1913....................	111,915,776

about $68 million, including holdings in the Peiping-Hankow Railway, the Peiping-Mukden Railway, the Tientsin-Pukow Railway, the Shanghai-Nanking Railway, the Hankow-Canton Railway (Hupeh-Hunan section) and the Canton-Kowloon Railway.

In communications other than railways, which included cables, telegraph and wireless telegraph, the British stake amounted to $1,960,834. Of considerably more importance were British holdings in "unsecured" loans. These amounted to $20,094,000. Finally, the British had $14,235,000 invested in the long-term obligations of those local governments in China in which foreigners had some degree of political control, especially the Shanghai International Settlement. The total of British holdings of government obligations in 1931 was $183,814,000.[6]

British business investments in China included, in the order of their importance, import and export and general trading, real estate, manufacturing, banking and finance, transportation, public utilities and mining. British real estate companies included the Shanghai Land Investment Company, which in 1930 had a paid-up capital and funded indebtedness of Ch$18 million and real estate holdings of Ch$22 million. In the field of manufacturing the most important firms were the Ewo Cotton Mills, Ltd. and the British American Tobacco Company. The Ewo Cotton Mills was the owner of the three British mills at Shanghai while the B.A.T. and its subsidiary, the British Cigarette Company, owned factories at Shanghai, Hankow, Tientsin, Mukden and Harbin. Other British manufacturing enterprises could be found in many fields, including cement, chemicals, bean oil, flour, ice, printing, rope, lumber, soap and candles. In addition, there were plants which prepared for export products like skins, furs, bristles and wool.

Banking and finance constituted another group of important investments. In this field the Hongkong & Shanghai Banking Corporation and the Chartered Bank of India, Australia & China predominated. The paid-up capital and reserves of the former were reported to be about £8 million on December 31, 1930, and its 160,000 shares, which had a nominal value of HK$125, were sold for as much as Ch$2,300 (HK$2,085.3) at Shanghai

[6] This figure is based on the place of issue. Professor Remer has arrived at the figure of $225,814,000 as the total British holding of the obligations of the government organizations in China, using the basis of actual holding.

during 1931. The amount of capital in banking and finance does not indicate the full importance of the British banking institutions in China. Not only did they finance British trade in China and have intimate relations with the most important business organizations in China, but they also performed special functions such as serving as depositories for Customs receipts.

The remaining fields were public utilities and mining. Among the larger public utilities in which there were British investments were the Shanghai Gas Company, the Shanghai Waterworks Company and the Shanghai Electric Construction Company. In 1931 British investments in mining were chiefly in three companies—the Chinese Engineering & Mining Company, Ltd., British participant in the Kailan Mining Administration, which owns the port of Chinwangtao for the export of its coal; the Peking Syndicate, which owned important coal mines in Honan province; and the Tung Hsing Sino-Foreign Coal Mining Company, owners of the Mentoukon Colliery in Hopei.

The total of British business investments in China was about £178 million, of which over £150 million was in Shanghai—an indication of the overwhelming importance of Shanghai to the British, whose total investment in China in 1931 amounted to about £236 million.[7]

Historical Development of British-Chinese Relations Before 1931

The economic interests which Great Britain had in China in 1931, coupled with the privileges and special rights which she enjoyed, were the products of a long process of development. An analysis of the policies which Britain had to pursue to achieve and maintain this position is essential both for the understanding of the British position in 1931 and for the full comprehension of the history of British relations with China after 1931.

The main historical periods of British policy in China before 1931 were three in number: (1) from about the Opium War to the Sino-Japanese War of 1894; (2) from the Sino-Japanese War to the anti-British movement of 1925-7; and (3) from 1928 to 1931. When the British Government in 1834 took over the management of the British trading community at Canton from

---

[7] This does not include about £2 million for British mission and philanthropic societies.

the East India Company, and began to have direct and continuous contact with Chinese authorities, the modern phase in Sino-British relations began. From 1834 to 1894 the prime interest of Britain was to find markets in China for the products of Britain's expanding industries, especially textiles. This motive, together with Britain's outstanding technological superiority, explain the main characteristics of British policy during this period. On the one hand Britain took the lead in opening up the China market and in building up the elaborate system of treaty rights and privileges, and on the other, she was quite content to allow other nations, by means of the most-favored-nation clause, to share in these gains. During this period, especially after the acquisition of Hongkong in 1842 which gave Great Britain the best port in South China as a base for naval as well as commercial operations, Britain was interested in the maintenance of China's territorial integrity as the best means of guaranteeing Britain's predominance in the China market. Free-trade Britain was able in China as elsewhere to secure the lion's share of the market and the British navy ruled the waves, including the western Pacific. The opening of China involved force on several occasions and in 1840, 1857 and 1860 military campaigns were launched. Whatever the immediate causes in each case, all intended to open up the China market and in each of the treaties which followed there were written new special rights for the foreign trader.[8]

By the end of this period, however, new forces began to operate in the relations between Great Britain and China. Economically, Great Britain was passing from the stage in which practically her sole interest in China was in its potentialities as a commercial market to the stage in which the possibilities of China as a field for long-term capital investment, particularly in railways and mining, were of major interest. Rivals were appearing on the scene. Russia, France, Germany, Japan and the United States now began to challenge the previously undisputed position of Great Britain. Henceforth, China's place in the world system of states became that of a chief subject of

[8] The Treaty of Nanking, 1842, provided for the cession of Hongkong and the establishment of a universal 5% tariff. The Treaty of Tientsin, 1858, provided for the creation of the Foreign Inspectorate of Chinese Maritime Customs, the right of navigation on China's rivers and the extension of extraterritoriality. The Convention of Peking, 1860, provided for the establishment of a permanent legation at Peking and the opening of Tientsin to foreign residence and trade.

international rivalry. With the appearance of these new factors there came corresponding major shifts in Britain's policies. The two main characteristics of British policy had been equality of access to commercial markets, sometimes called the open door, and the preservation of China's territorial integrity; in the period after 1894, the acquisition of special "spheres," with repeated violations of China's integrity, were characteristic. Furthermore, Britain now had to take into account the ambition and strength of her competitors, and out of this came a "balance of power" technique.

The dividing line between the two periods was the Sino-Japanese War. Japan, which had defeated China, was herself forced to surrender the spoils of victory by the combined pressure of Russia, Germany and France. Then began the Battle of Concessions and by 1898 even the territorial partitioning of China was considered a real possibility. Britain had marked out as her sphere the Yangtze valley and North China, and looked upon Russia as her most dangerous rival. Overtures to Germany were made first and when these led to nothing, Japan was successfully approached. The Anglo-Japanese Alliance (into which the treaty of 1902 was expanded at its renewals in 1905 and 1911) became the foundation of Britain's balance of power diplomacy in China until the Washington Conference of 1921. International rivalry in China now took the form of competition for loans and for railroad and mining concessions. It was at this time that the bulk of Britain's investments in China were made and the history of this period could be written around the rivalry of the Hongkong & Shanghai Banking Corporation, the Russo-Asiatic Bank, the Deutsch-Asiatische Bank, the Banque de l'Indo-Chine, the International Banking Corporation and the Yokohama Specie Bank. Hay's Open-Door Note attempted to maintain equal commercial access in China, but did not touch the issue of special "spheres." Financial penetration, whether by countries or banks acting individually or by consortiums, continued until the Washington Conference. The World War was merely an interlude during which Britain, unable to advance her own position, had to acquiesce in the aggressive policy of her ally Japan.

During this period China was in no position to resist the policies of the foreign powers. However, although both the Boxer Rebellion of 1900 and the Revolution of 1911 partly failed, there were indications of the development of a nationalist movement which was to become an increasingly important factor in China's foreign relations in the post-War period.

The Treaty of Versailles not only ignored Chinese demands for treaty revision, but even recognized the Japanese occupation of Shantung. However, it also introduced, by the Covenant of the League of Nations, a new element into China's foreign relations. China, along with the other members of the League, received the promise that her "territorial integrity and existing political independence" would be respected and preserved against external aggression.

British policy in China in the years immediately after the World War reflected the change in the balance of forces in the Far East. Russia and Germany, the two main pre-War rivals, were eliminated; Japan was making a bid for supremacy, and the United States strategically, economically and diplomatically was in an unprecedentedly strong position. Furthermore, the Anglo-Japanese Alliance, made less necessary by the elimination of Germany and Russia, was extremely unpopular in the United States and Canada. The net result of this changed situation was the Washington Conference Treaties. The Anglo-Japanese Alliance was dropped in favor of a Four Power consultative Pact and the Nine Power Treaty affirmed China's territorial integrity and the doctrine of the open door.

In one basic respect, however, the Washington Treaties did not effect any real change in China's foreign relations: the treaty structure remained practically untouched. China, seeking fiscal independence, received instead a promise in the Customs Treaty that a special tariff conference would be convened to consider minor increases in the Chinese import tariff. China had hoped that her administrative autonomy would be restored, that the foreign garrisons would be withdrawn and the concessions and leased territories surrendered. All that the Washington signatories conceded was the adoption of a resolution calling for the withdrawal of the foreign postal agencies, the sending of an international commission to investigate the issue of extraterritoriality, and indefinite offers to restore certain of the leased territories, including the British leased port of Weihaiwei. The old treaty system of which Great Britain had been the principal architect continued to exist. The foreign powers, including Great Britain, refused to depart from their fundamental policy that China should be kept under foreign tutelage.

The anti-British movement of 1925-7 was a turning-point in Sino-British relations. This movement was the result of the rise of Chinese nationalism, reacting to the policies pursued by the powers, especially Great Britain, after the World War, and the attitude of the Communist movement toward the Chinese nationalist movement and toward the British Empire. The nationalist movement in China under the leadership of Sun Yat-sen had grown up for the most part in the southern part of China, but by 1925 had gained adherents throughout China. Large sections of the population, including intellectuals, professionals, students, businessmen and laborers were eager that China should be completely independent of foreign control. Great Britain, as the leading foreign power in China, and Japan, because of the Twenty-one Demands, were regarded as the main obstacles to the achievement of this aim. The Nationalists pointed to the denial of the demands made by China at Versailles and at Washington, and to the failure of foreign powers to implement the promises made at Washington, as evidence that these powers intended to keep China in a "semi-colonial" status.[9] This anti-foreign feeling was given organization and direction as the result of the alliance effected in 1923 between the Kuomintang and the Communist Party of China. The structure of the Kuomintang by 1925 was completely reorganized and the Nationalist Party built up an effective army. Furthermore, the Communist International at this time regarded their aid to China not only as a logical consequence of their policy of supporting colonial nationalist movements, but as being especially aimed at Great Britain, which they regarded as their chief antagonist.

By 1925 anti-foreign feeling was running high throughout China. This sentiment came to a climax after a clash between the Shanghai Municipal police and Chinese demonstrators on May 30, 1925. May 30 became a slogan throughout China and the anti-British movement was on. The boycott weapon was used more effectively and consistently than ever before. Hongkong appeared to be on the verge of ruin and British shipping

---

[9] The only important exception to the general failure to implement the Washington Treaties were the withdrawal of the foreign post offices from China early in 1923 and the restoration of Shantung by Japan.

on the Yangtze seriously declined. The Nationalist armies under the leadership of Generalissimo Chiang Kai-shek marched victoriously from Canton to the Yangtze, and the capital of the Kuomintang Government was established at Hankow. Clashes between British forces and Chinese occurred, and war between Nationalist China and Britain seemed possible. The high point came in January 1927 with the taking of the British concession at Hankow by the Nationalists.

The British communities in China, especially those in Shanghai, demanded strong action. The British Government, however, adopted a dual policy. On one hand it dispatched a large expeditionary force to Shanghai; on the other it indicated its willingness to make concessions. In the Chamberlain Memorandum of December 18, 1926, it declared its willingness to negotiate on treaty revision and in February 1927 an agreement was signed providing for the rendition of the British concession at Hankow. At this time the Kuomintang was divided into three factions—the conservatives under General Chiang Kai-shek, the center, and the radicals who favored and practiced close co-operation with the Communists. The conciliatory policy of the British strengthened the position of those Nationalists who wanted to weaken or end the anti-British movement. By the summer of 1927 the anti-foreign Hankow Kuomintang Government had collapsed and Chiang Kai-shek's faction was in complete control. The anti-British movement came to an end and, as expressed by Sir Eric Teichman, "before the year was out it was more dangerous to be a Russian or a red in South and Central China than it had ever been to be the most die-hard of Imperialists."[10]

The period from 1928 to the Manchurian incident of 1931 might be called the Lampson period. During this time Sir Miles Lampson, who became British Minister to China in 1926, directed British policy in China in such a distinct fashion as to leave a marked imprint on the history of China as well as on Sino-British relations. Britain now took the lead in supporting the new Nationalist Government, which was no longer the anti-British Kuomintang of Canton and Hankow, and by pursuing a policy of concession and conciliation she built up British

[10] Sir Eric Teichman, *Affairs of China*, p. 49. During this period Sir Eric Teichman was Chinese Secretary to the British Legation at Peking.

prestige in China to a point it had not held since pre-World War days.

British concessions to China took place in several fields, but the most important was the recognition of China's tariff autonomy. Since the Treaty of Nanking in 1842, China's tariff had been bound by treaties to 5 per cent *ad valorem*. In 1902 Great Britain, followed by Japan and the United States, had concluded with China a new commercial treaty, according to which China was permitted to raise her import tariff by a further 7.5 per cent in return for the abolition of *likin* (internal transit dues). This agreement, however, came to naught. Both at Versailles and at Washington the Chinese representatives had unsuccessfully raised this issue. Although the Washington Treaty had provided for the assembling of a tariff conference within three months, it was not held until 1925. After months of futile discussion, the conference disbanded, with only a promise made by the powers that China was to secure tariff autonomy by 1929 in exchange for the abolition of *likin*. Little happened until the summer of 1928 when the United States, stealing a march on the British, suddenly concluded a treaty with the new Nanking Government conceding unconditional tariff autonomy as from January 1929. The British, not to be outdone, concluded a similar treaty on December 20, 1928. When Japan followed suit in 1930, China was finally free from treaty restrictions on her tariff-making power.

The grant of tariff autonomy was followed up by the restoration to the Nanking Government of the leased port of Weihaiwei in 1930, after 32 years of British rule, although the port was still to be used as the summer resort for the British Fleet. Furthermore, the British Government surrendered the British concessions at Kiukiang, Amoy and Chinkiang, while retaining those at Tientsin and Canton.

Another example of the new British policy was the agreement on the Boxer indemnity funds. The British share of the Boxer indemnities had originally amounted to £7.5 million, but in 1922, as a result of compound interest, £11 million were still outstanding. In December 1922 the British Government notified the Chinese Government of its intention to devote the funds accruing from all future installments to purposes mutually beneficial to China and Great Britain. Not until 1930, however, was an agreement for the disposition of the funds reached.[11] This provided for the investment of the funds in Chinese railways and other public works, as an endowment for cultural, educational and philanthropic purposes. The Chinese Government was to appoint a board of trustees, composed of Chinese and British members, to control and supervise the funds. Moreover, the "accumulated funds," the installments of which since 1922 had been paid into a special account amounting by 1930 to over £3 million, were to be remitted to London and expended through a "Purchasing Commission" on the purchase in the United Kingdom of materials and equipment for Chinese railways and other public works. Thus, the remission of the Boxer funds was calculated both to increase British prestige in China and to increase British exports to China in a period of declining world markets.

The new trend in Sino-British relations was also in evidence in less important matters. In 1931 the Chinese Salt Administration, which had been under foreign administration since 1913, passed into the control of the Chinese Government.[12] In 1929 the embargo on the shipment of arms to China, which had been maintained by the Treaty Powers since 1919, was dropped. Finally in 1931 an agreement was concluded with the British Government for a British naval mission to train and reorganize the naval forces of the Nanking Government.

Thus, as a result of the "Lampson policy" some changes in the treaty structure of China had been made in the matter of the tariff, concessions and Salt Gabelle. Extraterritoriality, however, continued, despite protracted negotiations to secure some change. In 1926, in accordance with the resolution adopted at Washington, an international commission visited China and made a report which visualized the gradual and progressive abolition of extraterritoriality. After much diplomatic wrangling, during which the Chinese Government twice unilaterally

[11] In 1925 the British Government established an Advisory Committee under Lord Buxton to consider the question and report. In 1926 this committee sent a delegation, under Lord Willingdon, to China. It drew up a report recommending that the funds should be devoted to cultural, educational and philanthropic works in China, partly by direct expenditure and partly by the creation of an endowment fund invested in China's public works.

[12] The Chinese Salt Administration was a result of the Reorganization Loan of 1913 of £25,000,000 to Yuan Shi-kai by Britain, Japan, France and Germany. The entire loan was made a direct liability of the Chinese Government and was secured "by a charge upon the entire revenues of the Salt Administration of China."

decreed the abolition of extraterritoriality, a tentative agreement was reached in the summer of 1931 based on the principle that any arrangements would have to be accepted by the other interested powers. The commencement of hostilities against China by Japan soon after put an abrupt end to the negotiations.

The "Mukden incident" of September 1931 opened a new chapter in Chinese history and in Sino-British relations. Henceforth the main threat to the British position in China no longer came from Chinese nationalism which aimed at an independent China, but rather from Japanese imperialism.

CHAPTER II

THE MANCHURIAN CRISIS: 1931-33

On September 18 Japanese troops seized Mukden, the chief city of Manchuria, and a new era in the history of the Far East had begun. The history of China and likewise that of Sino-British relations henceforth bears the name of Japan on every page. The attack launched against China in 1931 involved Great Britain both as a signatory of the Covenant of the League of Nations and also as the Western power with the greatest material interests in China.

The Manchurian incident came at a moment when a brief season of pacifist hopes and economic stability was fast disappearing amidst a gathering storm of economic crisis and political conflict, whose shadows were to grow darker during every year of the following decade. For British diplomacy, disarmament and reparations were ever-recurring problems. The failure of the Credit-Anstalt in Austria pulled down the big banks of Germany and with it the gold standard in Great Britain. In the midst of the financial crisis the Labor Government of Ramsay MacDonald gave way to the National Government also headed by MacDonald but representing a Conservative-Liberal-Labor coalition. An Austro-German customs union loomed, with implications of possible political unity, and while it was given its final blow by a World Court interpretation of a previous treaty, the 8-7 vote caused a serious loss of prestige to the peace-making structure of the Versailles system. India was in ferment and the Round Table conferences were being held. With these issues on her hands, Great Britain had to weigh her Far Eastern policy.

The history of British relations with China during the Manchurian crisis falls into two chronological divisions—the periods before and after the invasion of Shanghai in January 1932.

On September 18, 1931, an explosion took place on the tracks of the South Manchurian Railway near Mukden. The Japanese, claiming that this was the act of the soldiers of Marshal Chang

Hsueh-liang, the war-lord of Manchuria, immediately went into action. The Japanese forces at Mukden, under General Honjo, bombarded the Chinese barracks and within forty-eight hours took control of Mukden, Changchun, Antung and other points. In spite of the actions taken by the League of Nations, the Japanese continued their drives and by the end of December Marshal Chang was obliged to withdraw his troops behind the Great Wall. With the occupation on January 3, 1932, of Chinchow, the Japanese were in complete control of Manchuria and a new local administration was installed under the protection of the Japanese military.

British policy toward this invasion was best seen in her role in the League and in her relations with the United States. On September 21, 1931, China, through Dr. Alfred Sze, her chief delegate in Geneva, invoked Article 11 of the Covenant.[1] The Council was asked to take immediate steps "to prevent the further development of a situation endangering the peace of nations, to re-establish the *status quo ante,* and to determine the amounts and character of such reparations as may be due to the Republic of China." The Council on that very night sent identic cables to Nanking and Tokyo, calling upon them to withdraw their troops immediately. The British position was stated by Viscount Cecil at the Council meeting of September 25, 1931. He supported the Council's action, declaring that only when peace had been safeguarded would any question as to the settlement of the actual dispute arise.

In the meantime the Japanese military forces in Manchuria continued their advance. On September 28 the Chinese suggested the early dispatch of a neutral commission to determine the true facts of the situation. Lord Cecil expressed interest in the Chinese proposal, suggesting that it be put in writing, and voiced the hope that his Japanese colleague would give it

---

[1] Article 11 of the Covenant reads:

"(1) Any war or threat of war, whether immediately affecting any of the Members of the League or not, is hereby declared a matter of concern to the whole League, and the League shall take any action that may be deemed wise and effectual to safeguard the peace of nations. In case any such emergency shall arise the Secretary-General shall on the request of the Members of the League forthwith summon a meeting of the Council.

"(2) It is also declared to be the friendly right of each Member of the League to bring to the attention of the Assembly or of the Council any circumstance whatever affecting international relations which threatens to disturb international peace or the good understanding between nations upon which peace depends."

further consideration.² Furthermore, he hoped that some agreement for evacuation of the troops might be reached at a meeting between the Chinese and Japanese representatives. "If that meeting should prove fruitless, the Council would then have to consider if anything else could be done by it to bring about an agreement."³ The net result of the Council discussion was the resolution of September 30 which requested both parties to do all in their power to hasten the restoration of normal relations between them and to furnish the Council at frequent intervals with full information as to the development of the situation. The Council then adjourned.

The Council reconvened on October 13, 1931, in response to a Chinese request, for the Japanese were continuing their advance in southern Manchuria and had twice bombed Chinchow. China placed herself in the hands of the League and in the words of Dr. Sze "abides the issue with confidence in her destiny and in the moral forces of civilization."⁴ The Japanese delegate, Mr. Yoshizawa, in reply, charged the Chinese with infringements of Japanese treaty rights. On October 15 the United States, over Japan's objections, was invited by the Council to attend its sessions, and on October 16 Mr. Prentiss Gilbert took his seat at the Council table. Supporting the proposed invitation, Lord Reading, the British delegate, tried to reassure the Japanese that "the invited representative would sit, not as a Member, but merely for the purpose of making verbal communications to the Council and informing his Government." Above all, however, he pleaded, "the Council should not lose sight of, or relegate to the background, the real question which was responsible for the present meeting of the Council," i.e., the "putting into practice, with the assistance of the Japanese and Chinese representatives, all possible peaceful means for the purpose of preventing acts of hostility which might speedily become acts of war."⁵

A meeting of the Council was scheduled to take place on October 22, but it was decided by all the members of the Council except Japan that it was desirable to invoke the moral weight

---

² Professor Shotwell points out in his *Rim of the Abyss* that on September 23 the Japanese delegation at Geneva learned that Mr. Stimson was opposed to the sending of a commission of inquiry to Manchuria.
³ *Official Journal*, League of Nations, December 1931, p. 2292.
⁴ *Ibid.*, p. 2312.
⁵ *Ibid.*, p. 2326.

of the Paris Peace Pact in the Manchurian controversy. Accordingly, on October 17 the governments of Great Britain, France, Germany, Italy, Spain and Norway sent to China and Japan identic notes calling attention to their obligations under the Peace Pact, and the French Government undertook to notify the other signatories of the Pact.

While Japan was still protesting that she had no intention of making war upon China, her army continued its advance in Manchuria. The other members of the Council, especially Great Britain and France, sought to obtain from Japan a specific undertaking with regard to the cessation of her military operations in Manchuria and the withdrawal of her troops. These efforts proved unavailing and M. Briand, the president of the Council, on October 22 introduced a resolution which, it was known, would not receive the supporting vote of Japan. This resolution was passed on October 24 by a vote of 13 to 1 and called upon the Japanese Government "to begin immediately and to proceed progressively with the withdrawal of its troops into the railway zone," by the date fixed for the next meeting of the Council, November 16. In the discussion which followed, Lord Cecil stated the position of his government. The British Government he said, had been made extremely uneasy by the bombing incidents that had taken place and had found it extremely difficult to see how those incidents could be justified by any known principle of international law. Lord Cecil then called upon the Japanese delegate, Mr. Yoshizawa, to clarify what the Japanese Government had meant by its statement that certain "fundamental principles" regarding the relations between China and Japan needed to be determined before normal relations between the two countries could be resumed. Failing to receive a satisfactory reply from his colleague, Lord Cecil suggested that perhaps Japan desired "to enter into a discussion of treaty obligations with China concerning Manchuria before evacuation."[6] The Japanese delegate still refused to elucidate.

Lord Cecil, speaking again, commented on a Reuters press agency report which stated that the Japanese Government took the position that, unless the League was prepared to take some action which would imply recognition of the validity of the treaties which Japan had with China, it should not attempt to

[6] *Ibid.*, p. 2350.

force Japan to change its position before the Council. The British delegate pointed out that any dispute as to the validity or interpretation of a treaty could now be settled by the Permanent Court of International Justice. Furthermore, he held that evacuation must precede discussion of the treaties by the League.[7] The Council, after adopting the resolution calling for withdrawal of the Japanese troops, adjourned until November 16.

At the November 16 meeting of the Council in Paris, Sir John Simon represented the British Empire. Nothing of importance happened although the troops had not been withdrawn. At the next meeting, on November 21, the Japanese representative proposed the sending to the Far East of a "Commission of Enquiry." Lord Cecil, who had replaced Sir John Simon, urged the acceptance of the proposal. A resolution was finally drafted in a form acceptable to both China and Japan and it was adopted at the Council meeting of December 10.[8]

In addition to providing for a commission of five members, the resolution reaffirmed the resolution of September 30 and added in paragraph 2 that the two parties undertook "to adopt all measures necessary to avoid any further aggravation of the situation and to refrain from any initiative which may lead to further fighting and loss of life."[9] No mention was made of the October 24 resolution or of a definite date by which Japan should have its military forces withdrawn from China or at least within the railway zone. In this respect Lord Cecil's comments on paragraph 2 of the resolution are significant as indicating the British attitude at this time toward Japan's activities in Manchuria.

> There can be no doubt that the position in Manchuria is difficult and exceptional. It may well be that circumstances may arise there which will cause danger to Japanese lives and property from elements of the population out of control, and if an emergency of that kind should arise it might become inevitable that Japanese forces in the neighborhood should take action against bandits and the like. But I welcome the recognition by my Japanese colleague of the exceptional character of the situation and that the necessity for such exceptional action will come to an end as soon as normal conditions have been restored. In saying this, I do not mean to

---

[7] *Ibid.*, p. 2354.
[8] The resolution can be found in the *Official Journal*, December 1931, pp. 2374-5.
[9] *Ibid.*, p. 2374.

suggest that the Japanese declaration weakens the obligations set out in paragraph 2 of the Resolution to avoid any action which will lead to a recrudescence of fighting between the Chinese and Japanese troops, or a further aggravation of the situation.[10]

Thus the British Government was not only unwilling to commit itself to more than the expression of hope that Japan would not act in violation of her obligations, but also indicated a willingness to accept the Japanese contentions, at least in part.

The Japanese, despite all assurances to the contrary, continued their occupation of Manchuria, completing it by January 3. The center of diplomatic activity now shifted from Geneva to Washington, for on January 7, 1932, the American Government enunciated the "Stimson Doctrine."[11] From the beginning of the Manchurian incident the United States through its Secretary of State, Mr. Henry Stimson, had voiced its approval of the steps taken by the League, culminating in direct association with the League's efforts. The American Government, after consultation with the British and French ambassadors, addressed an identic note to the Chinese and Japanese Governments on January 7 invoking the Pact of Paris as a basis for the declaration of a policy of non-recognition.

> The American Government deems it to be its duty to notify both the Imperial Japanese Government and the Government of the Chinese Republic that it cannot admit the legality of any situation *de facto* nor does it intend to recognize any treaty or agreement entered into between those Governments, or agents thereof, which may impair the treaty rights of the United States or its citizens in China including those which relate to the sovereignty, the independence, or the territorial and administrative integrity of the Republic of China, or to the international policy relative to China, commonly known as the open-door policy, and that it does not intend to recognize any situation, treaty, or agreement which may be brought about by means contrary to the covenants and obligations of the Pact of Paris of August 27, 1928, to which treaty both China and Japan, as well as the United States, are parties.[12]

Mr. Stimson has written that he expected British support for this move and has openly voiced the disappointment which he felt when this was not forthcoming.[13] The official British view

[10] *Ibid.*, p. 2577.
[11] The Council had adjourned on December 10, 1931, until January 25, 1932.
[12] U. S. Department of State, *Press Releases*, No. 119, January 9, 1932.
[13] Henry Stimson, *The Far Eastern Crisis*, pp. 98-105. One of the important factors in determining the action of the United States at this time was the political situation in Japan. On December 12, 1931, a cabinet change took place. Mr. Inukai became prime minister and Mr. Yoshizawa replaced Baron Shidehara as

on the Stimson Note was expressed in a brief *communiqué* of the Foreign Office on January 8, issued to the press on January 11.[14]

> His Majesty's Government stand by the policy of the open-door for international trade in Manchuria, which was guaranteed by the Nine Power Treaty at Washington.
>
> Since the recent events in Manchuria, the Japanese representatives at the Council of the League of Nations at Geneva stated October 13th that Japan was the champion in Manchuria of the principle of equal opportunity and the open-door for the economic activities of all nations. Further, on December 28th the Japanese Prime Minister stated that Japan would adhere to the open-door policy, and would welcome participation and co-operation in Manchurian enterprise.
>
> In view of these statements, his Majesty's Government have not considered it necessary to address any formal Note to the Japanese Government on the lines of the American Government's Note, but the Japanese Ambassador in London has been requested to obtain confirmation of these assurances from his Government.

Mr. Stimson's comments on this Foreign Office *communiqué* indicate why this refusal of Great Britain to go along with the United States was so disappointing.

> The contents . . . were such as to be taken by most readers, including—what was most important—the Japanese Government, as a rebuff to the United States. . . . Its omissions were the most important feature of the communiqué. It was entirely silent as to the preservation of the sovereignty, independence and integrity of China, the Kellogg-Briand Pact, and the assertion of the principle of the non-recognition of the fruits of unlawful aggression. It thus ignored entirely the questions of world peace and China's integrity, which we had deemed the most important features not only of our note, but of the previous three months' negotiations in which we had been supporting the efforts of the League of Nations and the British Government.[15]

Sir John Pratt, then in the Foreign Office, has given the most authoritative British explanation of this *communiqué*. In a letter published in the London *Times* of November 30, 1938, Sir John wrote,

> I am not revealing any very closely kept secret when I say that the Foreign Office have never attempted to defend this communiqué and have always regretted that a slip was made which has, it would seem, proved a real obstacle in Anglo-American relations. The communiqué was drafted

---

foreign minister. This indicated a shift from the liberal to the more militaristic elements in Japanese politics.

[14] London *Times*, January 11, 1932.
[15] Stimson, *op. cit.*, pp. 101-2.

and approved in haste by the permanent officials at 1 o'clock on Saturday, and it was not realized until it appeared in the Press on the following Monday that it read like a rebuff to America. This is really all there is to it.

Sir John Pratt's version of this *communiqué* as an error in judgment does not explain, however, the leading article which appeared in the *Times* on January 11, 1932, which elaborated its view of the reasons for the *communiqué*.

The British Government have acted wisely in declining to address a communication to the Chinese and Japanese Governments on the lines of Mr. Stimson's Note. . . . In invoking its clauses [those of the Nine Power Treaty] the American Government may have been moved by the fear that the Japanese authorities would set up a virtually independent administration in Manchuria which would favour Japanese interests to the detriment of the commerce of other nations. It is clear that the Foreign Office does not share these apprehensions, and that, although the Nine Power Treaty provides for consultation between the interested powers, it was not in fact consulted before the Note was communicated to Nanking and Tokyo. . . . Nor does it seem to be the immediate business of the Foreign Office to defend the "administrative integrity" of China until that integrity is something more than an ideal. It did not exist in 1922 and it does not exist to-day. On no occasion since the Nine Power Treaty was signed has the Central Government of China exercised any real administrative authority over large and varying areas of its huge territory. Today its writ does not run in Yunnan and in other important provinces, and while its sovereignty over Manchuria is not disputed, there is no evidence that it has exercised any real administration there since Nanking became the Chinese capital.

This expression of attitude toward the Chinese Nationalist Government was not unique. On September 26, 1931, the *Times* had warned China that "the Council's championship of peace does not in the least mean that it has any sympathy with the 'pin-pricking' policy in which Chinese governments have indulged only too often in recent years." On November 14, 1931, on the eve of Sir John Simon's departure for Paris, the *Times* had stated that the League had "from the first made its own position more difficult than it would have been in any case by concentrating too exclusively upon the juridical framework of peace. When the matter came before the Council in September, it did not consider the rights and wrongs of the case or make any attempt to ascertain whether motives of unsatisfied practice had prompted the Japanese seizure of Mukden." Again on November 23, 1931, the *Times* had spoken of the League's "initial error of condemning out of hand a State that may be in the right, because it had felt compelled to fire the first shot in what it believed to be the defense of its own rights and the cause of justice."[16] The Foreign Office *communiqué* of January 8, even if it was an administrative blunder, was in accord with views prevalent in Conservative circles.

A similar attitude was shown by the *North-China Herald*, the most representative spokesman for British interests in China.[17] In the issue of January 12, 1932, it clearly indicated its position on the January 7 note:

> At the time when China's integrity is most menaced by the inherent defects of the internal administration of the country, it would be insidious to throw on one particular signatory of the Nine Power Treaty special responsibilities for preserving that elusive quality. . . . Let it be conceded that the Army in Manchuria has definitely led where it should have been directed, that Japanese propaganda has been singularly inept and unwise in certain aspects, and that the Government at Tokyo has allowed its case to be prejudiced by conflicting statements of policy, there still must remain the spectacle of Manchuria grossly misgoverned, bled white by reckless depreciation of currency to the point of imposing the servitude of a cruel, invisible taxation and helplessly caught up in the web of a system of administration which, by the circumlocutory methods of its neophytes, put a premium on irresponsibility and complete negligence. That is why the Council of the League of Nations, after the case had been brought to its cognizance, realised the danger of an out-of-hand judgment. . . . Having regard to the general position in China, Great Britain and France are content to believe that Japanese assurances will be forthcoming at the appropriate time. Here again the League's usefulness is revealed. It acts as a lightning conductor. . . . It is recognised by Great Britain that Japan's specific statements at Geneva on October 13 and, through the mouth of Mr. Inukai, on December 28, require only confirmation by the ordinary diplomatic channels for present satisfaction of anxieties over recent Manchurian developments. It will be recognised that, in some degree, this conveys a friendly hint to Tokyo. In view of the close identification of British with Japanese policy in China . . . it may be confidently expected that the hint will be taken in the spirit in which it is offered.

The willingness of the British Government to accept Japanese assurances was again seen in an announcement made by the Foreign Office on January 15. As a result of a conversation be-

[16] Such views were also expressed in such other Conservative newspapers as the *Daily Telegraph, Morning Post, Daily Mail* and *Daily Express*.

[17] From the beginning of hostilities in September 1931, the *North-China Herald* showed marked sympathy for the Japanese position, although it did support China's appeal to the League. It is interesting to note in this connection the great and unfriendly attention being paid at this time to the Communist movement in China and to the growing strength of Soviet Russia in the Far East. Obviously, the experiences of 1925-7 were still remembered.

tween Sir John Simon and the Japanese ambassador, Mr. Tsuneo Matsudaira, on January 8, the Japanese ambassador had called at the Foreign Office on the 14th and had conveyed from his government express assurances in reference to Japan's disclaimer of territorial ambitions in Manchuria and of her intention to respect the principles of the Open Door and the Nine Power Treaty.

The Japanese in their reply to the Stimson Note on January 16 completely ignored Article II of the Paris Pact which calls for the pacific settlement of all disputes. In paragraph 2 the Japanese Government boldly stated that, "The Government of Japan was well aware that the Government of the United States could always be relied on to do everything in their power to support Japan's efforts to secure the full and complete fulfillment in every detail of the treaties of Washington and the Kellogg Treaty for the Outlawry of War. They are glad to receive this additional assurance of the fact." The remainder of the note, written in the same vein, declared that the Open Door would be maintained in Manchuria, "as in China proper," and argued that China's "present unsettled and distracted state" might "modify" the application of the Washington Treaty.[18] The *Times* on January 19, in a tone strikingly dissimilar to that used in commenting on the Stimson Note, described the Japanese reply as "courteous," "reassuring" and "informative."

With the reconvening of the Council on January 25, 1932, at Geneva, the center of diplomatic activity again shifted to the League. A new situation, of special importance to the British, was now developing in the Far East. Shanghai, the hub of British interests in China, was in serious danger. On January 20, 1932, the Japanese consul-general at Shanghai had demanded a cessation of anti-Japanese agitation and had lodged a protest against a mob attack on five Japanese monks. On January 27 a twenty-four hour ultimatum was delivered by the Japanese authorities to the Mayor of Greater Shanghai, Wu Te-chen. The authorities of the International Settlement declared a "state of emergency" to exist, which meant that the foreign military forces were to be prepared to defend the sectors of the

---

[18] U. S. Department of State, *Press Releases*, Weekly Issue No. 120, January 16, 1932, pp. 68-9.

Settlement assigned to them in accordance with previous arrangements. The British, American, French, Italian and Japanese forces took the positions assigned to them, the Japanese sector consisting of the northeastern area of the Settlement where most of the resident Japanese nationals lived. On January 28 the Chinese unconditionally accepted the Japanese ultimatum but Shiozawa, the Japanese admiral in charge, announced that evening the dispatch of Japanese sailors to the native city of Chapei to enforce order and protect Japanese property. The Nineteenth Route Army, under General Tsai Ting-kai, decided to resist and clashed with the Japanese. On January 29 Chapei was bombarded and the "Shanghai War" had begun.

The British attitude toward the Sino-Japanese conflict changed considerably with the attack on Shanghai. At Geneva the Chinese delegation, in order to obtain, if possible, greater assistance from the League, decided to invoke Articles X and XV of the Covenant, instead of continuing to base its pleas on Article XI. When the Japanese representative tried to argue that the Council could not consider Article X to have been violated since the Council had "authorized" the Japanese Government "to take action to protect the property and lives of the Japanese nationals scattered throughout the vast territory of Manchuria," Lord Cecil rejected this construction. "I think it would be a rather more accurate statement to say that the Council recognized that the obligation to withdraw was dependent upon the safety of Japanese nationals."[19]

The *Times* reflected the change in attitude in Conservative circles in Great Britain after the bombardment of Shanghai. A leading article of January 29, 1932, commented on the dispatch of Japanese reinforcements to Shanghai.

> Such doubts about the expediency and the effect of the measures taken by the Japanese cannot, of course, obscure the fact that they have had serious provocation in the shape of attacks on Japanese subjects and the boycott of Japanese goods. Moreover, there has been in the recent past somewhat similar action taken by other Powers. In 1927 the British Government, after consulting other Powers, sent a strong expeditionary force to Shanghai to defend the International Settlement against attack: Japan, the United States, Italy and other Powers also sent naval contingents and warships; the French protected their own concession, and Sir Austen

[19] *Official Journal*, League of Nations, March 1932, p. 347.

Chamberlain, in reply to questions in the House of Commons made it clear that His Majesty's Government considered that they had the right to move troops beyond the limits of the Settlement if the Chinese authorities should prove unable to protect British nationals. In the present case the Japanese authorities on the spot consider the close proximity of a large and notoriously ill-disciplined force of Chinese troops to be a reason—and it is a good *prima facie* reason—for refusing to be satisfied by the promises of the Mayor of Shanghai, for expelling these troops as a precaution from the suburbs of the city and for seizing the headquarters of the boycotters of their goods. Their Government disclaim any intention of taking military action in the International Settlement, or of interfering with its administration, and there is no reason to fear that they wish to complicate or aggravate the situation any further than they have done already. But when all this is said, the situation at Shanghai must remain a delicate and a difficult one, and the responsibility of the fourteen Powers interested in the Settlement will be vastly increased by the drastic action of the Japanese Admiral.

On that very day Chapei was bombarded and in the following issue of January 30, the *Times* said:

> Collective international action of a more vigorous kind than has recently characterized affairs in the Far East will be required if order is to be restored in Shanghai, which is definitely an international town, and if the combatants on either side are to be restrained from wreaking further destruction on life and property. It is of the first importance that the two countries should not proceed to a state of formal war with one another. A foolish act of defiance by some irresponsible and transitory office-holder in Nanking might be made an adequate excuse by the Japanese to blockade the whole coast of China, with disastrous consequences for the large foreign communities and especially for the great trading centre of Shanghai. There must be a firm defence of foreign interests and an equally firm and united effort to separate the entangled combatant nations. . . . With all its limitations the League at least possesses convenient machinery for concerting international policy. It is also the proper organ through which an international inquiry can be carried out.

The Japanese attack on Shanghai also resulted in a period of Anglo-American co-operation. As early as January 25, Stimson had discussed with the British Ambassador in Washington the possibilities of a "co-operative solution" if difficulties arose in Shanghai. On January 29 the British Government sent a sharp protest to the Japanese Government in regard to the attack on Chapei and requested the United States to do likewise, as it did. During the following days the British representative made repeated *démarches* to the Japanese Government making it clear that his government "could not approve of the use of the Settlement except for defensive purposes."[20]

Anglo-American co-operation was also in evidence in the sending of naval forces. Mr. Stimson learned on January 31 that the British were sending two more 8-inch gun cruisers with additional marines and that they had suggested that the United States do likewise. On the same day the cruiser *Houston* and the transport *Chaumont*, with the 31st Infantry aboard, were ordered from Manila to Shanghai, together with the remaining American destroyers, thus collecting at Shanghai the entire American Asiatic Squadron.

In Shanghai itself, the British and American consular authorities were co-operating in trying to arrange a truce. The British suggested that a neutral zone should be created to protect the International Settlement and received the consent of the United States for such a move. On February 2 Britain and America made joint representations to the Japanese and Chinese Governments, proposing the cessation of hostilities, the withdrawal of troops by both sides and the protection of the International Settlement by the establishment of neutral zones to divide the combatants. Upon acceptance of these conditions prompt advances were to be made in negotiations to settle all outstanding controversies between the two nations in the spirit of the Pact of Paris and the December 10th resolution of the League of Nations. The House of Commons was informed of these moves on February 2 by Sir John Simon[21] and the Council of the League was informed by the British delegate, Mr. James H. Thomas.

These proposals were accepted by the Chinese but rejected by the Japanese, mainly on the ground that the proposals unacceptably linked the Manchurian and Shanghai affairs. The Japanese Government, however, published a statement on February 7 giving assurances that they cherished "no political ambitions in the region of Shanghai nor any thoughts of encroaching on the rights and interests of any other Power."

At Geneva the serious situation in Shanghai was reflected in the tone of the Council discussions. Mr. J. H. Thomas found

[20] Stanley Baldwin in the House of Commons on February 9, 1932. Mr. Baldwin also said: "Our aim all the time is to bring about a peaceful settlement between the Japanese and the Chinese and to avoid embroiling ourselves on either side."
[21] *Parliamentary Debates,* House of Commons, Vol. 261, cols. 17-19.

it necessary on February 2 to declare: "His Majesty's Government in the United Kingdom feel it to be impossible that the present situation in the Far East should be allowed to continue. . . . War in everything but name is in progress. To such a state of things the Members of the League of Nations cannot be indifferent. If it is allowed to go on, the Covenant, the Pact of Paris and the Nine Power Treaty must inevitably lose the confidence of the world."[22] This was the strongest statement which had yet been made by a British representative in criticism of Japanese behavior.

The situation in Shanghai, however, grew more acute, and efforts by the ranking British naval officer, Admiral Kelly, to bring about a settlement proved unavailing.[23] In Geneva the Council met on February 9 and in an inconclusive meeting decided to delay the detailed discussion of the situation until they had received further information from the Consular Committee in Shanghai. It was after this meeting of the Council that the Chinese Government decided to ask for the immediate convening of a special session of the League Assembly to consider the Sino-Japanese conflict.

At this time, too, the American Government approached the British Government on the advisability of invoking the Nine Power Pact. On February 9, 1932, Mr. Stimson indicated to the British ambassador his views on such action. On February 11, 1932, at the suggestion of President Hoover, Mr. Stimson telephoned Sir John Simon at Geneva and, according to Mr. Stimson, suggested a joint invocation of Article VII of the Nine Power Treaty.[24] The actual events of the next few days have been a matter of bitter dispute and the persons intimately involved disagree as to exactly what happened. The best American account is that given by Mr. Stimson in his *Far Eastern Crisis* and the most authoritative British version is contained in Sir John Pratt's letter to the London *Times* in November 1938.

Mr. Stimson's account asserts that on the day following the

[22] *Official Journal*, League of Nations, March 1932, p. 350.
[23] For a first-hand account of events in Shanghai, see British Foreign Office, *Miscellaneous No. 4* (1932), *Reports to the League of Nations by the Committee of Representatives at Shanghai of certain States Members of the League Council appointed to report on Events in Shanghai, Shanghai, February 6 and 12, 1932.*
[24] "The Contracting Powers agree that whenever a situation arises which in the opinion of any one of them involves the application of the stipulation of the present Treaty, and renders desirable discussion of such application, there shall be full and frank communication between the Contracting Powers concerned."

first telephone call to Geneva, he again spoke to Sir John Simon at Geneva. Then, at the British Foreign Secretary's request, he cabled to him a proposed draft of such a joint statement and explained that the main purpose of the proposed draft was to make clear America's intention to live up to the covenants of the Nine Power Treaty respecting the future sovereignty and integrity of China. On February 13 and 15, according to Mr. Stimson's version, he again talked with Sir John, then in London. Although he received no explicit refusal to his suggestion, Mr. Stimson finally became convinced that the British Government felt reluctant to join in such a *démarche*. Therefore, he pressed it no further.

Sir John Pratt in his letter to the *Times* of November 10, 1938, denied that the British refused to "go along" with the Americans.

> In making this statement Mr. Stimson's memory has deceived him. The facts are that on receiving the draft of Mr. Stimson's proposed joint invocation the Foreign Office telegraphed to Geneva a paragraph containing the non-recognition doctrine and this paragraph was embodied in the declaration issued by the twelve members of the Council on February 16, 1932. At the same time a written answer was handed to the American Embassy for transmission to Mr. Stimson stating that the British Government was most anxious to co-operate with America in this matter and that, in view of their adherence to this declaration, it was hoped that those of the League Powers who were signatories to the Nine-Power Treaty might also associate themselves with the proposed joint invocation. The Foreign Office, so far from refusing to "go along" with Mr. Stimson, did all they possibly could to further his proposal. To obtain the concurrence of several Governments in a particular draft is, however, always a cumbersome and sometimes a lengthy process. It is not in general the kind of procedure that commends itself to the State Department and Mr. Stimson preferred to drop the idea of a joint invocation and turn his draft into the letter from himself to Mr. Borah of February 24, 1932.

Which version, if either, is correct, it is impossible to say. However there are other indications of what the British position was at this time. Thus, Sir John Simon in a detailed statement to the House of Commons on February 22 on the Shanghai situation said that the Government would direct its full influence in support of the moral authority of the League, and it was ready to offer its good offices to both nations, with both of which it was friendly. This attitude of impartiality was re-emphasized as the Foreign Secretary went on to say that the duty of the League was to hear both sides after collecting all the information, and it would be quite improper for anyone to attempt to pronounce a partial or interim judgment in a matter where everything depended on the report which would have to be made by the League being recognized on both sides as proceeding from a complete sense of impartiality.[25] Anthony Eden, speaking for the Government in the House of Commons on February 29, 1932, in response to questions as to whether Great Britain would send notes to Japan and China indicating Britain's determination to adhere to the non-recognition doctrine, evasively said,

> I do not think that a further note on this subject would, even if it were addressed to both parties . . . serve any useful purpose. His Majesty's Government have already made their position sufficiently clear and the Japanese Government have given definite assurances that they will uphold the principle of the Open Door.[26]

At Geneva the Council of the League quickly reacted to the increasingly acute situation in Shanghai. On February 16 the neutral members of the Council, hoping to dissuade Japan from authorizing the great attack upon Shanghai which was known to be impending, sent an urgent appeal to the Japanese Government. In this appeal Japan, for the first time, was clearly pointed out as the responsible party. Japan's obligations under Article X of the Covenant and under the Nine Power Treaty were recalled and an appeal to Japan "to recognize the obligations of her special position and of the confidence which the nations have placed in her as a partner in the organization and maintenance of peace" was made.[27]

The President of the Council, M. Paul-Boncour, said that the sending of the appeal to Japan was not to be taken as a judgment against Japan by them, and this was repeated by the representative of the British Empire, the Marquess of Londonderry, who declared: "that appeal contained no indictment; it embodied no judgment: it was an appeal to the strength and to the honor of Japan."[28] The appeal, however, did contain an affirmation of the doctrine of non-recognition. Article X of the Covenant was invoked as a basis for asserting that "no infringement of the territorial integrity and no change in the political independence of any Member of the League brought

[25] *Parliamentary Debates*, House of Commons, Vol. 262, cols. 178-83.
[26] *Ibid.*, Vol. 262, cols. 359-60.
[27] *Official Journal*, League of Nations, March 1932, p. 384.
[28] *Official Journal*, League of Nations, March 1932, p. 369.

about in disregard of this article ought to be valid and effectual by Members of the League."

Japan rejected the appeal in a reply dated February 23, 1932, and declared China to be the aggressor. The United States, however, chose that very day (February 23) to make public its position on the Sino-Japanese controversy. Mr. Stimson in a letter to Senator William E. Borah, chairman of the Committee on Foreign Relations of the United States Senate, maintained that the Washington Nine Power Treaty was still in force and applicable to the events in Manchuria and Shanghai and that this treaty and the other treaties drafted in the Washington Conference were "interrelated and interdependent." The American Secretary of State emphasized for the benefit of his British readers the part which Britain had played in the formulation of the open-door policy and in the work of the Washington Conference. Mr. Stimson also invoked the Pact of Paris as being applicable to the existing situation. The intention of the American Government to adhere to the policy of non-recognition was affirmed for the present and for the future.[29]

On February 29 the Council held its last meeting before the transfer of the Sino-Japanese controversy to the Assembly.[30] It had convened in order to examine the Shanghai situation in the light of new information which Sir John Simon would present to it. Sir John said that he had been informed that a meeting between commanders or representatives of the Chinese and Japanese forces had taken place on board the British flagship *Kent* in the presence of the British admiral, at which had been discussed a mutual and simultaneous withdrawal of both the Chinese and Japanese forces and the controlling of the evacuated area with neutral assistance. No definite agreement had been reached, but the proposal had been forwarded to the Chinese and Japanese Governments.[31]

The president of the Council then made certain proposals which needed acceptance by both the Chinese and the Japanese Governments and the co-operation of the other principal powers

[29] See U. S. Department of State, *Press Releases*, No. 126, February 27, 1932, for complete text.

[30] On February 19 the Council had passed a resolution in accordance with China's request, referring the dispute to the Assembly and calling for a special session of the Assembly to convene on March 3, 1932. The author has it from a high authority who was present that the British delegation tried to persuade the Chinese delegation not to request the transfer.

[31] *Official Journal*, League of Nations, March 1932, p. 917.

with special interests in the Shanghai settlement. A mixed conference of all the powers concerned was to take place for the purpose of bringing about a final conclusion of fighting and the restoration of peaceful conditions in the Shanghai area. The conference would be undertaken on the basis (a) that Japan had no political or territorial designs and no intention of establishing a Japanese settlement in Shanghai or of otherwise advancing the exclusive interests of the Japanese, and (b) that China entered the conference on the basis that the safety and integrity of the International and French Settlements must be preserved under arrangements which would secure these areas and their residents from danger. Finally, the meeting of this conference was to be subject to the making of local arrangements for a cessation of hostilities.

> The Council trusts that this will very speedily be brought about. It is proposed that the military, naval and civilian authorities of the other principal Powers represented in Shanghai will render all possible assistance in consolidating the arrangements.[32]

Sir John in expressing his approbation of the plan informed the Council that the United States approved of the plan and would co-operate.

> America is not a member of the League of Nations, but none the less I am happy to be able to announce here at a meeting of the Council of the League that I have been in close consultation with the United States and I am authorised to communicate the assurance of the United States that it is prepared to associate itself with the step which we are now taking and to instruct its representatives in the Shanghai area to co-operate with us who are Members of the League in the fullest measure in carrying out the proposals which the President has put before us and which I hope we are about to adopt.[33]

China and Japan accepted the proposals and a meeting between Chinese and Japanese delegates was arranged by the British, French and American ministers to China. The negotiations broke down, however, because the Japanese insisted upon the prior unconditional withdrawal of the Chinese troops. This was the final effort made by the Council to bring the hostilities to an end. Henceforth, the Assembly assumed the main burden of dealing with the Sino-Japanese controversy.

At the meeting of the Assembly on March 3 the Chinese dele-

[32] *Ibid.*, p. 918.
[33] *Ibid.*, p. 919.

gate, Dr. Yen, severely condemned the Japanese invasion and emphasized the failure of the Council to remedy the situation. He appealed to the Assembly to bring about the cessation of hostilities, the withdrawal of Japanese troops and the peaceful settlement of the entire Sino-Japanese controversy. Mr. Matsudaira, in defense of his country's actions, pleaded the disordered conditions of China and the prevalent anti-Japanese feeling in China. The whole problem was submitted to the "General Commission" of the Assembly, corresponding to a "Committee of the Whole" in American practice.

At the first meeting of the General Commission on March 4, there was some discussion as to whether or not active hostilities at Shanghai had ceased and also as to what steps should be taken for the final liquidation of the situation. A resolution was adopted calling for cessation of hostilities and recommending negotiations with neutral assistance for the conclusion of arrangements which should render definite the cessation of hostilities and regulate the withdrawal of Japanese forces. The Assembly, in a plenary session held the same afternoon, unanimously adopted this resolution.

The second meeting of the General Commission was held the next day, March 5. At this meeting the delegates from the smaller states like Norway, Sweden and Mexico lived up to China's expectation that they would urge stronger action in defense of League principles than had been advocated by the great powers. These expressions of opinion continued also in the meetings of the General Commission. On March 7, at the fourth meeting of the General Commission, Sir John Simon rose to speak in behalf of the great powers. He began by recognizing that the Far Eastern situation involved not only the restoration of peaceful conditions but also "nothing less than the utility in the case of a major dispute of the League of Nations." The League, he declared, was "an indispensable instrument for influencing international relations, and the preservation of its useful, authoritative influence is the best hope for the future of the world." However, as to what was practical for the League to do with regard to the controversy before it, Sir John maintained that its first duty was mediation. Involved in this mediation, he said, was the duty of effecting a settlement of the controversy, and to this end it was the first duty of the League to persist in pursuing the procedure of conciliation by every means in its power. However, although the time had not yet come to pronounce a judgment on the matters in controversy, the Assembly might make a declaration at once as to the measures by which the solution of the controversy should be sought.

> Should not we take this opportunity now solemnly to reaffirm the fundamental principles on which the League is based, and by which every signatory represented in this room is bound? Should we not declare afresh that the Covenant does not authorize a State, however well-founded its grievances against another State, to seek redress by methods other than the pacific methods set forth in Article XII of the Covenant? Should we not make reference afresh to the Pact of Paris which, together with the Covenant, is one of the pillars of the peace organization of the world? . . . Should not we make reference therefore to Article X of the Covenant?

Such a declaration, he said, would reassert the conditions under which every member was obliged to conduct relations with every other member. "It would be far better for the League to proclaim its principles, even though it failed to get them observed, than to forsake those principles by meaningless compromise." The propositions contained in Article X were ones which every member of the League was bound to accept without regard to the merits of the controversy. Changes brought about, not as a result of methods of conciliation and peaceful adjustment, but by means contrary to the Covenant, manifestly could not receive the approval of an Assembly of nations which existed for the very purpose of observing these obligations and upholding these principles.[34]

The discussion in the General Commission continued until March 8, when a Drafting Committee was appointed whose function it was to present propositions in formulated terms. A draft resolution was finally presented to the General Commission on March 11, which invoked the Covenant of the League of Nations and the Pact of Paris and declared that it was incumbent upon the members of the League not to recognize any situation, treaty or agreement which might be brought about by means contrary to these international agreements. The resolution also called for the setting up of a committee of nineteen members, including the neutral members of the Council, the president of the Assembly and six other members to be elected by the Assembly. This Committee of Nineteen was to report on the

[34] *Official Journal, Special Supplement*, No. 101, pp. 62-3.

cessation of hostilities and was to regulate the withdrawal of the Japanese forces, following the execution of the resolutions adopted by the Council on September 30 and December 10, 1931. The resolution was unanimously adopted by the General Commission and that afternoon the Assembly did likewise, with, however, Japan and China abstaining from voting.[35] Immediately following the adoption of the Resolution, the Committee of Nineteen was created. The six members which were elected by secret ballot were Switzerland, Czechoslovakia, Colombia, Portugal, Hungary and Sweden.

The United States promptly gave its full approval to the resolution. Furthermore, the secretary-general of the League was informed that the American Government had already authorized its representatives in Shanghai to assist, in co-operation with the representatives of the other powers, in the settlement of the situation at Shanghai.

Shanghai now became the center of diplomatic interest and activity. The Shanghai Conference, in pursuance of the Assembly's resolution of March 4, opened its negotiations for the cessation of hostilities on March 24. The situation seemed to be improving, since fighting had largely ceased and the Japanese forces were already in the process of being withdrawn. By March 30 the Conference was able to announce that an agreement had been reached for a definite cessation of hostilities, but the signing of a formal agreement did not come until May 5. The delay was due largely to the Japanese unwillingness to agree to the Chinese proposal that a definite time should be fixed for the complete withdrawal of the Japanese troops to within the International Settlement. An armistice agreement was reached after Sir Miles Lampson, who had been active in attempting to mediate the conflict, devised a formula acceptable to both parties. The substance of the agreement was reported to the Assembly on April 29 by the Committee of Nineteen, and a resolution approving it was adopted by the Assembly on

[35] Under the practice of the Assembly, a member abstaining from voting is counted simply as not present. The Chinese delegate did not vote because he had not yet received formal instructions from his government. He later informed the Assembly of his approval.

The author has it from the same high authority previously quoted that the Chinese delegation was led to believe by the representatives of the great powers that this non-recognition resolution was to be the first in a series of increasingly strong acts to be taken by the League in defense of China.

April 30. The agreement, which was signed on May 5, 1932 by the representatives of China and Japan in the presence of diplomatic representatives of Great Britain, the United States, France and Italy, rendered definite the cessation of hostilities and the withdrawal of the Japanese forces. A joint commission, including members representing the four participating friendly powers, was provided for to "certify the mutual withdrawal." This commission was also to collaborate in arranging for the transfer of territory from the evacuating Japanese forces to the incoming Chinese police. The "Shanghai War" had come to an end.

In the period following the cessation of hostilities in the region of Shanghai, events in Manchuria and the work of the Lytton Commission took the center of the stage. In February the new "state" of Manchukuo had come into existence and on March 9, 1932, the Manchu boy-emperor Pu Yi became head of the new regime, with Japanese approval and support. In a note of March 12, the new state unsuccessfully asked the nations for recognition. Sir John Simon told the House of Commons on March 14 that such recognitions "would be premature."[36] In June 1932, the government of Manchukuo seized control of the customs and salt revenues, a move of obvious importance both to China and to foreign creditors of China since Manchuria had normally supplied one-third of the total customs revenue. At Harbin and elsewhere the British commissioners of customs were intimidated and forced from their offices by Manchukuo police. In September the Japanese Government formally recognized Manchukuo.

In the meantime the commission of five headed by Lord Lytton, which had been set up in January 1932 in accordance with the Council's December 10th resolution, was carrying out its duties. This commission had visited China, Japan and Manchuria and finally in October 1932 issued a voluminous report.[37] The report contained not only information on the situation in China and Manchuria but also made certain recommendations. It proposed that Manchuria should be given autonomy under Chinese sovereignty and that new Sino-Japanese treaties should safeguard the rights of both parties. It did not directly consider

[36] *Parliamentary Debates,* House of Commons, Vol. 263, March 14, 1932, col. 10.
[37] In July 1932 the Assembly granted the commission of inquiry an extension of time for the submission of its report.

the question whether Japan had violated existing treaties and did not recommend sanctions or any other coercion against Japan. The report was a thoroughgoing document, but Japan, as had been expected, refused to accept the report as a basis for a settlement.

The Lytton Report, as the report came to be known, came up for consideration by the Council on November 21, 1932. In the discussions which followed it soon became evident that there was little hope for any measure of agreement between China and Japan on the recommendations made in the report—the main bone of contention being the status of Manchuria. The Council on November 28 decided to transmit the report to the Assembly, and henceforth the Council ceased to play an active part in the consideration of the Sino-Japanese controversy.

On December 6, 1932, the Assembly began its discussions of the Lytton Report. The small states like Sweden, Norway, the Irish Free State and Czechoslovakia supported the report, stressing the necessity of upholding the principles of the Covenant and denouncing Japan's actions in Manchuria. The great powers were considerably more restrained. France, through its representative M. Paul-Boncour, praised the report as being able and impartial, but suggested only that it should be made the "center and pivot" of the Assembly discussions and that heed should be paid to its conclusions. Sir John Simon praised the Lytton Report because it made a "measured criticism" of both China and Japan. Without referring to the conclusions which were condemnatory of Japan's actions, he proceeded to call attention to those portions of the report that tended to cast discredit upon conditions in China or upon Chinese actions such as anti-foreign propaganda and the boycott. Sir John then stressed the necessity of being concerned with "realities" and indicated that a restoration of the *status quo ante* was no solution. Neither side he said, accepted the report in its entirety and both had something to concede. The principles of the League must be upheld and conciliation must be promoted. If direct negotiations gave promise of good results, they should be encouraged by all means. The League, he affirmed, might be able to assist in the work of conciliation and the Committee of Nineteen would, he thought, be much more effective for this purpose if means could be found to add to it representatives of the United States and Russia.³⁸ In light of the actual findings of the Lytton Commission, Sir John's speech was definitely pro-Japanese.³⁹ Italy and Germany followed the lead of Great Britain.

The outcome of the discussions at this time was a resolution adopted by the Assembly on December 9, 1932, calling upon the Committee of Nineteen to study the report and submit proposals to the Assembly. The Committee was unsuccessful in its attempts at conciliation because of Japan's objections to the participation of the United States and Russia and her insistence on recognition of the independence of Manchukuo. Considering all further efforts futile, the Committee prepared a draft of the report which the Assembly would be called upon to make under paragraph 4 of Article XV of the Covenant.

The draft of the report was finished by the Committee of Nineteen and circularized to the Members of the Assembly on February 16, 1933. The report was divided into four parts. The first accepted the findings of the Lytton Commission. Part II traced the course of the controversy before the Council and Assembly without any attempt to apportion blame or responsibility. Part III consisted of estimates of the character and significance of the events recorded in Part II. In this section, China's claim to Manchuria was upheld; the issues pending between China and Japan were declared to be capable of settlement by arbitral procedure, and the responsibility for the development of events after September 1931 was placed entirely on Japan. The final part made certain specific recommendations for the permanent settlement of the situation based on three general propositions: (1) "The settlement of the dispute should observe the provisions of the Covenant of the League, the Pact of Paris, and the Nine Power Treaty of Washington." (2) "The Settlement of the dispute should observe the provisions of Parts I and II of the Assembly Resolution of March 11, 1932." (3) "In order that a lasting understanding may be established between China and Japan on the basis of respect for the international undertakings mentioned above, the settlement of the dispute must conform to the principles and conditions laid down by

³⁸ *Official Journal, Special Supplement*, No. 110, p. 51.
³⁹ The *Manchester Guardian*, of December 8, 1932, reported that Mr. Matsuoka, the Japanese representative, remarked that Sir John Simon had said in half an hour, in a few well-chosen phrases, what he (Matsuoka) had been trying to say in his bad English for the last ten days.

the Commission of Enquiry." The most important specific recommendation was that the regime in Manchuria was not to be recognized by members of the League either *de jure* or *de facto*.[40]

The report came before the Assembly for its consideration on February 24, 1933. Dr. Yen accepted it for China, while Mr. Matsuoka rejected it for Japan. The report was unanimously adopted.[41] Mr. Matsuoka, after a brief declaration, withdrew with his entire delegation from the Assembly and on March 27, 1933, the Japanese Government gave notice of its intention to withdraw from the League. The League had suffered a blow from which it was never wholly to recover.

The pros and cons of British policy during this period have been a subject of much discussion, often bitter and recriminatory. Among those who have defended British policy, some have pointed to the critical world situation and to the political and economic crisis in Great Britain. Others have stressed the desirability of keeping Japan's friendship in case of another outburst of anti-foreign sentiment in China, or in case of Russia's becoming stronger and more influential in the Far East. Some have pointed to the historically predominant position of Japan in Manchuria, and nearly all have maintained that Britain could not rely on the United States for more than moral support. Others have attacked British policy either as weakening the League of Nations, or deserting the Chinese, or failing to bring about Anglo-American co-operation. These have argued that the Conservative Party was pro-Japanese and more concerned with the defense of material and immediate interests than with upholding Britain's obligations.

The debate still goes on. It can be definitely said, however, that whatever were the motives of British policy, Britain's actions during this period were on the whole favorable to Japan rather than to China. Furthermore, Britain acted more vigorously and promptly when Shanghai, the center of British interests, was attacked than when Manchuria, in which she had substantial but relatively less important interests, was invaded.

[40] *Official Journal, Special Supplement*, No. 112, pp. 73-5.
[41] Siam abstained from voting and therefore was considered not present. Japan's negative vote did not count as such because Japan was a party to the dispute.

CHAPTER III

FROM 1933 TO THE LEITH-ROSS MISSION

In the period after the subsiding of the Manchurian crisis, Great Britain's foreign policy had to reckon with an increasingly complicated and turbulent world situation. On January 30th, 1933, Adolf Hitler became German Chancellor. Diplomatic crises which in a few years became almost the "normal" situation were multiplied. The World Economic Conference met in 1933 and failed to offer any substantial relief to help the nations out of the depression. In 1934 France and Spain were rocked by internal political crises; Germany went through the purge of June 30; the Austrian Premier Dollfuss was assassinated in a Nazi putsch that failed, six months after Dollfuss had put down a last-stand uprising of the Vienna socialists. On the other hand the entry of the U.S.S.R. into the League of Nations offset the departures of Japan and Germany, and the Franco-Soviet pact offered a certain measure of stability. Finally, the constitutional crisis in India continued in 1933-4. Hence it is perhaps easy to understand why during 1933 and 1934 Great Britain continued her policy of maintaining friendly relations with Japan. Her prestige in China, which had fallen during 1931 and 1932 as a result of her attitude on Manchuria remained low, and her policy toward China in 1933 was characterized by its inactivity.[1]

[1] Britain's chief diplomatic activity during 1933 was the renewal of the Shanghai Provisional Court Agreement of 1930.

The Shanghai Special District Court and its appellate division, the Second Branch Kiangsu High Court, which had been established in 1930 to replace the unsatisfactory Provisional Court, were incorporated by 1933 into the judicial system of China as regular Chinese courts, preserving, however, considerable foreign control. The Municipal Council of the International Settlement shared in the appointment and dismissal of the judicial police, and the initiation and prosecution in criminal proceedings were assumed largely by the Municipal Police and the Municipal Advocate, foreign head of the Council's Legal Department. Since the Nanking Government and the foreign authorities were satisfied with this arrangement, the 1930 agreement was renewed for three years on February 8, 1933. The foreign powers concerned—Great Britain, France, United States of America, Brazil, Norway, and the Netherlands—exchanged notes with China, and the latter undertook to check undue delay in civil proceedings.

44   BRITISH RELATIONS WITH CHINA: 1931-1939

This inactivity contrasted sharply with the positive policy of Japan. Ignoring the moral censure of the League of Nations and the United States, Japan followed up the seizure of Manchuria with an advance into Jehol. On May 31, 1933, the Chinese signed the humiliating Tangku Truce. This capitulation carried Japanese power even beyond Jehol. It provided for the withdrawal of Chinese forces from virtually all of Hopei province north of Peiping and Tientsin, and also effectively added several thousand square miles north of the Great Wall to Manchukuo, while leaving Japanese garrisons within the so-called demilitarized zone. Japanese "co-operation" in China's internal affairs loomed as an imminent possibility. In March 1933 pro-Japanese Wang Ching-wei had become president of the Executive Yuan; the boycott of Japanese goods was at a low ebb, and by 1934 Japanese ships resumed their activities on the Upper Yangtze River.[2]

These developments, however, did not yet constitute a direct or immediate threat to British interests and did not effect any change in her policy.

The Amau Declaration

This attitude of *laissez-faire* was best illustrated by the British reaction to the Amau Declaration of April 17, 1934, which announced to the entire world the extent of Japan's aims in China.

Earlier, on January 22, 1934, in his annual review to the Diet of Japan's foreign relations, Foreign Minister Hirota emphasized the sole responsibility of Japan for the "maintenance of peace" in East Asia. However, the restrained and amicable manner with which he referred to Japan's relations with the great powers ("Japan's traditional amity with the British Empire remains unshaken even to these times") smoothed over his claim of a right to independent action in the affairs of China, and it passed almost without foreign comment.

On the other hand, the statement to the press of Mr. Amau, spokesman of the Japanese Foreign Office, aroused great interest and concern in the world's leading capitals. Although subsequent attempts were made to gloss over the April 17 declaration, it was never officially repudiated or retracted. A week before this, Mr. Amau had told the press that his department was anxious that foreigners should know that Japan was abso-

[2] Japanese shipping on the Upper Yangtze River had been suspended since 1931.

lutely opposed to foreign interference in China and to any plans of international co-operation with China. This *démarche*, which attracted little notice abroad, was followed on April 17 by a further statement to the press reiterating Japan's "special position" in her relations with China and emphasizing that no country but China was

in a position to share with Japan the responsibility for the maintenance of peace in East Asia. Any joint operations undertaken by foreign Powers, even in the name of technical or financial assistance, at this particular moment after the Manchurian and Shanghai Incidents are bound to acquire political significance . . . and . . . would have the most serious repercussions upon Japan and East Asia.

Japan, therefore, must object to such undertakings as a matter of principle, although she will not find it necessary to interfere with any foreign country negotiating individually with China on questions of finance and trade, as long as such negotiations benefit China and are not detrimental to peace in East Asia.

However, supplying China with war aeroplanes, building aerodromes in China, and detailing military instructors or military advisers to China, or contracting a loan to provide funds for political uses, would obviously tend to alienate the friendly relations between Japan, China and other countries and to disturb peace and order in Eastern Asia. Japan will oppose such projects.[3]

The Japanese Foreign Office, in an effort to allay the stir these statements evoked among the Nine Power Treaty signatories, insisted that the Declaration was merely an amplification of Mr. Hirota's speech in the Diet in January. Mr. Amau, however, on the following day not only reiterated his statement that it rested with Japan to determine whether foreign aid to China was or was not of a nature to imperil peace and order, but also insisted that the Japanese attitude was not in conflict with any treaties—treaties being susceptible to various interpretations.[4] According to the Rengo News Agency, then one of the two chief Japanese news agencies, Japan would not object to assistance to China of a cultural or non-political character financed by remitted Boxer Indemnity funds, or to other economic arrangements which might be free from political import.[5]

These statements created a stir on the surface but no deep

[3] For an authoritative version of the Amau Declaration, see statement made by Sir John Simon in House of Commons on April 23, 1934, *Parliamentary Debates*, Vol. 288, cols. 1368-9.
[4] The various Japanese statements can be found in the London *Times*, April 23-6 inclusive.
[5] This statement was later described as "unauthorized."

concern in Great Britain. When, on April 23, Sir John Simon was asked in the House of Commons whether the Foreign Office had received notification of Japan's intention to redefine her policy in the Far East with the object of claiming a controlling voice, he replied that he had received no such intimation. As for the Amau Declaration, he said, it had apparently been inspired by "an apprehension of certain dangers to peace, to good relations between China and Japan, or to the integrity of China which might follow from certain action by other Powers in China. None of these dangers is to be apprehended from the policy of His Majesty's Government which aims in fact at avoiding them." Nevertheless, because of the broad nature of the Amau Statement, the British Government, he said, would make its position clear to Japan.[6] On April 30, the Foreign Secretary outlined for the House of Commons the steps which the British Government had officially taken. Sir Francis Lindley, the British Ambassador to Tokyo, had called on Mr. Hirota to make a "friendly inquiry" and to remind him of China's position and of British rights as guaranteed by the Nine Power Treaty. Since Japan's anxiety regarding China, expressed in the April 17 statement, could not apply to Great Britain, whose aim was to avoid dangers to the peace and integrity of China, the British Government could not admit the right of Japan alone to decide whether any particular action, such as the provision of technical and financial assistance, promoted such danger. The British Government assumed that Japan did not intend to infringe upon the common rights of the other powers in China or upon Japan's own treaty obligations, but was merely exercising her right, under articles 1 and 7 of the Nine Power Pact, to call the attention of the signatories to any action in China inimical to her security.[7] Mr. Hirota's reply of May 1 was taken to indicate that the British Government had been correct in that assumption, for it gave assurances of Japan's observance of the provisions of the Nine Power Pact and of her adherence to the "open-door" principle.

The London *Times*, which had refrained from comment on the Amau Declaration until April 26, also indicated a willingness to put the best light on Japanese policy. "The latest development at Tokyo suggests that to condemn Japanese policy

---

[6] *Parliamentary Debates*, House of Commons, Vol. 288, cols. 1366-7.
[7] *Ibid.*, Vol. 289, cols. 13-14.

towards China unheard is just as premature as to applaud it
. . . there is every desire to remain on the best of terms with
our old Ally and to assist the growth of peace and order in China.
. . . The Japanese Government seem now to wish to allay the
anxieties which their spokesmen have aroused. Surely they can
best achieve this end, and obtain a hearing for their views on
Chinese affairs, by cooperation rather than friction with other
civilized nations."[8]

The British position reflected the strong desire of the Government to maintain cordial political relations with Japan, as long as Japan's China policy and her attitude toward the naval treaties did not force a shift in British policy.

Oil Monopoly in Manchukuo

The establishment of an oil monopoly in Manchukuo in 1934 clearly implied what Japanese domination of China would mean to British interests. While Western adherence to the non-recognition doctrine did not result in trade discrimination against the nationals of the non-recognizing powers during 1932 and 1933, in 1934 Manchukuo established state regulation over various industries, specifically oil, coal, gold and steel production, of which oil was of most importance to the British. In March of the same year, the Manchuria Petroleum Company, capitalized at ¥5,000,000, was established by a decree issued by the Government of Manchukuo.[9] The open-door principle was evaded by making no shares available to foreign companies.

In the summer of 1934 Great Britain, the United States and the Netherlands, aroused by rumors of the intention of the Manchukuo Government to enforce an oil monopoly, protested informally to the Japanese and Manchukuo Governments. They asserted that the note of March 12, 1932, in which the Govern-

[8] London *Times,* April 26, 1934. The Amau Declaration was perhaps not intended to apply to Great Britain, but rather to the United States and the League of Nations. The Declaration itself omitted from interference by Japan "any foreign country negotiating individually with China on questions of finance and trade, as long as such negotiations are not detrimental to peace in East Asia"; and in the listing of activities which would tend to disturb peace and order in East Asia, the type of British activities in China at this time—participation in China's economic reconstruction by use of the Boxer Indemnity Funds and the sending of a naval mission—were not mentioned. This perhaps lends added significance to the previously quoted statement of the Rengo News Agency.

[9] The Manchukuo Government subscribed 1,000,000, the South Manchuria Railway Company, 2,000,000, and the Nippon Oil, Ogura Oil, and the Mitsui and Mitsubishi interests 500,000 each.

ment of Manchukuo had invited the recognition of the foreign powers, had given assurance that the principle of the open door would be observed with regard to economic activities. This admission that the continuance of the open door did not depend on recognition had been repeated on several later occasions. The Japanese Foreign Office in its reply to these protests disclaimed any responsibility for the acts of the Manchukuo Government. Nevertheless, it maintained that, while the purport of the decree was to make the sale of oil a government monopoly, it by no means intended to monopolize the manufacture and the import and export of oil. The articles of incorporation of the company had not excluded foreign participation and, moreover, the Manchukuo Government really had no intentions of enforcing even a monopolization of sales. The Manchukuo Government, however, replied to the above protests on October 30, 1934, by issuing a statement announcing its decision to enforce a monopoly of the sale of oils in Manchukuo. Simultaneously the detailed organization of the Manchuria Petroleum Company was published. This was followed by the promulgation of an ordinance on November 13, 1934, which was to go into force in April 1935, making the sale of oil a government monopoly, and requiring government permission for its importation and exportation.

The potential loss to the British and American interests involved was considerable. In 1933 the Asiatic Petroleum Company, a British concern, had supplied nearly a third of the 700,000 barrels imported during that year. British and American interests had controlled approximately 80 per cent of the retail trade and, as a result of the new laws, faced the loss of their distribution facilities. In the House of Commons on April 29, 1935, the British Secretary of State for Foreign Affairs, Sir John Simon, outlined the notes which had been exchanged by Japan and Great Britain since November 1934 and took the Japanese Government to task for its failure to use "their undoubted authority to ensure the fulfillment of assurances given by themselves and by the Manchurian authorities regarding the maintenance of the principle of the Open Door in Manchuria and the fulfillment of Treaty obligations." A new note, he said, had been dispatched to the Japanese Government reminding it of its responsibility for losses to British interests resulting from the oil monopoly.[10] The Japanese were not deterred by the protests and the oil monopoly went into effect.

The passage of the Japanese Petroleum Industry Law in June 1934 received more attention than the Manchurian situation and helped to arouse concern over Manchuria as well as over Japan. It came into effect on July 1. Foreign oil companies in Japan, Dairen and Korea were now to maintain in stock an amount equal to one-half of their annual imports of each item during the previous year and such stocks were to be sold to the Japanese Government at its own price in case of emergency. Refineries were required to have the necessary equipment to manufacture a minimum of some 300,000 barrels. At the same time the Japanese Government was given price-fixing powers, depriving the companies of any security as to future sales. Oil production, refining and importation were all made subject to government license. Quota limitations were placed upon petroleum imports. The foreign companies objected to these regulations, and ineffective protests on their behalf were made by the American, British and Netherlands Governments.[11]

The oil monopoly laws in Manchukuo and Japan were a clue to the future of foreign interests in a Japanese-dominated China and a blow to those who held that the maintenance of British interests was compatible with Japanese rule. It was with this as a background that Britain viewed Japan's North China policy during 1935.

Japan in China, 1935

In 1935 Japanese and Manchukuoan forces advanced into the demilitarized zone between Chahar and Jehol and by May were south of the Great Wall. In May and June, Japanese military authorities in North China demanded the suppression of anti-Japanese activities, abolition of the Peiping Political Council, disbandment of the Kuomintang branches in Hopei and of the Blue Shirt organization, and the withdrawal of the Nanking Government from the Peiping and Tientsin areas. By the Ho-Umetsu Agreement of July 1935 Nanking accepted these de-

[10] *Parliamentary Debates*, House of Commons, Vol. 301, April 29, 1935, cols. 5-8.

[11] The *Economist* of November 3, 1934, commented as follows: "Are American, Dutch and British oil companies really to pay through the nose in order to provide facilities for the Japanese Navy to operate against the Philippines or Netherlands Indies or British Malaya in the event of war?"

mands. A Japanese dominated North China in the immediate future thus loomed as a threat to British interest in China.

Their anxiety was increased by Nanking's further concessions to Tokyo. Chiang Kai-shek had personal interviews with Japanese diplomatic and military officials in January 1935 (for the first time since 1931), and on June 10, 1935 the Chinese Government, in accordance with the Ho-Umetsu Agreement, felt compelled to promulgate the "Good-Will Mandate," a blanket injunction forbidding anti-Japanese activities.[12] Lin Yu-tang described this summer of 1935 as "the darkest period of China's political history."[13] In Great Britain this was taken to indicate that, voluntarily or involuntarily, Nanking itself was becoming the instrument of Japan.

The fears aroused by Japan's China policy were increased by her denunciation of the Washington and London Naval Treaties in December 1934. The *Round Table*, in a remarkably farsighted analysis, wrote:

> If she denounces or ignores the Washington Naval Treaty, she will be free to build what ships she likes and will be rid of the prohibition against fortifying or creating naval bases in the Pacific islands as provided by Article 19 of the treaty. If she denounces or ignores the Nine-Power Treaty relating to China as well, she will be free from her international obligations to respect the integrity of China, and to maintain therein the open door for the trade and commerce of all nations—a principle already impaired by the Manchoukuo affair. She will then be able to carry out that policy of indirect control in China which was recently outlined by Japanese official spokesmen in a number of capitals, in accordance with which those who want to trade in China will have to negotiate in Tokyo and not in Nanking. She will further be able to lease a naval base in the south of China (as European nations have done in the past) and to squeeze British trade out of the Yangtze valley if Great Britain opposes her desires. Finally, if she ignores her obligation not to fortify bases in the mandated Caroline and Marshall Islands, which she took over from Germany at the end of the war, she can acquire submarine and possibly fleet bases just north of the equator, next door to Borneo and the Australian territory of New Guinea, and between the Philippines and Hawaii. If she can do all these things with impunity, she will obviously both have closed the back door to the Far East and nullified the collective system established for that area at Washington in 1922, and she will have done so in the most effective way, not only by having the power to defend her own interests but by being able to menace Hawaii and Singapore.[14]

[12] The complete texts of the Ho-Umetsu Agreement and the "Good-Will Mandate" can be found in T. A. Bisson, *Japan in China*, pp. 55-8.
[13] Lin Yu-tang, "China Prepares to Resist," *Foreign Affairs*, April 1939.
[14] "Power Politics in the Pacific," *Round Table*, December 1934, pp. 8-9.

The visit of the Japanese naval training squadron to Germany in the summer of 1934 and their hearty welcome by Hitler was another portent of possible future developments.

The Silver Question in China

Another source of the concern aroused in Great Britain by Japan's foreign policy was the fear that China's economic difficulties would make her incapable of withstanding Japanese pressure. Since Nanking's financial stability and economic strength seemed to depend on silver, the silver question was of key importance.

The existence of a currency depreciating with the price of silver had enabled China to mitigate the effects of the depression for two years. Great Britain had gone off the gold standard in September 1931, and Japan had followed in December. Silver began to rise in terms of sterling, of the rupee, and of the yen (and of the dollar after the United States left the gold standard in 1933). The silver agreement of July 1933,[15] made in accordance with the unanimous recommendation of the World Economic Conference, was ratified by the United States in December, and in the following June the Silver Purchase Act was passed. In August, as the American Government began to purchase silver from abroad, the price of silver rose sharply and the flow of silver from China increased.[16]

The American action accentuated an already existing trend. More important and basic in accounting for the outflow of silver were the decrease in China's foreign trade and the reduction of her income from emigrant remittances. China's imports fell from Ch.$ 2,233,000,000 in 1931 to Ch.$ 1,030,000,000 in 1934, while exports declined from Ch.$ 1,417,000,000 to Ch.$ 535,000,000. China's foreign trade was financed largely by foreign banks. With the decrease in foreign trade, there was a shrinkage in the demand for commercial credits and correspondingly less need of silver holdings as reserves against these credits. The banks, therefore, began to dispose of their holdings, which were

[15] The signatories were Australia, Canada, China, India, Mexico, Peru, Spain and the United States.
[16] The outflow of silver from China began in 1932 before the American silver purchase policy. In 1932 China experienced a net export of 10 million, in 1933, 14 million, and in 1934, 257 million. This coincided with a steady shrinkage in China's foreign trade.

in the form of forward contract purchases and physical silver holdings. The American silver policy gave them the opportunity of selling their physical holdings in a favorable market in exchange for foreign currencies which could always be used to repurchase silver.[17] America's buying of silver at the very time that the foreign banks in China were disposing of it actually served to prevent a slump in the silver market.

The other important factor responsible for the outflow of silver was the decrease in emigrant remittances from approximately Ch.$ 360,000,000 in 1931 to about Ch.$ 250,000,000 in 1934.[18]

The Chinese Government, though concerned over the rapid outflow of silver, delayed action until September 9, 1934, when the Ministry of Finance took interim action limiting purchases and sales of foreign exchange to normal business requirements for contracts entered into on or before September 8, 1934, and for traveling or other personal requirements. The decree was ineffective. On September 23, 1934, a communication was sent to the American Government, seeking a change in the policy of the United States. The American reply, though cordial and appreciative of China's difficulties, did not promise any cessation of the silver purchase program. The Chinese Government, desirous of preventing a further fall in internal commodity prices, announced on October 14, 1934, an increase in the tax on the export of silver and variable equalization charges equal to the difference between the theoretical parity of London silver and the rate of exchange fixed by the Central Bank of China.[19] No longer was the external value of the Chinese currency exclusively linked to the price of silver. China's exchange was brought down to 15s. 3½d., as compared with a bullion value of about 15s. 8d. The increasing disparity between the London silver price and the Shanghai exchange rate of the Chinese dollar would have made the export of silver profitable during the months of April to October 1935, but a "gentleman's agree-

---

[17] Silver stocks in the foreign banks in Shanghai declined from Ch.$ 275,660,000 in 1933 to Ch.$ 54,672,000 in 1934.

[18] This figure includes remittances from Manchuria.

[19] An *ad valorem* duty amounting to 7¾ per cent on silver dollars and mint bars (10 per cent less 2¼ per cent minting charges) and 10 per cent on other forms of silver (in lieu of the then 2¼ per cent effective since April 6, 1933) was imposed.

ment" between the National Government and the banks, foreign and Chinese, stopped the legal export of silver.

Shanghai, center of British interests, was seriously affected. The increase in the supply of silver stocks and silver's favorable position between 1931 and 1933 had enabled the maintenance of an artificial prosperity, which collapsed in 1934. Many lending concerns, banks, trust companies, real estate companies and individuals found themselves with loans secured by real estate for which there was no market. Business reorganizations and failures in Shanghai rose sharply. The monthly average of reorganizations in 1933 was 5.08, by 1934 it was 107.50, and for the first six months of 1935, 155.17. The monthly average number of failures was 17.83, 30.50 and 41.67 for 1933, 1934, and 1935, respectively. The number of new buildings constructed in the International Settlement fell from 8,699 in 1931 to 4,571 in 1934, while the assessed value of these buildings fell from Ch.$ 64,466,532 to $27,600,350. The general index of wholesale prices in Shanghai (1926=100) declined from 126.7 in 1931 to 97.1 in 1934. The foreign trade of Shanghai amounted to Ch.$ 1,428,510,650 in 1931; in 1934 it was Ch.$ 868,385,264. The Shanghai Stock Exchange did 10,650,892 shares of business during the first half of 1934 compared with 4,429,710 shares during the first half of 1933, but this increase was due to intense speculation caused by the rise in rubber shares and increasing uncertainty over the future of Chinese currency.

The British colony of Hongkong was experiencing an even more serious crisis than Shanghai. A continuous decline in trade was accompanied by a fall in the price of shares.[20] Moreover, Hongkong, still adhering to the silver standard, was seriously out of equilibrium with China, to which she had always been tied. Shanghai's acute shortage of money was making it difficult to obtain funds even at 20 per cent and to remit one hundred dollars to Hongkong in Hongkong currency was costing Shanghai $124. This disparity in exchange interfered with Hongkong's *entrepôt* trade between North and South China. In May 1935 the official rate of exchange of the Hongkong dollar rose from 2s. 1¾d. to 2s. 6d., with business done at 2s. 7d. A year earlier

[20] With the exception of the Hongkong & Shanghai Banking Corporation and the leading insurance companies. For the twelve months ending March 31, 1934, imports were Hk.$ 463.9 million as compared with Hk.$ 586.1 million for the previous year, while exports dropped from Hk.$ 450.2 million to Hk.$ 357.2 million.

it had been 1s. 4¾d. Since the Chinese dollar was out of all relation with the Hongkong dollar (which stood at 54—a premium of between 40 and 50 per cent), Canton buyers sought their requirements in Shanghai rather than in Hongkong and were relying more upon internal products or upon those of Japan. The importance of maintaining Hongkong's *entrepôt* trade was indicated by the report of the Economic Commission appointed by the governor of Hongkong in June 1934 to study the economic situation. It inquired into the causes of the trade depression and concluded that Hongkong's *raison d'être* was the *entrepôt* trade of South China. The Commission therefore opposed any departure from free trade, although they did favor coming to an understanding with China which would enable Hongkong to have free preferential entry into China in respect of goods manufactured within the Colony. Nothing concrete, however, was done at this time to alleviate the situation.

Anglo-American versus Anglo-Japanese Co-operation

In Great Britain unofficial debate of British policy at this time largely centered around Anglo-American versus Anglo-Japanese co-operation.[21] At a discussion held at the Royal Institute of International Affairs in the summer of 1934 both positions were presented. Professor G. C. Allen urged a friendly and sympathetic attitude and policy toward Japan on the ground that the prosperity of both countries rested on greater freedom of international trade. Mr. C. V. Sale, chairman of the Japan Society, maintained that the future of British trade and industry would greatly depend on the extent to which Great Britain could co-operate with Japan in raising the standard of living in the densely populated regions of the East. He described the lapse of the Anglo-Japanese Alliance in 1922 as "a calamity for both nations and for the peace of the world" and claimed that it had driven Japan into isolation. Professor Zimmern, one of the leading advocates of Anglo-American co-operation, retorted that the end of the Anglo-Japanese Alliance did not drive Japan into isolation. On the contrary, it had resulted in "the concert of

[21] The Anglo-American groups usually were also pro-League of Nations, though emphasis was placed on the desirability of acting with the United States rather than on the necessity of acting through the League of Nations. Discussion on the Far East fell under these two headings, but two separate and distinct schools of thought consciously debating the issue did not exist as such.

Four Powers," and it was the breach of the Washington Treaties by Japan which had brought about her isolation.[22]

The *Round Table* also entered the discussion. The issue of June 1934 pointed out the fundamental changes which had taken place in the relations between the Western Powers and China and discussed past, present and possible future British policy. It pointed out that the old questions of extraterritoriality and the status of Shanghai had disappeared from the forefront of the scene. Now it was "growing more likely that the ultimate loss by the westerners of their privileges will come rather from Japanese than from Chinese pressure."[23] This did not mean, however, that a policy of resistance to Japan was advocated. Instead international co-operation including Japan was urged as the most desirable means of developing China's potentialities as a market for British goods and as a field for capital investment. In the Amau Declaration, the author of this article found, not a bar to securing Japanese co-operation for such a scheme, but rather the suggestion that her participation with other countries was possible.

Another *Round Table* article clearly and unequivocally advocated Anglo-American co-operation. It held that Britain was unable to stop Japan by unilateral action since she could not make her power effective beyond the Straits in the Far East. Her Yangtze trade and Hongkong were "hostages in the hands of Japan." The central question, therefore, which is being asked in the Far East today is "will the United States and Great Britain stand together?" Such a combination could, especially with Russian support, "easily frustrate Japan's larger ambitions," though Japan and her home waters could not be attacked or entered. In the United States, however, isolationist sentiment was stronger than ever and Great Britain, increasingly pre-occupied with Europe, could not act in the Far East except in concert with the United States "and after the experience of the last fifteen years she has lost confidence that the United States will enter into any specific obligation or will take action rapidly and decisively." This explained why "the present British Government has never been at pains to conceal from Japan that it was not really so very hostile to the Manchoukuo

---

[22] G. C. Allen, "The Political and Economic Position of Japan," *International Affairs*, July-August 1934.
[23] "China and the World Depression," *Round Table,* June 1934, p. 535.

adventure, that it does not wish to join in any combination against her and that, if possible, it is anxious to be friends with her. . . . The British Foreign Office, convinced that no definite obligation will be undertaken by the United States, has not varied from its determination not to form part of an Anglo-American front against Japan even though it is Japan who is proposing to tear up the Washington Treaties." There was, however, "clearly no passable road in the direction of a special understanding with Japan," for this could only be bought at the price of the destruction of the Washington principles, China's integrity and the Open Door. Such action would be unfavorably received in the United States and in the Commonwealth, as well as hurt British prestige throughout the world. "Great Britain cannot embark upon any active policy which may induce Japan to use force by herself, beyond the line Singapore-Borneo-New Guinea-New Zealand."[24]

As usual, the *Economist* was pro-League and pro-American, but, at the same time, it stressed the fact that the economic development of China presented "the greatest opportunity ever offered for international collaboration." While it opposed granting "Japan a free hand to exploit for her own benefit the resources of China," it did favor an understanding with Japan through the League of Nations.[25]

The arguments of the pro-American group were strengthened by Japan's denunciation of the naval treaties. Lord Lothian warned that war might result from the failure of the Washington signatories to act together if it enabled the Japanese military party to fulfill its ambitions. As for the belief held by some that Great Britain should come to terms with Japan, the country "best able to damage her vital interests in the Far East," Lothian held the view that such was "a feeble and delusive policy." The only condition upon which Japan would guarantee British interests and possessions in the Far East would be a condition which would reduce Great Britain to dependence on Japan. Britain should not repeat the "mistake" of 1932, of driving the United States back into isolation, for "together we can succeed; divided we are each impotent." More concretely he suggested a policy of actively supporting and assisting China. Although he claimed to be in no way hostile to Japan and expressed the belief that

[24] "Power Politics in the Pacific," *Round Table,* December 1934, pp. 10-15.
[25] *Economist,* May 19, 1934.

Japan ought to have a predominant influence in the Far East, he added the basic qualification, "if she follows the line of good-will and moderation."²⁶

Such views, however, did not meet with unanimous approval. Admiral Sir Sydney Fremantle denied that Anglo-American co-operation would make it possible, if necessary, to suppress Japan. "Nothing of the sort was the case." In the first month of war, Hongkong, the garrisons at Shanghai and Tientsin, the China trade and British prestige in the East would have been destroyed. "That was a thing that could not be contemplated and no assistance from the United States, in the remote possibility of their coming in, would be of the smallest value." Great Britain should be friends with everybody and take no hostile action until her own honor or material interests were threatened. Great Britain need not fear Japan unless she interfered in matters which did not concern her.²⁷

The increased pace of Japanese activities in China in 1935 aroused correspondingly more interest and concern in Great Britain. Sir Frederick Whyte and other adherents of the Anglo-American school insisted that Great Britain must take a more active stand in support of China and in collaboration with the United States.

> If Japan were quite sure that Great Britain and the United States were ready to approach the problem of stabilizing the Far East in a spirit which showed that they appreciated the true nature of Japan's own problems, the readiness to cooperate with us might begin to appear. And, in the immediate future, we may find that the present predicament of China will provide the first opening.²⁸

Influential voices, like that of Sir Francis Lindley, former ambassador to Japan, could still be heard favoring agreement with Japan.²⁹ In January 1935 the *North-China Herald*, representative of British business interests in China, recommended "Anglo-Japanese co-operation in developing the backward markets of the world." Commenting on a pro-Japanese speech by

---

²⁶ Lord Lothian, "The Crisis in the Pacific," *International Affairs*, March-April 1935.
²⁷ Discussion following address by Lord Lothian, *ibid.*, pp. 171-3.
²⁸ Sir Frederick Whyte, "The Far East in 1935," *International Affairs*, May-June 1935. Was this, perhaps, a reference to the coming, though still unannounced, Leith-Ross Mission?
²⁹ See discussion following address by Sir Frederick Whyte, *ibid.*

Wang Ching-wei in February, this authoritative journal remarked:

> Great Britain will be the first to recognize the importance of Japan's economic contributions to China's development. Her own commitments may preclude political, but they need not necessarily prevent commercial cooperation in the general task of ensuring Far Eastern stability.[30]

The *Economist*, though still expressing fears (March 1935) that Japan was "putting China into her pocket," was still quite willing to allow Japan "a reasonable share" of world trade and of the reconstruction of China, on condition that China's independence and the existing Western interests in the Far East were simultaneously secured. If Japan refused these terms, "concerted and determined resistance" should be taken.[31]

The Federation of British Industries Mission to Japan and Manchukuo

Britain's actual policy during 1934 and the early part of 1935 approximated the desires of the Anglo-Japanese co-operation group but, at the same time, attempted to increase British participation in China's economic reconstruction and to rehabilitate Britain's diplomatic position at Nanking.

The outstanding attempt to achieve Anglo-Japanese co-operation was the dispatch of the Federation of British Industries Mission to Japan and Manchukuo, which took place in October-November 1934.[32] It was to study conditions in Manchukuo and to ascertain whether British industry could co-operate with local interests in its development.[33] The Mission was also charged with the task of paying a short visit of courtesy and good will to Japan, with the object of establishing friendly contact with representative organizations of Japanese industry and commerce. The

[30] *North-China Herald*, January 16, 1935; February 27, 1935.
[31] *Economist*, March 23, 1935.
[32] *Times*, August 10, 1934.
The personnel of the Mission consisted of: Colonel Lord Barnby, past president of the Federation of British Industries; Sir Charles Seligman, senior director of Seligman Brothers, Ltd., bankers; Sir Guy Locock, director of the Federation of British Industries, and Mr. Julian Piggot, representing the British Iron and Steel Federation.
[33] The London *Times*' comment of August 10, 1934, on the F.B.I. Mission is interesting in this connection. "Naturally, the circumstances being what they are, British enterprise in Manchukuo will fare the better the more it is able to work in friendly cooperation with the Japanese. . . . To promote a better understanding between British and Japanese industry may well have valuable results over an area much wider than Manchukuo or even the whole of the Far East."

FROM 1933 TO THE LEITH-ROSS MISSION

Mission, which was regarded in some quarters in Japan as a possible preliminary to British recognition of Manchukuo and as a move toward a general world-wide Anglo-Japanese rapprochement, was warmly received there.[34] It consulted with the outstanding financial, industrial and commercial leaders of Japan and Manchukuo. The chairman, Lord Barnby, as a result of meetings with the Manchukuoan authorities, received written assurance that "the principle of British collaboration in the development of Manchukuo was definitely accepted." The Mission considered this assurance justification enough for its visit. It was also able to report that an agreement had been reached with regard to the supply of steel products to Japan and Manchukuo during 1935.[35]

The Mission also published its views on Manchukuo:

> We do not propose to express any opinion of the events which led up to the foundation of the new State of Manchukuo. Our task was to form an appreciation from the business point of view of present conditions. The inhabitants of Manchukuo enjoy an increasing measure of security and ordered government. They are free from depredations and exactions by the military. They are subject to a reasonable system of taxation which is fairly administered, and they have the advantage of a sound currency. Plans are being laid, and are being executed, for improvements in transportation, communications, inland navigation, flood control, sanitation, hospitals, medical training, and the provision of school buildings hitherto lacking. From this it is easy to visualize the scope which Manchukuo offers as a market for industrial products.
>
> A modern State is in process of creation. Although difficulties still lie before it, we believe that they will be overcome and that economic prosperity will gradually be achieved to the benefit of Manchukuo and of the trade of other countries.

The *Economist*, usually favorable to trade missions, commented:

> The economic advantage which Great Britain may expect to derive from this F.B.I. Mission is less easy to discern than the political advan-

---

[34] The information on the F.B.I. Mission has been taken from the *Report of Mission to the Far East, August-November 1934*.

[35] These orders never materialized.

Manchukuoan-British Trade Relations: 1934-1936

(in 1,000 yen)

	1934	1935	1936
Imports from England	9,299	9,485	7,419
Exports to England	16,190	24,231	27,521
Total	25,488	33,989	34,940

Compiled from *Manchuria Economic Year Book, 1938* (Japanese edition).

tage to Japan. For the Japanese, the F.B.I. Mission offers an opportunity of obtaining what may be called "a semi-official British recognition" for the *de facto* regime which Japan has illegally set up in Manchuria.³⁶

British Boxer Indemnity Funds

The F.B.I. Mission, though fruitless in itself, did not end British efforts to obtain Japanese co-operation. At the same time, however, Britain was attempting to strengthen her position at Nanking and was increasing her participation in China's economic reconstruction. The use of remitted Boxer Indemnity funds provided the main opportunity for this.

In accordance with the Indemnity Agreement of 1930, the National Government of China had promulgated regulations for the constitution of the Board of Trustees on March 28, 1931.³⁷ The Indemnity Funds were apportioned in the following manner:

Railways.............................		⅔
Huai River Conservancy...............	40	per cent of ⅓
Pearl River Conservancy...............	20	per cent of ⅓
Yellow River Conservancy.............	13.33	per cent of ⅓
Ministry of Industries..................	13.33	per cent of ⅓
National Construction Commission.......	13.33	per cent of ⅓

When the Board of Trustees began to function, funds held in London amounted to £3,442,131 plus interest, while the sum still receivable until 1945 aggregated £7,744,416, making a total of £11,186,547. Of this amount £3,872,208 was to be paid to a purchasing commission in London for the acquisition of materials in Great Britain, while an equal amount was to be paid to the trustees in China. The interest derived from the investments in railway construction, river conservancy and electrical and mechanical works was to defray the cost of educational and cultural purposes.³⁸ Actual use of the funds began in 1933 and increased in 1934 and 1935.

The outstanding undertaking was the advance in July 1934 of £1,500,000, at the rate of 6 per cent redeemable by January 1, 1947, for the completion of the Canton-Hankow Railway. Loans were also made for the construction and rehabilitation of other

³⁶ *Economist*, August 18, 1934. See also November 3 and 10, 1934.

³⁷ Before the Commission was duly appointed, two small advances were made by agreement between the British and Chinese Governments in 1930, when £40,000 was advanced for the construction of a new Foreign Office building in Nanking, £20,000 for a British hospital in Peking and £500 for administrative expenses.

³⁸ In 1931, £265,000 was paid to the University of Hongkong for the education of Chinese students, and £200,000 was granted for the maintenance of Chinese students in London.

railways, including the Nanking-Pukow railway ferry, the Kiaochow-Tsinan, the Tientsin-Pukow, the Hangchow-Kiangshan, the Lunghai and the Shanghai-Hangchow-Ningpo railways. In addition, funds were made available for public works and utilities (including electrical works, conservancy, radio, telegraph, and telephone), and for industrial and commercial development (including the sanctioning of the expenditure of £400,000 by the China Merchants' Navigation Company for the purchase of four ships from England).

The accumulated interest derived from these loans, amounting at 5 per cent per annum to Ch.$ 1,646,200 by July 1934, was allotted for educational and cultural purposes. Among the beneficiaries of the allotments were the Central Museum, the Central Library, the Academia Sinica, National Peiping Institute, National Wuhan University, Chekiang University, Nankai University, the College of Medicine in Shanghai and the Sino-British Cultural Association. In addition, scholarships were made available for study in England.

The use of the Boxer Funds helped finance the sale of Britain's capital goods, especially railway supplies. In the period 1930-4, China purchased railway supplies to the value of 110 million yuan, of which 26 per cent came from Great Britain as against 18 per cent from the United States and 10 per cent each from Belgium, Germany and Japan.[39] By 1935 the purchasing commission in London had spent £3,000,000.

Private British interests also showed renewed interest in the possibilities of sharing in China's economic development. For example, in 1934 the Shanghai-Hangchow Railway 5½ Per Cent Loan of Ch.$ 16,000,000 was proposed by the China Development Finance Corporation jointly with the British and Chinese Corporation, Ltd. for the completion of the line from Hangchow to Ningpo. The unfavorable turn in the Shanghai money market, however, prevented the flotation of the loan. Successful Sino-British railway financing did not come until 1936.

Although Britain's main activity in China at this time was railway reconstruction and rehabilitation, China's increasing financial and economic difficulties, and their dire effects on British interests, resulted in proposals for direct financial aid to

[39] In 1935 Germany's sales of railway materials to China (1,686,788 Gold Units) were slightly larger than those of Great Britain (G.U. 1,644,300). In 1934 the Yuping Railway 6 Per Cent Loan of Ch.$ 12,000,000 was raised jointly by a syndicate of German industrialists (headed by Otto Wolff) and Chinese banks for the construction of the Yushan-Pinghsiang Railway.

the Nanking Government. The British Government, in the early months of 1935, entered into conversations with the governments at Washington, Paris and Tokyo with a view to obtaining their co-operation in granting assistance to China. The British Government did not indicate the exact nature of this contemplated aid, but it was widely assumed that an international loan was intended. While the United States indicated that it was sympathetic, the Japanese Government vetoed the loan, seeing in it an attempt to checkmate a Sino-Japanese entente. On March 6, 1935, Mr. M. Shigemitsu, vice-minister for foreign affairs, stated the Japanese position on foreign loans to China:

1. The improvement of Sino-Japanese relations contributes much to the maintenance of peace and order in the Orient. It also has a great bearing upon the stimulation of world peace. Therefore, there is no reason whatsoever for it to be looked upon with suspicious eyes by Britain, the United States and other Powers.

2. The rapprochement between Japan and China was brought about as the result of the mutual discovery that there is a perfect concurrence between the Greater Asia doctrine of the late Dr. Sun Yat-sen and the Oriental doctrine of the Japanese people. In other words, Japan and China, as two good neighbors, are now returning to their normal relationship. It is no matter for other Powers to make intervention, and we hope they will maintain a calm attitude until they see what Japan actually does.

3. Japan's plan to give economic assistance to China is, after all, no more than the attempt to make cooperation with China in China's efforts to accomplish economic recovery. For that purpose, Japan is ready to give assistance in men and materials. At the same time, Japan aims at the enhancement of trade between the two countries, which will assist largely in bringing normal recovery.

4. Japan has so far not received any overtures from China regarding loans and she has no intention at present to give consent to any such proposals, but there may be room for consideration if China approaches Japan with a request for loans which will be used for recovery purposes.

5. The United States[40] is advocating joint investments in China through the Four Powers Consortium of 1920, but it is a well-known fact that the Consortium since its inception, has never been utilized. It is not too much to say that it has been in existence in name only. China, herself, is opposed to getting assistance from the organization. Therefore Japan cannot help opposing the plan of joint investments in China. It is another question however, that the Powers make investments in China individually which carry no political meaning.

6. Japan will flatly refuse to participate in a discussion to give international economic assistance to China, as such a step will be tantamount to

[40] The emphasis in this statement on the American role in the international loan is interesting since Britain had taken the initiative in the loan negotiations. (See London *Times*, June 10, 1935.)

making China a colony of the senior Powers. Only when the Powers make negotiations individually for the giving of assistance to China, Japan will gladly take part.[41]

In the face of this Japanese opposition, the British Foreign Office disclaimed any intention of promoting an international loan. Three weeks later the House of Lords was informed that China had originally inquired whether Great Britain would support her by means of a loan, but that the British Government, after sympathetic consideration, had come to the conclusion that the projected scheme offered no real and lasting solution of China's difficulties.[42] This acceptance of the Japanese position was the last occasion on which Britain allowed her desire for Anglo-Japanese co-operation to obstruct her desire to act in active support of her position in China. Japan's co-operation was henceforth requested but her refusal—for instance, when, despite her expressed willingness to consent to individual negotiations, she objected to the Leith-Ross Mission, a clear example of individual aid—no longer acted as a veto.

Britain's growing interest in China's economic position, coupled with increased activity in her economic reconstruction and aid to her cultural and educational institutions, helped to reverse the downward trend of Britain's popularity and prestige in that country. Britain further improved her diplomatic position at Nanking by the agreement over the Yunnan-Burma border. The long-standing dispute (since 1897) over the border at Panhung moved toward a settlement when notes were exchanged at Nanking on April 9, 1935, by Wang Ching-wei and Sir Alexander Cadogan, agreeing on the formation of a joint boundary commission of five, two to be appointed by each side and a neutral commissioner to be appointed by the president of the Council of the League of Nations.[43]

[41] *China Year Book, 1935*, pp. 136-7.
[42] Statement by Earl Stanhope, *Parliamentary Debates*, House of Lords, April 3, 1935, Vol. 96, col. 557.
[43] The complete texts of the notes may be found in the *China Year Book, 1935*, pp. 148-9.

Another step in the rehabilitation of Britain's position at Nanking was the final settlement of the British Concessions in Hankow and Kiukiang, which had been retroceded to China in 1927. By the exchange of notes late in 1934 (published in March 1935) between the Chinese Foreign Office and Sir Alexander Cadogan, the agreements of March 1861 and August 1898, which had granted the concessions, were considered as having been canceled. In return, the annual land tax to be paid by former holders of British Crown leases in the Hankow and Kiukiang districts, was to remain at the existing rate for the time being.

CHAPTER IV

FROM THE LEITH-ROSS MISSION TO LUKOUCHIAO

By the summer of 1935, British diplomacy in China was on the threshold of a new policy. Since it was now recognized that Britain's position depended on an independent Nanking and since failure to obtain Japanese co-operation had been accompanied by Nanking's increasing subservience to Japan, it was necessary that individual assistance be given to China to relieve her economic crisis and thus strengthen her vis-à-vis Japan. China's economic difficulties were both the immediate reason and an excellent opportunity for carrying through such a policy. The Leith-Ross Mission marked this shift in British policy which came just at the time when diplomatic crises were beginning to give way to slowly but surely spreading war. In the fall of 1935 came the Italian invasion of Ethiopia, and the Hoare-Laval fiasco followed by the failure to apply sanctions decisively. In the spring of 1936 the Rhineland was remilitarized, dealing a deathblow to the Locarno treaties. Hard upon the heels of this crisis came the civil war and intervention in Spain, and the formulation of the non-intervention policy of M. Blum and Mr. Chamberlain.

The Leith-Ross Mission

The dispatch of Sir Frederick Leith-Ross, Chief Economic Adviser to the British Government, to the Far East was announced on June 10, 1935. He was to visit China "in order that his expert advice may be available to His Majesty's Government for the purpose of discussing with the Chinese Government and with the other Governments concerned the problems to which the present situation gives rise."[1] The proposed visit received much comment. For example, the *Round Table*, in a searching article in the September 1935 issue, indicated what it considered to be the reason for the visit. China's integrity was gone and with it had gone "the Washington corollary—the Pacific balance of power." "A new theory and a new policy will have to be discov-

[1] Foreign Office announcement, London *Times*, June 10, 1935.

ered to meet the changed conditions of 1935. . . . The new Far Eastern situation can best be expressed as the new position of Japan." Japan was getting complete control over China and was now in a position to bring "almost irresistible pressure to bear upon Chiang Kai-shek." The financial crisis had made the problem prominent again and had resulted in discussions of a possible British initiative in extending foreign credits to China. "In this connection Sir Frederick Leith-Ross has left England upon a visit of investigation to the Far East in behalf of the British Government." Japanese co-operaton was to be sought and could be obtained in the long run because of Japanese need for British capital, even though "Japanese policy and Japan's new position in China have today become a source of danger to the British trading and investment stake there."[2]

Mr. George E. Taylor wrote in *Pacific Affairs*: "Few have been blind to the purpose of the Leith-Ross Mission and its attempt to safeguard the interests of British bondholders and preserve what remains of British financial hegemony in China, not only against Japan but against the United States."[3] Most of the commentators, although disagreeing on the basic motives of the mission, agreed that more than mere discussion with the Chinese Government was intended.

The British Government requested the American, Japanese and French Governments to take action similar to their own, but the invitation received no response. There are indications that the Mission was viewed with favor by people close to the American State Department, but officially the relations of the Mission with the United States were cool. Sir Frederick chose to go to the Orient via Canada, although Secretary Hull issued an "open invitation" to him to stop at Washington. The Mission did not go to the United States but it did stop at Tokyo, where it met representatives of the Japanese Government. There Sir Frederick's proposals for joint action were declined. In the Japanese press the visit and rumors of a proposed loan were openly condemned. Said *Asahi*: "Japan holds the view that Japan should not cooperate in China on an equal footing with Great

[2] "Japan in China. The Far Eastern Problem," *Round Table*, September 1935, p. 695.
[3] G. E. Taylor, "The Powers and the Unity of China," *Pacific Affairs*, December 1936. Asiaticus has made a similar analysis stressing the rivalry between the United States and Great Britain in "The Financial Cutting Edge in the Partition of China," *Pacific Affairs*, June 1936.

Britain and the United States. Japan should consider cooperation only when she is recognized as being in a position of leadership."[4] *Nichi-Nichi* wrote: "To do anything important in China without Japanese understanding will be hopeless to attempt for Great Britain, because this will be attended by great risk and uncertainty."[5] The Japanese press reported that the Japanese authorities had demanded not only British recognition of Japanese supremacy in China but also British agreement to the open door for Japanese trade and capital within the British Empire.[6] Nevertheless, the Japanese, faced by Britain's unyielding determination, did not raise any formal objections to the Mission.

Sir Frederick arrived in Shanghai on September 21, 1935, to discuss the situation with the Chinese bankers and was joined by Mr. E. Hall Patch of the British Treasury and by Mr. C. Rogers of the Bank of England. It was at this time that the Chinese Government announced decrees on currency stabilization and the nationalization of silver.[7] The role which Sir Frederick played in this move was not publicly known but Mr. Leonard T. K. Wu's statement in the *Far Eastern Survey*, that "it is practically certain that he [Leith-Ross] acted as the tie between the sterling bloc and China on the one hand, and between official London, Tokyo and Nanking on the other," was typical of the common opinion.[8] Sir Frederick himself maintained that Nanking was solely responsible for the new policy, the success of which would benefit both British and Japanese trade.

The Japanese voiced bitter resentment at China's action and

[4] Quoted in "Japan in China: The New Far Eastern Problem," *Round Table*, September 1935.

[5] Quoted in H. B. Elliston, "China Dethrones Silver," *Foreign Affairs*, January 1936.

[6] It was generally supposed in Japan that Sir Frederick was engaged in a scheme for floating a £50,000,000 loan, with the co-operation of the British Government, to be secured on the Chinese Government's railway revenues.

[7] All silver coins in banks and in circulation were nationalized and the notes issued by the Central Bank of China, the Bank of China and the Bank of Communications were made sole legal tender. All obligations, including former debts and also taxes, could be discharged in the new money. Foreign exchange rates were stabilized at a basis of 1s. $2\frac{1}{2}$d. (average for the past five years) and the three government banks were ordered to sell and buy any amount of foreign moneys at $\frac{1}{8}$d. below and $\frac{1}{8}$d. above the basic rate of 1s. $2\frac{1}{2}$d. The export duty on silver was raised from $14\frac{1}{2}$ per cent to 65 per cent.

[8] L. T. K. Wu, "China's Monetary Dilemma," *Far Eastern Survey*, December 4, 1935.

what seemed to be Britain's role. The Japanese War Minister announced: "that China should suddenly take such a course without consulting Japan can only be interpreted as a complete lack of interest on the part of China in improving her relations with Japan. The army will take no action at once, but, when the time comes, it will not hesitate."[9] "If this is true," ran a Japanese War Office *communiqué* of November 9, 1935, "the leaders of the Nanking Government cannot escape criticism for selling their country to foreigners for their own aggrandizement. Japan, as a stabilizing influence in the Far East, cannot overlook any attempt on the part of Great Britain to place a semi-colonial China under the domination of British capital."[10]

The available evidence indicates that the currency scheme was drawn up before the arrival of Sir Frederick Leith-Ross, but it is clear that it was the support given to it by the British Government that guaranteed its success. On November 4, the very day the financial reform became effective, the British ambassador issued an order-in-council prohibiting British subjects from making payment in silver of any debt or other obligations, and making the offender liable to imprisonment with or without hard labor for a period not exceeding three months, or to a fine not exceeding £30, or to both.[11] The readiness with which the British banks transferred their silver stocks to the custody of the new currency Reserve Board contrasted sharply with the refusals of the Japanese banks to take similar action.[12] Britain's prestige and influence at Nanking had now been definitely reestablished.[13]

Sir Frederick Leith-Ross on June 23, 1936, preparatory to his

[9] Quoted in "Japan Moves On," *Round Table*, March 1936.
[10] Quoted in *Survey of International Affairs, 1935*, p. 323.
[11] The action did much to help a situation that might have been greatly complicated by the extraterritorial rights enjoyed by many British residents and institutions. The existence of the extraterritorial rights and special privileges and the special position enjoyed by foreign banks had been generally regarded as a great obstacle to the introduction of any form of monetary control.
[12] The Japanese banks did not hand over their silver stocks to the Nanking Government until the spring of 1937.
[13] On November 9, 1935, Hongkong prohibited the export of silver, and on December 5, 1935, a Currency Ordinance was passed, calling in silver coin from circulation and setting up machinery to control the exchange value of the Hongkong dollar. This machinery consisted of an Exchange Fund, with power to buy and sell foreign exchange, which took over the silver formerly held against their issues by the note-issuing banks, in return for certificates of indebtedness against which the Fund was permitted to hold silver or foreign exchange.

departure, issued a detailed statement outlining the future trends of British policy as well as the aims and accomplishments of his mission.

> His Majesty's Government in the United Kingdom sent me out to examine the financial and economic difficulties of China and the possibilities of our assisting her, in conjunction with the other Powers interested, to overcome these difficulties . . . It had been the hope of my Government that the U.S.A., Japan and France would appoint experts to collaborate with me, but this did not prove possible. However, an important Economic Mission from the United States recently visited China and I have found their report of great interest. I have maintained contact with the Japanese Government representatives and bankers here and have paid two visits to Tokyo so as to obtain first-hand information of the views of the Japanese Government. . . .
>
> The first question to which my attention was directed was naturally the position of the currency. . . . I did not bring any cut and dried scheme out with me to "put over" the Chinese Government. There were several possible alternatives, and the decision between them, depending as it did largely on Chinese psychology, could only be taken by the Chinese Government. I was examining the situation with a view to the preparation of a detailed programme with adequate safeguards and, if possible, with international support. But before any such scheme could be devised, the exchange market became dangerously weak and the Chinese Government decided to adopt an inconvertible managed currency on the basis of their own resources.
>
> I had no responsibility for this bold step, but I have of course closely followed the situation and I have no hesitation in saying that the action taken has been fully justified by the success which it has achieved. . . .
>
> Confidence in the currency is growing. But much has still to be done before it can be solidly assured as a basis for long-term trading and investment plans.

For example, it was necessary "to carry through efficiently the programme of internal reforms including especially the reorganization of the Central Bank and the reform of the Budget."

The currency reforms would stimulate trade, he said, and added,

> I have dealt at length with the currency position because financial security is the basis of trade. Erratic exchanges and contraction of credit strangle enterprise. The currency reform has laid the foundation for an increase of trade activities. But the export trade could still be further stimulated if the burden of local taxes, inter-port duties and export duties could be reduced and if the standards of production, manufacturing and handling could be improved. It rests with the Chinese themselves to promote exports by such means.

Closely related to the trade problem and of great importance to British interests was the tariff question. Sir Frederick urged a downward revision so far as this was possible without reducing revenue. He ended this plea with a reference to the Maritime Customs, in the administration of which the British had always had predominant influence,

> The Maritime Customs is the basis of Chinese Government credit, and it is in the first interests of China both to maintain that service in all its traditional efficiency and to adjust the tariff so as to secure the maximum revenue.

Britain, he maintained, could profit greatly by the new developments in China, especially since the Chinese were showing a marked willingness to co-operate with the British in making this possible.

> The development of China will require the importation of much capital goods and this is probably the most promising field for British exports. . . . In the past the United Kingdom has done much to develop the railway system of China, but unfortunately many of the loan obligations thus incurred have not been fully met. . . . The national Government appear genuinely anxious to settle outstanding obligations, within the limits of their financial possibilities, and also to remedy the serious defects in the administration and management of the railways with a view to enabling them to meet their charges. It must be borne in mind that the defaults are, in the main, a heritage of years of civil strife and social disorganization. If a reasonable settlement could be reached in regard to these old debts, the way would be open for financing extensions to the present railway system, and thus opening vast stretches of country to foreign trade. . . . Apart from railway financing, which calls for long-term credit, the possibilities of arranging middle-term credit deserve exploration. Such credits would be of particular value for financing public utility schemes. . . .
>
> There are also many openings for the investment of private capital in properties or undertakings in China. But if investors are to be attracted to such ventures confidence must be re-established by abrogating any measures that have the effect of discriminating against foreign capital, and, as regards real estate, by securing that the legal rights of mortgages are fully protected. Foreign capital cannot be expected to assist China unless it is assured of fair treatment.

Sir Frederick concluded by speaking of the great potentialities for trade in China and by reaffirming the British desire for international co-operation in the task of developing China. "There is room for all to assist her in this task."[14]

[14] London *Times,* June 23, 1936; *China Year Book, 1936,* pp. 178-80.

Subsequent British policy in China was in general accord with his recommendations. Just as Japan's policy had led Great Britain to act in support of China, Japan's activities in China during and after the visit of the Mission influenced Great Britain to continue support to Nanking. Moreover, British prestige was now tied up with the success of Nanking's financial program and British interests were becoming more involved in China's economic reconstruction.

The Leith-Ross Mission had roused great hostility in Japan, especially in military circles, and there was friction and ill-feeling in Anglo-Japanese relations until the spring of 1937. Japan's spokesmen began to emphasize the necessity of driving out the Western powers from China. On September 24, 1935, Major-General Hayao Tada, commander of the North China Garrison, issued the "Tada Statement" demanding the elimination of Western interests in China and the overthrow of the Nanking Government, the Kuomintang and Chiang Kai-shek. On October 28, Foreign Minister Hirota placed before the Chinese ambassador to Japan a three-point proposal for Sino-Japanese rapprochement, known later as Hirota's "three principles."[15] Consular and military pressure on Chinese officials in North China was increased and Japan's determination to separate the five northern provinces from Nanking's jurisdiction became evident. However, Nanking did not capitulate to Japan. She was bolstered up by British support and was under increasing pressure from a rising anti-Japanese nationalist sentiment, which culminated in the attempted assassination of Wang Ching-wei, leader of the pro-Japanese clique. The influence of this pro-Japanese group began to decline. The inauguration of the "East Hopei Autonomous Council" on November 25 was more effective in arousing anti-Japanese sentiment than as a step toward the "independence" of North China. The Hopei-Chahar Political Council, inaugurated on December 18, 1935, was a poor substitute for Doihara's strongly advocated five-province autonomy scheme. Soon thereafter Chiang Kai-shek replaced Wang Ching-wei as president of the Executive Yuan, and Wang's cabinet resigned.

[15] As originally presented to China, these were: (1) China must abandon her policy of playing off one foreign country against another. (2) China must respect the fact of the existence of Manchoukuo. (3) China and Japan must jointly devise effective measures for preventing the spread of Communism in regions in the northern part of China." T. A. Bisson, *Japan in China*, p. 126.

Smuggling

The Japanese, however, did not relinquish their aggressive North China policy and made repeated efforts—diplomatic, military and economic—to thwart Nanking's new strength. Smuggling, which had been carried on under private initiative, now became a state policy.[16] British interests were doubly affected by the existence of smuggling, indirectly by the weakening of Nanking's financial and political position, and directly by injuries to duty-paying British trade.

By the early part of 1935 the activities of the Preventive Secretariat of the Maritime Customs had succeeded in breaking the large smuggling organizations which had been operating in North China, and comparatively little was escaping the customs authorities. But during the latter part of 1935 "the Japanese authorities saw fit to take the action which destroyed the foundation of the work accomplished and rendered all customs preventive efforts abortive."[17]

By the summer of 1936 the situation was entirely out of control. The customs staff had remained at their posts, but all their

[16] The problem of smuggling foreign goods into China had been a serious one for many years. Increases in import duties after 1928, which had been made possible by China's recovery of tariff autonomy, had made smuggling profitable and the government was not able to cope with the greatly enlarged smuggling trade which soon grew up. At first smugglers were especially active on the south China coast and continued to be a serious problem there, though the center of activity shifted to North China. (See Chen Han-seng, "Japanese Penetration in Southernmost China," *Far Eastern Survey*, November 4, 1936.) The Japanese occupation of Manchuria gave rise to extensive operations both by sea from Dairen to the Shantung coast and across the land frontier along the Great Wall. Concerned by the serious losses of revenue, the government took measures to remedy the situation. A Customs Preventive Secretariat was inaugurated in 1931 and began to build up an organization for the suppression of smuggling. In 1934, its fleet contained twenty-six sea-going units as well as many smaller craft. The establishment of many new coast and frontier stations, the division of the coast into patrols, the promulgation of more stringent regulations (including the establishment of a twelve-mile limit in 1934), and other measures enabled the authorities to deal more vigorously with the problem. Proceeds from fines and confiscations amounted to Ch.$ 7.9 million in 1934, against Ch.$ 6.4 million in 1933, Ch.$ 3.7 million in 1932 and Ch.$ 2.7 million in 1931. But the smuggling continued. According to the customs report for 1934, nearly one-third of the rayon and over one-fourth of the sugar imports recorded in that year consisted of confiscated goods. In the Chefoo district about one-fifth of the volume of imports and one-third of the revenue came from intercepted cargoes. In the Bank of China's estimate of China's balance of international payments for 1934, an allowance of Ch.$ 154.5 million, or 15 per cent of the recorded merchandise imports, was made for proceeds from the smuggling trade.

[17] Report of the Customs Preventive Secretary, issued in June 1936.

prerogatives and means of enforcing the laws were taken from them. Citing the Tangku Truce as their authority, the Japanese authorities had reduced the Customs Administration to a state of impotence. Preventive patrols were not allowed on the Great Wall at Shanhaikwan and Customs officers within the demilitarized zone had to go without protection against the armed Korean and Japanese elements engaged in illegal activities. The armed preventive ships had to remain outside a three-mile limit from the coast of this zone, and Japanese naval authorities informed the custom officials that the latter could be considered as pirates and treated accordingly if a Japanese vessel, or an unidentified vessel which could be shown to have a claim to Japanese protection, was stopped at a point beyond three miles from the coast. This rendered all sea work in this area impossible and futile, since Japanese-owned or chartered vessels, which were not obliged by Japanese law to fly their flags or carry any mark or emblem denoting their nationality, could and did proceed from Dairen to any point on the Chinese coast of the demilitarized zone without risk of molestation of any kind, and other vessels, including Chinese, had only to avoid carrying distinguishing marks and, by thus placing themselves within the unidentifiable category, reduced risk of seizure to a minimum.

On land, customs officers, lacking any protection, were browbeaten and violently assaulted. The Japanese consular police and other Japanese authorities, even when eye-witnesses to these assaults, refused to come to their aid and on occasion the Customs Administration was completely humiliated by being compelled under threats of force to meet demands made by the Japanese authorities for redress and compensation for alleged illegal action and assault by customs officers, the charges being based on the statements of Japanese and Korean smugglers. "The results," wrote the Customs Preventive Secretary, "are deplorable. Commercial order has been reduced to chaos by the staggering amounts of illicit cargo thrown daily into the area, quantities of which are gradually finding their way through the media of the railway to other parts of China, undermining trade and depleting the national revenue on which China's loan services and credit depend."[18]

[18] See China Maritime Customs, *The Trade of China, 1935*, Introductory Survey.

The position of the Customs Administration in Eastern Hopei was aggravated after March 1936 by the action of the East Hopei Autonomous Government in levying its own taxes on the illicit cargo landed.[19] Here the Japanese gendarmerie, under the control of the Kwantung Army, rendered every assistance to the tax collectors in "persuading" the smugglers to pay the duties. This resulted in a truly unique situation. At Nanlichuang, some two miles from and in full view of Chinwangtao, an important customs port, and at places along the coast near the railway stations of Nantassu, Peitaiho, Liushouying and Changli, vessels of all kinds could be seen daily discharging vast quantities of sugar, artificial silk yarn, cotton and woolen piece goods, kerosene oil, sea products, dyes, cigarette paper and many miscellaneous articles (including those paying low duty rates) under the supervision of Japanese and Koreans, armed and ready to attack any customs officer who appeared in the vicinity. Taxes were col-

REVENUE FROM CUSTOMS, 1928–35
(in Chinese dollars)

Year	Total	Amount from import duty	Per cent of total revenue	Total value of imports	Per cent of import duty to total imports
1928	128,274,076	72,446,056	56.25	1,863,332,000	3.35
1929	238,109,285	167,098,564	70.17	1,972,083,403	8.66
1930	281,405,583	211,639,119	75.21	2,040,599,446	10.37
1931	385,002,673	314,686,596	81.74	2,233,376,164	17.24
1932	311,976,210	236,291,686	75.74	1,634,726,298	14.45
1933	339,524,490	265,610,812	78.23	1,345,567,188	25.23
1934	334,645,408	260,215,093	77.76	1,029,665,224	25.26
1935	315,519,712	250,165,356	79.28	919,211,322	27.21

COMBINED MARITIME AND NATIVE CUSTOMS REVENUE AND AMOUNTS THEREOF PAID ON FOREIGN LOANS AND INDEMNITIES
(in pounds sterling)

Year	Total	Amounts paid on foreign loans, etc.
1927	7,737,726	7,665,381
1928	10,012,913	7,526,151
1929	18,191,695	7,774,180
1930	15,529,200	7,762,280
1931	16,062,730	8,262,460
1932	15,457,668	6,144,797
1933	16,264,877	5,291,919
1934	17,666,997	5,066,901
1935	18,912,237	4,910,916

[19] EAST HOPEI GOVERNMENT AND CENTRAL GOVERNMENT TARIFFS COMPARED
(For three principal articles)

Article	Customs Tariff	East Hopei Government Tariff
Sugar (1 bag at 135 ctts.)*	Ch.$ 19.70 plus surtax	Ch.$ 6
Artificial silk yarn (100 ctts.)	Ch.$ 72.00 plus surtax	Ch.$ 26.67
Compoy (100 ctts.)	Ch.$ 48.00 plus surtax	Ch.$ 15

* 1 catty equals 1⅓ pounds.

lected by the East Hopei Tax Office and the goods then were transported by carriers, pack-mules, carts and all kinds of conveyances to Chinwangtao and the four above-mentioned railway stations, where they were accepted for shipment on payment of freight to other places, chiefly Tientsin. At Chinwangtao, which was the railhead for illicit cargo from Nanlichuang, the Customs made an attempt to exercise control, but the customs officers were assaulted and received no protection from the police.

Railway invoices, such as the following statement of arrivals at the Tientsin East Railway Station during the period from August 1, 1935, to May 6, 1936, indicated the amount of illicit cargo, mainly of Japanese manufacture or origin, and its distribution through the agency of the railway companies:

Artificial silk yarn: 95,632 bags at 45 kgs. per bag totaled 4,303,400 kgs.
White sugar: 622,081 bags at 90 kgs. per bag totaled 559,972 quintals.*
Cigarette paper: 6,407 bags at 20 bobbins per bag and 3.11 kgs. per bobbin totaled 398,515 kgs.
Piece goods: 26,023 packages, quality and quantity unknown.
Sundries: 30,329 packages, contents uncertain, but included in this figure were 12,692 cases of kerosene oil and 999 cases of gasoline.
* 1 quintal equals 200 lbs.

During the earlier stages illicit cargo had been confined to the high-duty-paying goods, but as stocks of such goods accumulated, more kinds of merchandise, e.g., apples, soda water, wine, electrical materials and even prohibited goods like arms began to to find their way in.

The railway companies did little or nothing to prevent the shipment of illicit cargoes. At Tientsin these goods were discharged and later loaded for shipment elsewhere. By this means the area of illicit goods was not confined to Eastern Hopei and Tientsin, but also extended southwards along the Tientsin-Pukow and Peiping-Hankow lines. The virtual extinction of the demand for duty-paid foreign goods throughout the provinces north of the Yangtze seemed likely. By May 1936 the Preventive Secretary had come to the conclusion that the preventive system in the north had been entirely wrecked.

The illicit trade directly threatened Western as well as Chinese interests, especially when contraband goods began to find their way into the Yangtze region. Hankow business was seriously affected by the smuggled goods which arrived via the

Peiping-Hankow Railway. Rayons, toys, bicycle parts, oleaginous products, piece goods, etc. were flooding the Wuhan markets. The Hankow Chamber of Commerce petitioned the central and local Chinese authorities, demanding that effective measures be taken promptly to deal with the serious situation. Even Shanghai suffered the effects of the smuggling. Smuggled goods were trickling into the Settlement and local companies, unable to meet the competition of contraband commodities, were progressively losing customers. A survey of the situation was made by a representative of the *Shanghai Evening Post and Mercury*. He reported:

> Each office visited was in a flurry of excitement when the reporters called, managers and their assistants eagerly unburdening their worries. We don't have any figures, and can't tell precisely how much smuggling is going on, but we do know it's hell for the legitimate importer, was the gist of their introductory remarks.
>
> Questioned as to the exact type of business affected, they revealed that valuable commodities, easily concealable, such as rayon, cosmetics, and pharmaceuticals, are the strongest invaders of the Settlement itself, while all sorts of foodstuffs in bulk and tins have flooded the interior, along with paper, cloth, and manufacturered articles, thus wiping out the trade in these commodities that formerly passed through the port of Shanghai.

The *North China Daily News* of May 14, 1936, told a similar story. Demands from the interior, especially from the north, were declining rapidly. In addition the northern markets were felt to be so near the saturation point that Shanghai would become the overflow region for goods smuggled into the north. Price differentials between North China and Shanghai brought about by the smuggling offered inducements for the illicit goods to find their way to Shanghai. Artificial silk, selling in Tientsin for Ch.$ 170 a bale, was commanding Ch.$ 400 at Shanghai. Sugar could be obtained at Tientsin for Ch.$ 14.50, while the Yangtze valley was paying Ch.$ 30. The chief sufferers among the foreign commodities in China were British and American kerosene and British sugar. Between May 1 and August 15, 1936, there were smuggled in 1,370,000 gallons of kerosene and 170,-000 gallons of gasoline, causing the North China business of the British and American firms to drop 40 per cent. British sugar sales in North China ordinarily amounted to over Ch.$ 20,000,-000 a year, but between October 1935 and August 1936 "not one pound of legal sugar was sold." On September 1, 1936, the smugglers were holding 300,000 bags of sugar in Tientsin, a six-months supply for North China.

Losses in trade were not the only possible injury from smuggling, for "unless there is an improvement in a comparatively short space of time not only the integrity of the Customs but the whole financial structure will be imperilled."[20] Although the reduction in Customs revenue did not yet jeopardize the service of the foreign loans, Nanking's financial position was injured and the prestige and authority of the Customs Administration were being undermined.[21]

The British press in Shanghai sharply denounced Japan's role in the smuggling, rejected all evasions of responsibility and clearly indicated its annoyance and anxiety.[22] The British Chamber of Commerce in Shanghai sent the following cablegram to the home government on June 1, 1936:

> Smuggling in North China has assumed enormous proportions. Lost revenue April Tientsin Chinwangtao estimated eight to ten millions and unless steps taken enable Chinese preventive service function monthly loss revenue liable increase. Position seriously jeopardizing foreign loans and obligations secured Customs and distribution smuggled goods seriously affecting legitimate trade throughout the country. Smugglers are Japanese subjects and receive support from Japanese military. Danger of wrecking China's finance and commerce due to assumed deliberate intention Japanese military achieve this objective.[23]

In London, Mr. D. G. M. Bernard, the chairman of the China Association, the most important organization in Great Britain representing British interests in China, addressing its annual meeting on May 15, 1936, also condemned the smuggling. The London *Times*, in less restrained terms than usual when dealing with Japan, declared,

[20] *Finance and Commerce*, May 13, 1936.

[21] The Chinese statements issued at this time exaggerated the damage done to the revenues and foreign loans, although not the actual extent of the smuggling. The weekly loss to the revenue of the Customs Administration at Tientsin was placed at Ch.$ 2,400,000, but in 1935 the average weekly revenue of the Tientsin office was only about Ch.$ 787,000. They were technically correct in reckoning as losses what revenue would have been if customs rates had been paid on the smuggled goods, but 85 per cent of these goods had not come into China at all before the smuggling began. An authoritative estimate of the actual losses in customs revenue in 1936 set the figure at Ch.$ 25,000,000, or 8 per cent of the total collections in 1935.

[22] *Finance and Commerce*, April 15, May 13 and June 3, 1936; *North China Daily News*, May 12, 1936.

[23] A similar cablegram was sent to Washington by Mr. James M. Howes, secretary of the American Chamber of Commerce in Shanghai.

The evasive answers of the Japanese authorities to diplomatic protests concerning the smuggling in North China indicate that connivance in this shoddy swindle is not merely an affair of the local military action, but a stroke of government policy.[24]

The question of smuggling came up frequently for discussion in the House of Commons.[25] On May 19 the China Sub-Committee of the House met to discuss the problem. Representatives of the British Residents Association and the China Association were invited to give their views on the situation. After lengthy discussions it was decided to offer constructive help to the Chinese Government for its effective carrying out of the preventive measures.

However, the situation in North China suddenly cleared as the result of diplomatic protests by Great Britain and strong action by the Chinese Central Government. On May 2, 1936, the British Government made representations to the Japanese Foreign Office concerning the smuggling. Foreign Minister Arita "categorically repudiated" reports that Japan was encouraging smuggling in North China or that Japanese military pressure had anything to do with the weakened sovereignty of the National Government in customs matters. He offered, as a counter-explanation, the lack of adequate tariff enforcement rendered more difficult by a high level of duties and the cessation of subsidies from Nanking. The whole matter, he said, was really an internal affair of the Chinese Government.[26] After these diplomatic exchanges, some improvement did take place, but more effective was the widely publicized action taken by the Nanking Government. The fight against the smugglers in the demilitarized zone north of Tientsin was abandoned and instead hundreds of emergency revenue guards were dispatched along the railways, roads and rivers leading south from Tientsin in an attempt to bottle up the illegal imports in the small area of Northern Hopei, Chahar and Suiyuan.

By mid-summer, apparently on a tip from Tokyo that the Japanese Foreign Office was withdrawing protection from the smugglers, the Chinese 29th Army broadswordsmen drove the smugglers out of the Central Station at Tientsin, and they were never seen again on the Tientsin-

[24] London *Times*, May 18, 1936.
[25] On April 29, May 11, 13, 20, 25 and June 9, 10, 15, 1936.
[26] Rumors were prevalent that Great Britain was discussing with the United States and other interested powers (Germany has been suggested) the possibility of joint action to check the influx of smuggled goods.

Pukow Railway. Illegal imports then dwindled to only 5 per cent of their former volume.[27]

The improvement in the situation was, however, only temporary, for motor trucks replaced the railways as means of transportation and considerable quantities of illicit goods again penetrated into adjoining provinces. In the spring of 1937, when the Japanese civil authorities and some of the military authorities lent their support to the Customs Administration, smuggling again declined. The outbreak of hostilities in the summer of 1937 destroyed the gains which had been made, and the illicit traffic revived. Smuggling thus remained as a constant irritant in Anglo-Japanese relations during the period from the Leith-Ross Mission to the war.

Japan's Policy in China

Smuggling was not the only method of attack on the Customs Administration used by the Japanese for the dual purpose of gaining control over North China and coercing Nanking. Japanese advisers to the Hopei-Chahar Political Council in Peiping, who were anxious to obtain financial independence, advised its chairman, General Sung Cheh-yuan, to stop the remittance to Nanking of the Central Government's revenues, including the customs receipts. The customs officials were ordered to pay revenue into the account of the Government in Peiping, but Sir Frederick Maze, the Inspector-General of Customs, promptly issued counter orders. The Peiping authorities dropped the issue. Later in the year the illegal establishment of local offices for the collection of a surtax on customs revenue gave rise to such wide public protests that it too was given up.

Other Japanese activities in North China also proved unsuccessful. An attempt to divorce the currency of North China from that of the rest of the country by setting up a separate central bank closely allied to the Bank of Chosen failed. Japanese pressure for concessions to exploit the resources of Hopei and Chahar and to construct public works resulted in evasions or unfilled promises.[28] Private Japanese interests were only a little

---

[27] Haldore Hanson, "Smuggler, Soldier and Diplomat," *Pacific Affairs*, December 1936. Another factor in the decline of smuggling in the summer of 1936 was the glutting of the North China market, making smuggling temporarily less profitable.

[28] Only in the case of air lines did the Japanese receive and operate a concession. These were to operate between Peiping and certain points in Manchukuo and Jehol.

more successful in strengthening their position in North China. At Tientsin they obtained a share of control over salt production, important to the Japanese chemical industry. A Sino-Japanese combine was founded for the purpose of exploiting cotton cultivation and the production of wool in North China, but the outbreak of war in Suiyuan brought it to a stop. Some gains were made in coastal navigation. Thus the attempt to achieve a Japan-Manchukuo-North China economic bloc failed. The Hopei-Chahar Political Council did, nevertheless, accept Japanese diplomatic and economic advisers and in August 1936 the former Japanese consul-general in Tientsin was appointed adviser on foreign affairs.

Japan's slight success in Hopei and Chahar compared favorably with her complete failure in Inner Mongolia, where General Fu Tso-yi's Suiyuan troops decisively defeated the Japanese puppet, General Li Shou-hsin. The net accomplishment of this Mongolian venture was to strengthen anti-Japanese feeling and to guarantee the failure of Japanese diplomacy at Nanking. The effect on Nanking of the Japanese reversals and the diplomatic support of Great Britain was clearly seen in the stiffening of its attitude toward Japan.

Hirota's three-point program, outlined in September of 1935, restated in his speech to the Diet on January 21, 1936, and providing for Sino-Japanese "co-operation," was the basis of Japan's China policy in 1936.[29] Arita, newly appointed Japanese Ambassador to China, came to China at the end of February 1936 to effect "a fundamental solution of outstanding issues" by means of normal diplomatic negotiations. Soon after his arrival he initiated a series of conversations with General Chang Chun, the Chinese foreign minister. Instead of capitulating, the Chinese demanded a cessation of Japan's North China policy and Japanese unwillingness to accept caused the collapse of the negotiations.

Arita's successor, Kawagoe, was even less successful. By interfering in the North China situation, by flying to Peiping and participating in the negotiations with General Sung Cheh-yuan concerning economic co-operation in North China, he set off serious anti-Japanese demonstrations during the summer of 1936. The Japanese then, it was reported, redefined their demands:

[29] For the complete text of this speech, see the *Japan-Manchoukuo Year Book, 1937*, pp. 103-8.

China was to assume responsibility for anti-Japanese activities; agitation against Japan was to be suppressed; Japanese inspectors were to visit the schools; the Chinese Government was to accept Japanese advisers; the customs tariff was to be revised; "joint defense" against Communism, or the brigading of Japanese troops with Chinese, was to be instituted, and Japan's "special position" in North China was to be recognized. The Chinese Government met the Japanese demands with counter demands of their own: smuggling in North China must cease; the East Hopei autonomous area must be abolished; the Tangku Truce and the demilitarized zone around Shanghai, created after the Shanghai Incident of 1932, must be annulled, and Japanese troops withdrawn from North China. The defeat of the Japanese puppet revolt in Mongolia strengthened the hand of Nanking and in December 1936 the Chinese foreign minister broke off the negotiations.[30] This indication of China's new confidence was generally appreciated and the accumulated effect of British diplomatic support in bringing this about was recognized by Chinese and Japanese alike.

The significance for British interests of Japan's China policy at Nanking as well as in North China, was heightened by the events in Manchukuo, for they indicated what might be expected in a Japanese dominated or controlled China. Foreign trade, commercial enterprise and investments in almost every case were being reduced by such means as currency reform and the formation of governmental and semi-governmental monopolies. The open door was proving to be a "one-way passage outward."[31]

[30] The immediate cause of the breaking off of negotiations was the landing of Japanese marines at Tsingtao to assist in suppressing a disturbance which had arisen out of a lock-out in some Japanese-owned mills.

[31] J. R. Stewart, "The Open Door in Manchoukuo," *Far Eastern Survey*, Dec. 1, 1937. Two important instances of investment of foreign capital since the establishment of Manchukuo were the expansion by the British-American Tobacco Company of its operation in Manchuria and the obtaining by French interests of a ¥300,000 contract to construct two government buildings at Hsinking. The B.A.T. built new factories at Liaoyang and Yinkow.

After the elimination of the oil companies, the B.A.T. was the largest foreign company operating in Manchuria. For many years it had enjoyed a virtual monopoly of the Manchurian market. After the creation of Manchukuo, however, it began to face serious competition from two officially supported Japanese tobacco companies, and, in addition, there were hints of a tobacco monopoly. The B.A.T., in order to preserve its position, "recognized" Manchukuo by incorporating its two Manchurian subsidiaries—the Chi Tung Tobacco Co., Ltd., capitalized at M¥52,325,000, and the Robert Tobacco Co., Ltd., capitalized at M¥3,500,000—

British Investments and Trade in China after 1936

The treatment which British interests were receiving in Japanese controlled Manchukuo was in sharp contrast with the encouragement being given by Nanking to British capital. On its return to England the Leith-Ross Mission had reported very favorably on China's progress toward political unity and financial stability and its recommendation for further reforms seemed to be the prelude to a large-scale British financing program in China. The Chinese were quick to show their willingness to accept British co-operation and suggestions. Thus, when Dr. H. H. Kung, the Chinese finance minister, prior to his departure as head of China's delegation to the Coronation, announced a number of financial measures, they were in full accord with the recommendations of the Leith-Ross Mission. Most important were the establishment of a Central Reserve Bank, the balancing of the national budget for the coming year, the revision of the Banking Law, and the continuation of the program for re-servicing outstanding foreign obligations. In addition, Dr. Kung announced three new sources of revenue which were expected to yield an additional income of some Ch.$ 90,000,000 annually, sufficient to cover ordinary interest charges on a substantial foreign loan.

The opportunities in South China, especially Kwangtung and Kwangsi, for British capital received particular attention at this time. Cordial relations were established between Hongkong and Canton for the first time since 1931. In October 1936 the governor of Hongkong, Sir Andrew Caldecott, called on Chiang Kai-shek in Canton, and the visit was returned by the mayor of Canton, who acknowledged China's indebtedness to Great Britain for her support of the currency stabilization scheme and for the promise of assistance from the export credit guarantee scheme. Reports were common of a Sino-British agreement for British co-operation in the economic development of South China, including British financing of a railway in Hainan, the establishment of an airdrome on Tungsha Island southeast of Hongkong, an oil depot in the Sesha Islands southwest of Hainan, and the development of mines in South China. The interview given to Mr. T. V. Soong by the governor of Hongkong, speeches of Chinese leaders, and the visits of the British

---

under Manchukuoan laws on August 1, 1936. Previously they had been Hongkong corporations.

ambassador and Mr. Kirkpatrick of the British Export Credits Guarantee Department to Hongkong and Canton early in 1937 gave rise to numerous rumors that China was to be given a substantial loan by Great Britain to be used for the economic development of Kwangtung. The Japanese press went so far as to publish full details of a reputed Ch.$ 100,000,000 British loan to be expended in the construction of a number of railways in south China and in the previously described development of Hainan Island.[32]

The validity of the rumors of these large undertakings cannot be established, and the outbreak of hostilities in July 1937 ended the possibility of their developing into anything concrete, but it is clear that British firms were taking a lively interest in south China. Nanking's success in September 1936 in gaining political control over Kwangtung and Kwangsi had brought these two provinces within the scope of the new currency scheme. The consequent stabilizing effect on foreign exchange was encouraging foreign firms to grant more favorable credit terms for construction projects. British capital was to be invested in a large iron and steel plant near Canton and it appeared probable that British credits would be granted for the purchase of materials and equipment for the proposed railway between Canton and Swatow. Negotiations were proceeding with regard to the linking of the Canton-Kowloon Railway with the Canton-Hankow line—an arrangement which would enable more of the production of the southern provinces to be exported via Canton and Hongkong rather than via Shanghai and would be a boon to Hongkong's declining trade.

British firms profited by the new Hongkong-Canton amity. Two large contracts were awarded to British firms by the municipality of Canton. Malcolm & Company secured a contract for the extension and improvement of the Canton waterworks, providing for the installation of a new waterworks system at a total cost of £81,000, and for a loan to cover it of Ch.$ 1,400,000.[33] The General Electric Company of China was given a contract, amounting to Ch.$ 3,200,000, for a new trolley-bus system for Canton. The municipality agreed to purchase the whole of

---

[32] Mr. O. M. Green, writing for *Pacific Affairs* in June 1938, says that an agreement had been reached in principle between Dr. H. H. Kung and London financial interests for a loan of £20 million.

[33] A six-year loan at 6 per cent, amortized monthly.

the equipment and mechanical plant required for the first section of the trolley-bus scheme. The company agreed to give the municipality credit extending over a period of six years.

The British Boxer Indemnity Funds began to take on new importance. British financing of railway development in China was being largely confined to loans from the British Boxer Indemnity Fund. The completion of the Canton-Hankow Railway in 1936 was made possible by the use of remitted Boxer funds. This project had been recommended in 1926 by the Willingdon Mission as the most important work which could be undertaken with Boxer funds. With the exception of a mile-long stretch across the Yangtze at Hankow, it was now possible to travel by direct rail communication from Canton or Hongkong to Tientsin, Peiping, etc.[34]

The progress made by the Chinese Ministry of Railways in adjusting a number of railway loans long in default[35] and the

[34] During the year ending June 30, 1936, cash loans aggregating $8,580,861, were granted to the following organizations:

Ministry of Railways	$8,040,000
Hwai River Conservancy Commission	405,861
Ministry of Industries	100,000
National Construction Commission	35,000

Apart from cash loans, three loans in materials amounting to $13,837,580 were transferred from the Chinese Government purchasing commission on completion of contract purchases for the Ministries of Railways and Communications, the Chekiang Provincial Government, the Hwai River Conservancy Commission and the China Merchants Steam Navigation Company. Although by December 31, 1936, the orders placed through the Chinese Government purchasing commission in London for British products reached a total of £4,225,881, Germany superseded Britain in 1935 and 1936 as the chief supplier of railway materials to China.

[35] The magnitude of the financial obligation which China had incurred for railway construction in the past was indicated by the statement of total capital obligations outstanding in connection with railway loans as of January 1, 1937: £19,881,656; U.S. $2,334,598; ¥93,600,000; Frs. 49,084,887; Belg. Frs. 137,743,000; Glds. 30,750,000, and local Ch.$ 112,075,456. A large number of these loans had been in default for twelve years or more and the Ministry of Railways was anxious to make some adjustment which would provide at least partial payment on loans in arrears. During 1936 loan service was resumed on, among others, the Tientsin-Pukow loans, the Lunghai loans, the Canton-Kowloon loan and the Honan Railway loan. The terms of settlement involved a considerable scaling down of interest rates and a cancellation of most of the interest in arrears, but the adjustment represented at least a partial "unfreezing" of the investment of foreign bondholders.

On April 4, 1937, the re-servicing of the Hukuang railway loan of 1911 was announced. This loan, originally underwritten by a four-power consortium (Great Britain, France, Germany and the United States), issued to the amount of £6,000,000 in four equal parts, with interest at 5 per cent, maturing in 40 years and amortization beginning in 1922, was outstanding to the total of £5,656,000 in 1937. The loan had been in default with respect to principal and half the interest substantial increase in railway revenues during 1936 stimulated renewed confidence among British firms that new capital investments in railway construction and the supplying of railway materials might be safely undertaken. The announcement was made that British materials would be purchased for the proposed Canton-Meihsien railway, a distance of 350 miles, which was to connect with projected lines in Fukien and Chekiang. In addition, it was authoritatively reported that British capital was likely to be invested in the following projected lines in South China: the Canton-Whampoa railway; the Samshui-Hohsien railway (to link Kwantung and Kwangsi), and the Kweilin-Henshow railway (to connect Kwangsi's new provincial capital with the leading commercial center in southern Hunan). It was also reported at this time that an agreement had been reached between the Ministry of Railways and Innis & Riddle Company, Ltd., a British company in Shanghai, whereby all-British engineering equipment (to a value exceeding Ch.$ 2,500,000) was to be supplied to the Chuchow Central Locomotive and Rolling Stock Repair Shop.

British investors in China were not only impressed with the possibilities for profit in China but also with the strength of the Chinese financial group. This was indicated in the numerous proposals for joint participation with Chinese capital. The successful Six Per Cent Sterling Shanghai-Ningpo-Hangchow Railway Completion Loan of 1936 served as a model for this type of enterprise.[36] This loan was not only the first joint Sino-British undertaking in railway finance but also the first foreign rail-

---

since 1926. The terms of the Hukuang adjustment were generally similar to those effected in the case of the loans mentioned above. Interest payment was to be at the rate of 3 per cent thereafter. Interest in arrears was to be calculated at 1 per cent, for which non-interest-bearing scrip was to be issued. Redemption of the scrip was to begin in 1942 and be completed in about twenty years. Redemption of principal was to begin in 1941 and be completed in 1976. Payment of interest was to be made out of the net earnings of the railway (the Canton-Hankow line) and guaranteed out of the salt revenues. Amortization was to be met out of the earnings of the railway with an undertaking by the Minister of Finance to produce adequate funds from other sources if the earnings were not sufficient. A loan service committee was to be established, consisting of representatives of each of the foreign groups and of the Chinese Government. By May 1937 final quotations of the Hukuang Loan bonds advanced from the 1936-7 low of 43 to 71 in London and 71½ in Shanghai.

[36] Earlier in 1936, a People's Banking Corporation was incorporated in Hongkong with a capital of Ch.$ 100,000,000 contributed by British and Chinese. Its plans were to establish a branch for industrial loans in Szechwan, a province in which the British had long been interested.

way loan to be offered without collateral security of any kind. Under the terms of an agreement with the minister of railways, the £1,100,000 issue was underwritten by a syndicate made up of the British and Chinese Corporation and the China Development Finance Corporation.[37] The loan was secured on the entire revenue of the railway which was already operating profitably.[38] In addition, a loan service committee was to be set up with foreign representation and with budgetary control over the railway. The existing system of joint administration with the Shanghai-Nanking Railway, with a British chief accountant and engineer-in-chief was to be retained. The loan was floated in Shanghai, but early in 1937 the bonds were introduced on the London market at 94½. Gross traffic receipts from this line for the first eight months of the year ending June 30, 1937, amounted to Ch.$ 4,462,270, an increase of 25.6 per cent over the same period in the preceding year. The feasibility of such capital investments was being clearly demonstrated when hostilities broke out in July 1937.

The Leith-Ross Mission had not merely pointed out the opportunities for increased long-term investments in China, but had also indicated the commercial possibilities opened to British firms taking advantage of the many contracts for railway materials, public utility equipment and machinery of all kinds which could be financed by middle-term credits. The credit issue was of primary importance because of the reluctance of many of the British companies exporting to China to assume credit risks involved in the contracts offered, while German firms with a large-scale organization supported by government subsidies were able to grant exceptionally easy credit terms and to underbid their British competitors. The Chinese saw in the appointment of Mr. W. M. Kirkpatrick, as Shanghai representative of the Export Credits Guarantee Department of the British Treasury—a direct result of the Leith-Ross Mission—an indication of the possibility that British credits amounting to £10,000,000 would be forthcoming for the purchase of British goods. But they were disappointed. Officials of the Export

---

[37] See *China Year Book, 1936,* pp. 278-80, for the terms of the contract.

[38] About a third of the proceeds of the loan was to go to repay advances already made to the Shanghai-Hangchow-Nanking Railway during 1934-6 by the syndicate. Most of the remainder was to be used to build a rail and highway bridge across the Chien Tang River and to finance the long-delayed completion of the rail line between Hangchow and Ningpo, two of the principal cities of Chekiang.

Credits Department tended to minimize the importance of Mr. Kirkpatrick's appointment by pointing out that the opening of the Shanghai bank was intended merely to make it easier for British firms to make use of the department's facilities.[39] There was reason to hope, however, that with a representative on the spot, a certain relaxation in credit terms might be made to meet local conditions. British merchants in China pointed out how extremely difficult it would be to provide proof of bankruptcy in China in a form acceptable to a British government department. It was hoped that Mr. Kirkpatrick's personal investigation of credit risks might lead British manufacturers to undertake business which would have to be refused if there were inflexible insistence upon regulations wholly inapplicable to local conditions. Though the arrangements might even lead to a rise in the selling price of British goods because of the charges levied by the Export Credits Guarantee Department, British export trade was expected to benefit by the reduction of the credit risk of the individual manufacturer or exporter.

These British economic activities not only meant profits for the British trader and investor, but also increased pro-British sympathy in Nanking. This sentiment was further strengthened by British aid to Chinese educational and cultural institutions through the Boxer funds. During the year ending June 30, 1935, nearly Ch.$ 1,400,000 was spent in educational allowances, mainly for the Central Museum in Nanking, for the National Library there, for equipment in educational institutions, for scholarships and for rural education. By the end of June 1936 the total amount of interest received on loans made by the board of trustees, available for distribution, approximated Ch.$ 3,356,000, which was about Ch.$ 1,700,000 more than that of 1935. Consequently, grants were appropriated for the preservation of historical and cultural sites; education in Kansu, Tsinghai, Ninghsia and Suiyuan; the construction of a new middle school, and the establishment of a higher vocational and technical school in Nanking in collaboration with the Ministry of Education and

---

[39] The Export Credits Guarantee Department acts as an insurance company. If it is satisfied that the risk is a good one, it will agree to underwrite a loan, possibly to the extent of 60 or 70 per cent, though never to the full amount. There is a charge for this service and the department rules are strict and rigidly applied. Thus, no payment can be expected under its guarantee unless satisfactory proof is forthcoming that the buyer has been declared bankrupt.

the municipal government of Nanking.[40] In this fashion Great Britain was building, as the United States had already done, a more solid basis for future Sino-British cordiality than economic ties alone could establish.

Britain's diplomacy continued to display her desire to obtain Nanking's good will. The doctrine of non-recognition was reaffirmed. The Yunnan-Burma Boundary Commission completed its labors on April 24, 1937,[41] and the report was understood to have recommended that China retain sovereignty over about three-fifths of the disputed area, or some 6,000 square kilometers. The Kuling Estate on January 1, 1936, passed from foreign control, in the form of the Kuling Estate Council, into the possession of the National Government.[42]

Anglo-Japanese Friction, 1936

The cordiality which marked Sino-British relations was not evidenced in Anglo-Japanese relations during 1936. Japan's with-

[40] The details of the disposal of interest and distribution of grants made in accordance with the established regulations may be described under the following five classes:

Class A	National Central Museum, construction	Ch.$300,000
	National Central Library, construction	300,000
	Preservation of historical and cultural sites and antiquities	100,000
Class B	Including professorships to National Central, Sun Yat-sen, Wuhan and Chekiang Universities, Peiping Engineering College, and Central Field Health Station, and grants to Academia Sinica and twenty-five other educational institutions	978,000
Class C	Scholarships on the basis of competitive examination to assistant professors with good academic records or university graduates who have rendered useful public service or published works of technical value, and subsidies for deserving educational activities abroad and other activities tending to promote cultural relations between China and Great Britain	417,000
Class D	Comprising (1) prizes to authors of textbooks of middle, primary and vocational school grades, and (2) prizes to authors of technical works of especial value	28,000
Class E	Grants appropriated for (1) the establishment over a period of years in every province of one model middle school and elementary school, and/or one school of agriculture or other means of promoting rural education, and/or one school of midwifery, and (2) the establishment over a period of years of one industrial vocational school in each large industrial center throughout the country	672,000

[41] The personnel of this commission consisted of a neutral chairman, Colonel F. Iselin (of the Swiss Artillery), Messrs. J. Clague (secretary of the Burmese Government) and F. S. Grose (Superintendent of the Shan States), with Mr. W. Stark Toller (British consul at Tengyueh) as adviser; and Messrs. Liang Yu-kao and Yin Ming-teh (Chinese commissioners).

[42] The British consul-general at Hankow, Mr. G. S. Moss, represented the Estate Council and an agreement was signed by him and by the director of the Bureau of Administration for Lushan. Leases in perpetuity to the lot-holders of all nationalities were granted, and an advisory committee, consisting of seven lot-holders, three of whom were to be foreigners nominated by the foreign lot-holders, was established to advise the director of the Bureau of Administration for Lushan.

drawal from the London Naval Conference and the expiration of the naval treaties on December 31, 1936, were followed by increased haste in completing the Singapore base, the strengthening of Hongkong's fortifications and the announced intention of building a "two-hemisphere" fleet. Japan's adherence to the so-called Anti-Comintern Pact aroused anxiety in Great Britain where in some circles it was regarded as anti-British.[43] Even *Asahi*, which was critical of the pact, interpreted it on March 1, 1937, as an anti-British step.

> By reason of its failure to promote Anglo-Japanese friendship the Japanese Government had no alternative but to conclude the Agreement. It was not the Agreement which made Anglo-Japanese friendship impracticable, but rather the failure of Britain to extend the hand of friendship towards Japan, since she knew she had nothing to gain by doing so, which brought the Agreement into being.

In addition to this friction in the international sphere, the Japanese in Shanghai were agitating against the predominant British control of the International Settlement, causing uneasiness among the British residents there who were anxious about Britain's ability and desire to look after them.

The situation was aggravated by the trade wars which Japan was waging with Australia and Canada. In Japan these self-governing dominions were considered to be "colonies" of Great Britain, and their restrictive policies toward Japanese goods (in addition to the long-standing grievance of their Japanese-exclusion policies) were taken as evidence of the hostility and opposition of British "imperialism" to Japanese ambitions.

Anglo-Japanese Rapprochement, 1937

Nevertheless, in 1937 a distinct improvement did take place. Having re-established her position in China, Britain was in a better position to negotiate with Japan, who now showed a more conciliatory attitude than had been usual since 1934. In January 1937 Foreign Minister Arita, in his speech to the Japanese Diet, emphasized the effect on Japan of the increasing restrictions on Japanese exports and suggested arrangements with Great Britain, the head of the world's largest colonial empire. Moreover, there was a growing need for funds to finance

---

[43] It is interesting to note that the same military groups in Japan who favored eliminating Western interests from China had successfully advocated adherence to the pact.

the economic development of Manchuria, for which purpose access to the London money market was important, if not essential. Mr. Sato, the new foreign minister in General Hayashi's administration (which came into office in February 1937), continued this trend. Japan was to adopt an economic approach to her fundamental problems and reliance was to be placed in trade arrangements for freer markets rather than in a Japan-Manchukuo-China economic bloc. Although he was denounced for being over-conciliatory, there was little disagreement among parliamentary circles with his fundamental plea for a revival of Anglo-Japanese friendship.

A Japanese economic mission headed by Mr. Chokuro Kadono, the president of the Chamber of Commerce and Industry of Japan and an influential leader of the pro-British group in Japan, left Yokohama on April 28, 1937, for the United States and England for the given purpose of returning the visits of Lord Barnby in 1934 and Mr. W. Cameron Forbes in 1935. In the United States the Mission was received by prominent business men and by President Roosevelt. On June 16 the Mission left for England, where similar conversations toward increasing trade between the British Empire and Japan were carried on.

Japan also made diplomatic approaches to Great Britain which resulted in *pourparlers* in London in the early part of 1937.[44] Foreign Secretary Anthony Eden told the House of Commons on March 24 that Mr. Sato's speeches were gratifying

---

[44] Mr. G. E. Hubbard has suggested what the Japanese conceived to be the basis for an Anglo-Japanese rapprochement. "The Japanese conception of such an agreement—provided that any agreement was possible in the state of British public opinion toward Japanese aggression in China—was easily discernible. For Japan an undertaking with Great Britain might open a door by which she might be able to re-enter the society of Western nations without having to renounce her objections to the League of Nations system; it might provide a means of improving her economic conditions and her financial prospects; and above all, it might lead to a recognition of her 'special position' in North China. In return, Japan could offer to conform to British desires by halting in her encroachment upon China's territorial integrity, by respecting British interests in Central and Southern China and by a pledge of non-interference with Chinese plans for economic reconstruction. Apart from China there was room for concessions on both sides, in Great Britain's part by lowering the barriers against Japanese goods in her Crown Colonies and, on Japan's part, by meeting the British wish for an understanding on the subject of the limitation of naval armaments. These, with the exception of the last, were actually the bases for an agreement between Japan and Great Britain which the Japanese Press anticipated when, in April 1937, it predicted the early opening of negotiations in London." *Survey of International Affairs, 1937,* p. 165.

and that Great Britain was equally anxious for friendly and harmonious relations. In the first week in May it was admitted, through official Japanese agencies, that Mr. Yoshida, the Japanese Ambassador in London, was engaged in general conversations with the British Foreign Office as a preliminary to more formal negotiations. In Great Britain, the possibility of an Anglo-Japanese understanding concerning the Far East aroused apprehension in pro-Chinese circles and the government was called upon to deny any intention of reviving the possibility of spheres of influence, and to affirm that no alterations would be made in treaties affecting China without the willing consent of China. In Japan, there were also denials of any intention to re-create spheres of influence, though here the distinction was carefully drawn between "spheres of influence" and "spheres of special interest," which Japan claimed to possess in North China.

The conversations made rapid progress. On June 24 the announcement was made that the Japanese Ambassador had received instructions enabling him to commence discussions on concrete issues in regard both to China and to Anglo-Japanese commercial relations. On the 25th Mr. Eden informed the House of Commons that the conversations which had been going on had encouraged the hope of further progress in the direction of better mutual relations. The outbreak of hostilities in China, however, interrupted these informal conversations, and as announced by Mr. Butler, the Under-Secretary of State for foreign affairs, the Japanese Government was informed that the British Government considered the initiation of the proposed negotiations as inopportune so long as the existing conditions in China persisted. The conversations were adjourned *sine die*.

The Chinese were made anxious by the possibility of an Anglo-Japanese rapprochement,

> for there were palpable loopholes in the assurances which were given of respect for the interests of China. It was difficult, indeed, to conceive any possible basis for an Anglo-Japanese understanding other than one which would imply at least a partial recognition by Great Britain of the *de facto* situation which Japan had created for herself in Manchuria and North China, in return for Japanese renunciation of further aggression. A situation was, in fact, developing in July 1937, in regard to China which bore at least a superficial resemblance to that which would have resulted from the Hoare-Laval agreement in respect to Italy and Abyssinia in 1935.[45]

[45] *Survey of International Affairs, 1937*, Vol. I, p. 167.

Wang Chung-hui, foreign minister of China, expressed surprise at the opening of discussions on matters affecting China without prior consultation of his government, which was watching the conversations with the closest interest and anxiety. Any new international arrangements in the Far East must, he said, if they were to serve peaceful ends, provide for the territorial and administrative inviolability of China and for non-interference in her economic and political development. Other Chinese spokesmen insisted on American participation in any new international understanding for the economic development of China.

These abortive informal negotiations did not succeed in overcoming friction between Japanese and British policies in China. Not only had Great Britain helped to make the Chinese Government more capable of resisting Japanese pressure, but there was obvious contrast between the halting, obstructed progress of Japanese economic expansion in North China and the steady advance which British interests were making in Central and South China.

There is little doubt that China's growing prestige abroad and especially its intimacy with Great Britain—in flat defiance of the "Monroe Doctrine for China" which Japan had announced in the spring of 1934—was a large ingredient in the soldiers' decision that they must strike before China became too strong.[46]

[46] O. M. Green, "Great Britain and Japan's War on China," *Pacific Affairs*, June 1938.

CHAPTER V

FROM LUKOUCHIAO TO THE BRUSSELS
CONFERENCE

The outbreak of hostilities in China in the summer of 1937 raised many immediate and long-range problems for the British. How long would the war last? What parts of China would be involved? What rights had the contending parties who were not technically belligerents? What of Britain's obligations under the Covenant of the League of Nations and the Washington treaties? What would other parties, especially the United States, do? What were the relations between the hostilities in China and the threatened hostilities in Europe? Should the diplomatic policy being applied in Europe be automatically applied in the Far East? If not, what were the alternatives? These and other questions were answered along two general lines—immediate measures to meet immediate problems, and general principles, especially neutrality, strict impartiality, and the maintenance of Britain's legal rights. These questions had to be answered at a time when the Spanish war had become the focus of world-wide attention, when Austria was seized by, and Czechoslovakia in imminent danger from, the Third Reich. To the European situation the British Government continued to apply the "non-intervention" and "appeasement" policies which neither checked aggression nor appeased the aggressors.

British Reaction to Fighting in North China

When hostilities broke out at Lukouchiao on July 7-8, 1937, there was reason to suppose that they might be localized. Clashes between Japanese and Chinese troops had occurred before without developing into general hostilities. That China would fight before making concessions was little suspected by the British communities in China. "No one can seriously believe that the Chinese government desires to engage in hostilities with Japan," stated the *North-China Herald*.[1] The Shanghai Municipal police

[1] *North-China Herald*, July 14, 1937.

took the precaution to increase patrols in districts with a large proportion of Japanese residents but nearly two weeks after the outbreak in the north, a peaceful settlement was still considered possible.[2]

In Great Britain, the danger that the North China incident would develop into general hostilities was considered small, and the Government indicated that it desired the localization of the conflict. It also made clear that it was neutral and impartial toward the contending parties, and it offered to mediate the dispute. Foreign Secretary Anthony Eden assured the House of Commons on July 12, that his latest information was that Peking was quiet. He refused to pronounce upon the merits of the dispute, but said he fully recognized its possible repercussions on British interests and hoped there would be a chance of discussing these matters with the Japanese Ambassador. On July 14 he stated that he had been in touch with the Chinese and Japanese Governments, and had made clear to them that the British Government was watching the situation closely and was much concerned lest hasty action on their side should lead to a conflict.[3]

Mr. Eden, surveying international affairs for Parliament on July 19, said that neither government had deliberately provoked the conflict and there were assurances from both sides that they wished it localized. Moreover, His Majesty's Government had been in communication with the French and the United States Governments, and had made it clear in Nanking and in Tokyo that it was ready to help in any useful form of mediation. A real settlement, however, he maintained, could not be secured without a change of method by the contending parties.

The *Times* on July 22, although in general accord with the government's position, was more hostile to the Japanese. The

[2] *North-China Herald*, July 24, 1937. A concrete manifestation of the optimism in Shanghai was the report that the Chinese Government had concluded, with British and Chinese corporations, contracts for two 5 per cent loans of £3,000,000 and £4,000,000, respectively, for the construction of two railways—one from Shelstan, on the Canton-Kowloon Railway, to Meihsien in Kwangtung; the other from Pukow to Hsiangyang. The loans were to be secured on the revenues of the railways and on the Salt Gabelle.

[3] The Chinese Ambassador, two days later, submitted to the Foreign Secretary a memorandum setting forth "the status and circumstances of the present threat from Japan in North China." It declared that the attack on Lukouchiao and the Japanese invasion constituted a clear violation of China's sovereignty and the Nine-Power Treaty, the Kellogg Treaty, and the League Covenant.

unfriendly attitude now taken toward Japanese "saber-rattling" contrasted sharply with the attitude which had prevailed in 1931.

> It is no exaggeration to say that if Japan went to war with China the best thing—the only good thing—that could happen to her would be a prompt and decisive defeat by the Chinese forces: which is inconceivable. . . . There exist, in short, no strategic, political, or economic objectives which a military adventure in North China could make good.

Again on August 6 the *Times* said:

> It now seems certain that the *status quo* in North China will not be restored—not, at least, for a century or two; and it also seems probable that Japan will shortly make a localized but strenuous military effort to make good her position. . . . Meanwhile the world awaits developments with anxiety. The Governments of this country and of the United States have made strong representations in the cause of peace, but Tokyo has intimated that she will not welcome intervention. Since effective intervention is scarcely possible, Tokyo's attitude in this matter is of purely academic interest. But Japan is mistaken if she thinks that her actions during the last month, and the "punitive" policy which she now contemplates, have impressed the world with anything save her irresponsibility. It is possible to pick your enemies, but it is not possible to pick your friends; and Japan seems bent on a course which must do grave damage to her standing in the eyes of other countries.

The statements of *Finance and Commerce*, an authoritative spokesman for British economic interests in China, shed light on the attitude of the British in China. Although expressing sympathy for China and condemning the Japanese for their aggressive policy, it counseled China to capitulate once again.[4] Thus, *Finance and Commerce* wrote,

> if the Central Government reaches the conclusion that the time has come to fight for its existence, war will spread from North to South. For a short while there will doubtless be great demonstrations of patriotic fervour, but, however stubbornly China may resist, she can scarcely hope to win a military victory, and the loss in trade and treasure will be enormous.

It commented in the same vein on Madame Chiang Kai-shek's appeal to the women of the country to support the army's rear.

> It is not difficult to sympathize with the appeal. . . . At the same time it would perhaps be wiser statesmanship if the country were advised to bear one further humiliation if need be, rather than risk, at this stage, the complete destruction of everything which has been done towards national rehabilitation during the past two decades. . . . We are satisfied that

---

[4] *Finance and Commerce,* indicated on July 21 that it realized that the issue involved was whether the Central Government would acquiesce in the gradual whittling down of its authority.

Japan has no desire to see an extension of the area of hostilities, although it may be taken for granted that she is prepared for all eventualities, which China is not. . . . Admittedly, China is being coerced, but her only way to salvation is to make the best terms she can for a settlement in the North . . . No feeling of humiliation or exasperation should be allowed to turn her from that one great objective.[5]

In the same spirit the British Government made continuous representations for a peaceful settlement.[6] That the situation in the Far East was steadily growing worse, however, was noted by the foreign secretary. On July 28 the British *chargé d'affaires* at Tokyo called upon Mr. Hirota, the Japanese foreign minister, to express his government's concern. Mr. Hirota replied that he had not yet abandoned hope that the crisis might be localized and added that every effort would be made to protect foreign nationals in North China.

Fighting in Shanghai

The clash between Japanese and Chinese Central Government troops at Nankow, and the extension of the scene of warfare to Shanghai, ended the question of localizing the conflict in North China. On August 12, 1937, when the Chinese 88th Division from Nanking moved into the Shanghai area to reinforce the local forces, the Japanese authorities convened a meeting of the Joint International Truce Commission. This commission had been appointed to supervise the 1932 Agreement guaranteeing the neutrality of Shanghai.[7] At this meeting the Japanese lodged a protest as the result of which the Joint Commission requested the mayor of Greater Shanghai to withdraw the 88th Division from the Shanghai area. He refused, declaring that such a request should be referred to Nanking. The meet-

[5] *Finance and Commerce*, Aug. 4, 1937. See also Aug. 11, 1937, for similar statement.

[6] Mr. Eden in the House of Commons, July 27, 1937. The United States and France made similar representations.

[7] The 1932 Agreement provided that all Chinese regular forces should be replaced by the Peace Preservation Corps, but, when they signed it, the Chinese declared—in an annex regarding the positions in which their troops should remain—that nothing in the agreement implied any permanent restriction of the movements of Chinese troops in Chinese territory. The commission had held no meeting since 1932, but in the intervening years the Japanese had on several occasions drawn the attention of the commission to alleged breaches by China. The other powers refused to accept Japan's broad interpretation of the agreement and were prone to consider the agreement as designed to meet the particular situation existing in 1932. Since it could enable the powers to exercise a restraining influence on both parties in the event of a crisis, the agreement was not formally terminated.

ing adjourned after both sides undertook not to attack unless fired upon. The British Government followed this with representations to both sides, expressing the hope that foreign lives and property in Shanghai might not be exposed to danger from military operations. But on August 13, 1937, the Japanese bombardment of Shanghai began and the British authorities were called upon to protect British residents and interests.[8] Thus, the British ambassador protested the accidental bombing by the Chinese of the International Settlement and H.M.S. *Cumberland*. Evacuation of British women and children was begun. At home, the cabinet issued a statement on August 17 declaring that the ministers had considered all possible steps "in an endeavor to ensure a peaceful solution to the situation at Shanghai," but had decided to "adopt all possible measures to protect British lives and interests there."[9] The *Times* of August 20, 1937, wrote, "it is time for Japan to learn that the free hand which she desires in Eastern Asia will in no circumstances include licence to play havoc with the lawful interests of Great Britain."

Anti-British Incidents

The first major Anglo-Japanese incident was the serious wounding of the British Ambassador, Sir Hughe Knatchbull-Hugessen, on August 26, 1937, when Japanese aviators fired on the automobile in which he was traveling from Nanking to Shanghai. The Japanese ambassador in London immediately expressed his personal regrets and sympathy, but the Japanese Government reserved its attitude, while the Japanese press suggested that the Union Jack upon the car had not been large enough, and that the ambassador had not notified the Japanese authorities of his intention to visit Shanghai, or of the route he proposed to take. The implication that the ambassador of a

[8] The Japanese Foreign Office issued a statement on August 16th regarding the suggestion that Japan should refrain from military operations at Shanghai. It said that 30,000 Japanese were in the city and could not be abandoned. "In 1927 it was a mob of anti-British demonstrators who invaded the International Settlement. The Municipal Council then took forceful measures to suppress the disturbance, and not a word was said about the legal or moral responsibilities of the British in the matter. Britain sent 17,000 men to protect her interests and the Settlement. It now happens to be a large force of Chinese regulars who are attacking the Settlement with the Japanese as their objective. The two cases do not differ except in their scope and Japan cannot be held responsible for damages the Chinese have caused or may cause." (The *Times*, August 17, 1937.)

[9] The *Times*, August 18, 1937.

friendly foreign power had to account for his actions and whereabouts to a third power was, of course, without legal foundation. This acceptance by Japan of the rights of a belligerent without the corresponding duties was to become characteristic of her relations with Great Britain. After the British authorities had carefully investigated the case, the British Government addressed a note of protest to the Japanese Government, which was handed to the foreign minister in Tokyo on August 29. In the light of the outrage, the protest was mild indeed. The Japanese Government was to make a formal apology; those responsible were to be punished, and an assurance was requested that measures would be taken to prevent a recurrence. The Japanese Government, in an *ad interim* reply on September 6, expressed its regrets, and these were repeated in a formal reply on September 21. The question of punishing those responsible for the attack was evaded on the ground that responsibility had not been established. As for the prevention of recurrences, the Japanese said that they had renewed instructions to their forces to exercise care in "safeguarding non-combatants." Though only one of the three demands of the British note had been fulfilled, the British Government accepted the answer as satisfactory and declared the incident closed.

The fighting in and around Shanghai lasted until about November 9, 1937. During this period several Japanese actions caused the greatest concern and injury to British lives and property. Of outstanding importance were the declaration of the "pacific blockade," the seizure of the Pratas shoals off Hongkong, interference with the Customs Administration, the refusal to withdraw Japanese troops from the Shanghai area and the destruction of British property during the bombing of Chinese cities. The British Government replies to these measures indicated their conciliatory attitude toward the Japanese.

On August 25 the commander of the Japanese naval forces at Shanghai proclaimed a blockade against Chinese shipping all along the coast from Shanghai southward to a point below Swatow. On September 5 the blockade was extended to all coastal waters from Chinwangtao on the border of Manchukuo to Pakhoi, with the exception of Tsingtao. The blockade was not to apply to foreign shipping but the right was reserved to hail all merchant vessels within Chinese waters in order to ascertain their identity.[10] Foreign shipping companies were requested to inform the Japanese authorities of the movements of their vessels in Chinese waters. The British Government acceded to these declarations and on September 11 proposed that British merchant captains should be advised to submit to examination of their papers in the forbidden zone, on two conditions: (1) if a British warship were in the vicinity, the permission of her captain should be obtained; and (2) in the absence of a British warship, the result of the Japanese inquiry should be reported to the British naval authorities at once. The Japanese Foreign Office welcomed the British proposals and expressed the hope that other governments would follow the British example in co-operating with the Japanese Navy.

On September 4, Japan began the seizure of the islands off the China coast. Pratas Shoal, eighty miles southeast of Hongkong, was seized; the meteorological and wireless stations there were wrecked, and, according to the crew of the Hongkong Clipper, Japanese destroyers immediately began to use it as a naval base. The British Government chose to take no action.

The Japanese also seriously interfered with the Customs Administration, in whose functioning the British had always shown great concern. Thus on September 6, Japanese warships seized two Chinese customs preventive launches near Hongkong waters. According to Sir Frederick Maze, they had been deliberately bombed and machine-gunned by Japanese aircraft. The customs preventive fleet had not taken any part in the hostilities; they possessed no military value and were used solely for customs enforcement. Moreover, the bombing of these vessels seriously jeopardized the lives of the foreign officers in command—both of whom were British—who were engaged in the peaceful performance of their duties as customs officers. The Hongkong Government announced that the incident had been reported to London and to the British Embassy in Tokyo for diplomatic negotiations. The British Government did nothing effective to prevent the recurrence of such incidents.

British Attitude toward "Incidents"

Great Britain did, however, show more concern for the International Settlement in Shanghai, but this did not prevent im-

---

[10] On September 2 Mr. Hirota had informed the foreign correspondents that the exemption of foreign ships from the naval blockade would not be extended to those carrying munitions of war.

portant losses to British interests there. The dispatch of the 2nd Battalion of the Royal Welsh Fusiliers and the 1st Battalion of the Royal Ulster Rifles considerably strengthened the military position of the Settlement and made possible the return to a more normal existence by the end of August.

This did not mean, however, that the International Settlement was henceforth secure from the effects of the hostilities. British nationals and property within the Settlement continued to suffer injuries from the Japanese bombardment. The British official position on the losses caused by the hostilities was that the Chinese and Japanese Governments would be held responsible. When an attempt was made by the British, French and American naval commanders to relieve the International Settlement and the French Concession of the perils arising from the military operations by requesting the withdrawal of the Japanese warships and of the Chinese troops from the section of Pootung immediately opposite the International Settlement and the French Concession, the Japanese refused.

The extension of the bombing to Nanking on September 19 indicated that the Japanese did not intend to refrain from bombing civilians. The British Government instructed its ambassador in Tokyo, Sir Robert Craigie, to make representations to the Japanese Government against the bombing of anything but military objectives in Nanking, on the ground that such attacks would endanger the lives of civilians. The British Government reserved the right to hold Japan responsible for any loss of British lives or damage to British property. On September 25 the British Ambassador made further representations concerning the bombardment of Canton as well as Nanking. The bombardments of Shanghai, Nanking and Canton continued and on September 29, the Japanese Government indicated its refusal to cease the bombardment of Nanking. More effective for the protection of British interests was the dispatch of H.M.S. *Diamond* to Amoy.

Those attacks on British lives and property could not be effectively countered as long as Britain regarded herself as a potential mediator. An acceptable mediator must have the confidence and friendship of both parties. "Deploring though they do her present policy of aggression, the British people are anxious to maintain their friendship with Japan no less than with China," wrote the *North-China Herald*. Japan and China were urged to make peace and if the "services of a third party are required, both China and Japan can count on friends who would be willing to offer such services should they be likely to lead to practical results."[11] The Japanese official veto on October 1 of the British mediation offer ended this possibility for the time being. With the rejection of this individual mediation offer, British diplomacy began to center around the League of Nations in an effort to achieve the same end.[12]

League of Nations Discussion

Dr. Wellington Koo had addressed the Assembly of the League of Nations on September 15 on the subject of the Sino-Japanese hostilities, asking it to denounce Japan's policy.[13] The Council on September 15, in private session, decided to refer the Chinese appeal to the Far Eastern Advisory Committee which had been set up on February 24, 1933. This proposal was accepted by Dr. Koo.[14] On September 21 the Advisory Committee met and was attended by a United States observer. The Committee decided to invite four more states—China, Japan, Germany and Australia. Mr. Bruce of Australia suggested that the League should arrange for a conference of the powers most vitally concerned in the Far East, whether members of the League or not, with a view to attempting to find a settlement of some kind.

The Far Eastern Advisory Committee met again on September 27. Lord Cranborne, presenting the British position, expressed the hope that the committee "in unmistakable terms" would express its opinion on the practice of indiscriminate bombing. The British Government had reserved all their rights as regards holding the Japanese responsible for the consequences of such bombing but this was a matter which went "far beyond the interests of any single nationality. The extension of air bombing in China represents a menace not only to the unhappy people who are suffering so grievously from it today, but to the whole world." The Committee then passed a resolution regarding "the aerial bombardment of open towns in China by Japanese aircraft" in which it expressed "its profound distress

[11] *North-China Herald*, September 15, 1937, p. 395.
[12] *North-China Herald*, September 29 and October 6, 1937.
[13] *Official Journal*, League of Nations, 1937, Special Supplement, No. 169, p. 46 ff.
[14] *Official Journal*, League of Nations, 1937, Special Supplement, No. 177, p. 13 ff.

at the loss of life caused to innocent civilians, including great numbers of women and children as a result of such bombardment, solemnly condemns such acts, and declares that they have aroused horror and indignation throughout the world." On September 28 the Assembly unanimously adopted this resolution of the Far Eastern Committee.

The Far Eastern Advisory Committee reconvened on September 29 and October 1, when it adopted a French proposal to set up a sub-committee.[15] The United States was invited and agreed to participate in the sub-committee as an observer. The terms of reference were "to examine the situation arising out of the Sino-Japanese conflict in the Far-East." The sub-committee was also entrusted with the preparation of reports on questions arising out of the situation and the formulation of any proposals which it might see fit to submit to the Advisory Committee. Lord Cranborne said that the British Government would accept Mr. Bruce's suggestion for a Pacific powers conference, if other interested parties also did so.

The Far Eastern Committee reassembled on October 5 and two reports were laid before it. The first found no indication from either side that there was anything in their relations which could not be settled amicably, but declared that the military operations being carried on by Japan against China by land, sea and air were out of all proportion to the incident. It also stated that the Japanese actions were in contravention to Japan's obligations under the Nine Power Treaty of February 6, 1932, and under the Pact of Paris of August 27, 1928. The second report suggested that further efforts had to be made to secure restoration of peace by agreement, and recommended that the Assembly should invite those members of the League who were parties to the Nine Power Treaty to initiate at the earliest practicable moment the "full and frank communication" and consultation provided by that Treaty. Other states with special interests in the Far East might be associated with this work. Moreover, the Assembly should

express its moral support for China and recommend that members of the League should refrain from taking any action that might have the effect

[15] The members of this sub-committee were Australia, Belgium, China, Ecuador, France, the Netherlands, New Zealand, Poland, Sweden, the United Kingdom and the U.S.S.R. The Polish delegate announced that pending instructions from his government he would not attend the meetings.

of weakening China's power of resistance and thus increase her difficulties in the present conflict, and should also consider how far they can individually extend aid to China.

The Far Eastern Committee adopted these reports and decided to communicate them to the Assembly, to the members of the League, and to the American Government. The Assembly also adopted these reports and requested the president to take the necessary action with regard to the proposed meeting of the members of the League who were parties to the Nine Power Treaty.

In the United States the proceedings of the League were followed with great interest. President Roosevelt chose the same day on which the Far Eastern Committee presented its two reports to make his Chicago "quarantine the aggressor" speech, and the text of the speech was in the hands of the League Assembly when it acted on October 6. On that day the American State Department issued a statement agreeing with the conclusions of the Assembly.

Great Britain was quick to sound out the implications of the American position. The British ambassador in Washington was instructed to inquire in what ways the American Government contemplated giving effect to the co-operation with the "peace-loving nations" to which the President had referred. In London Mr. Eden received the American *chargé d'affaires* to inform him of the British Government's gratification at President Roosevelt's speech and on October 8 Mr. Chamberlain, addressing the Conservative Party Conference at Scarborough, referred to Mr. Roosevelt's speech as "a clarion call from the other side of the Atlantic" and declared that the British Government would gladly co-operate in any effort to secure the restoration and maintenance of peace.[16]

Brussels Conference

Isolationist sentiment in the American Congress, however, prevented the implementation of the October 5th speech and the Administration rapidly retreated. The president in a "fireside chat" on October 12 and in a statement to the press indicated that the purpose of a proposed conference would be solely mediation. This was borne out in the announcement on October 15 that the Belgian Government, as a result of con-

[16] London *Times*, October 9, 1937.

versations which had taken place between the United Kingdom and American Governments, had accepted the mission of convening a conference in Brussels. On October 16 invitations were sent by Belgium to all the signatories of the Nine Power Treaty and to the five adherents to the Treaty (Norway, Sweden, Denmark, Bolivia and Mexico) and to Germany and the U.S.S.R. The invitations were explicitly stated to be "at the request of the British Government and with the approval of the Government of the United States," and the purpose of the conference to be, in conformity with the Nine Power Treaty, "to examine the situation in the Far East, and to study peaceable means of hastening the end of the regrettable conflict which prevails there."[17] The possibility of either military or economic sanctions was considered extremely remote by the British and American press.

Mr. Eden, in a statement on foreign policy made to the House of Commons on October 21, gave an account of the efforts which had already been made to settle the Far Eastern conflict. The British Government had from the first made it clear that their good offices were available at any time and when hostilities began at Shanghai, they had offered to undertake the protection of Japanese nationals jointly with other powers, in exchange for the withdrawal of the Japanese troops. In all this they had kept in close touch with the other governments, including the United States. He then summarized the events at Geneva which resulted in the approaching Brussels Conference. The same day, the Earl of Plymouth, stating the Government's present position to the House of Lords, emphasized the fact that the primary object of the Conference was to find a way of restoring peace by general agreement.

The speech from the Throne, delivered by the King on October 26, further indicated that the British Government would "persist in their policy of attempting, in cooperation with other Governments, whether members of the League of Nations or not, to mitigate the suffering caused by the conflict and to bring it to a conclusion." Mr. Eden, however, in an address to the House of Commons on November 1, indicated clearly that American co-operation was the *sine qua non* for any British action regarding the Far East. The foreign secretary, in view of the recognized isolationist feeling in the United States, was

[17] Text of notes in *New York Times*, October 17, 1937.

really undertaking very little when he said that Great Britain would "go as far as the United States in full accord with them, not rushing ahead and not being left behind." His willingness to travel, "not only from Geneva to Brussels but from Melbourne to Alaska" to obtain American co-operation indicated a penchant for traveling, rather than for leadership.[18]

The British press in China regarded the Brussels Conference as serving a mediatory and conciliatory function.

For the Far East, the significant point is that the United States of America, with the concurrence of European powers, has been moved by the crisis here to restart a method of appeasement which in recent years has been so disappointingly ineffective. Amid their other preoccupations these powers would not have so exposed themselves to the danger of futility had they not the conviction that a real opportunity for constructive mediation had offered. . . . To Brussels, therefore, the world looks with restrained optimism; past experience urges avoidance of extravagant expectation. It is enough that an approach to sanity is being attempted.[19]

The Brussels Conference, foredoomed to failure, opened on November 31. Japan and Germany refused to attend. Italy attended and defended the position of Japan.[20] The British position, following the American, stressed conciliation and defended the right of the powers directly interested in the Far East to consult together and see if there was any way in which they could assist toward an early cessation of hostilities and the restoration of stable conditions.

The Conference, in private conversations and meetings held

[18] In China the Japanese had continued to do serious injury to British interests. Thus, the Chinese fishermen of Hongkong, in spite of their British nationality, were not exempt from the attacks of Japanese warships, and, in an appeal which they made for British naval protection early in October, their representatives declared that two hundred boats had failed to return from the fishing-grounds and were believed to have been sunk by the Japanese. The Japanese defended their action by declaring that these boats were armed and therefore open to the suspicion of hostile intent. (Their armament, it was well known, consisted of small and antiquated cannon as protection against pirates and had no military significance.) A more probable explanation was the desire to open the field to Japanese fishermen. Moreover, the promises given by the Japanese after the Knatchbull-Hugessen incident did not prevent a second attack on British Embassy motor cars on the road from Nanking to Shanghai on October 12. The Japanese authorities had been notified beforehand of the intended journey and route and the cars were marked on the roof with the British colors. The occupants escaped injury. In this case, as in the case of the attack on the British ambassador, an apology was accepted by the British Government.

[19] *North-China Herald,* October 20, 1937.

[20] Italy adhered to the German-Japanese Anti-Comintern Pact of November 25, 1936, on November 6, 1937.

on November 4th, discussed questions of procedure, including the advisability of setting up a small committee to act in a mediatory capacity and the desirability of dispatching to Tokyo a second note of invitation, recalling the provisions for consultation in Article 7 of the Nine Power Treaty and suggesting, as an alternative to participation in the Conference, the establishment of direct contact with the proposed committee. Such a letter was dispatched to Tokyo on November 6.

Japan again refused to co-operate with the powers at the Conference. The Conference then gave up its attempts to conciliate Japan and began the drafting of a declaration setting out their rights and views in relation to the conflict. Mr. Eden declared that not only British national interests, but British belief in the necessity for upholding international law, explained the co-operation of his country in the Conference. It was impossible, he said, to assent to the doctrine that the conflict was a matter for Japan and China alone.

The Conference finally adopted on November 15, by a vote of 15 to 1 (Italy), a long declaration submitted by the American, French and British delegations.[21] It embodied the conviction of the Conference that a just and desirable settlement was not to be expected of direct negotiations between the parties. A cessation of hostilities, it pointed out, might offer a chance for negotiating a satisfactory settlement and the hope was expressed that Japan would not persist in her refusal to participate. On November 24 the final session of the Conference adopted another declaration, from which Italy alone dissented, which affirmed the Nine Power Treaty as an instrument for the safeguarding of international peace and security. It also expressed its conviction that force could provide no just and lasting solution for disputes between nations. The declaration concluded by strongly urging a prompt suspension of hostilities as being in the best interests of all concerned. Then, instead of going out of existence entirely, the Conference declared that it was merely adjourning its sitting, i.e., having a recess, and provided for its being recalled should the chairman or members so recommend. This left the door open for a future session of the Conference.

Mr. Norman Davis, the American representative, said the adjournment in no way meant that the problem was to be dropped, or that interest in its solution had lessened. He was

[21] Norway, Sweden and Denmark abstained from voting.

returning to the United States to consult his Government. Lord Cranborne associated himself with Mr. Davis's remarks and expressed the view that the conclusions incorporated in the declaration represented the limit of existing possibilities.[22] This indicated the failure of the Conference since the declaration did not go even so far as the report which the Far Eastern Advisory Committee had adopted on October 5.

[22] *The Conference of Brussels, November 3-24, 1937*, issued by the United States Government Printing Office.

CHAPTER VI

FROM SHANGHAI TO NANKING

While the futile Brussels Conference was in session, a far-reaching change for foreign interests had taken place in China. The capture of Shanghai had been completed and the drive toward Nanking begun. This raised the immediate and vital problems of the future relations between the International Settlement and the Japanese surrounding it, the future of the Customs Administration and the difficulties arising from the military situation.

The Japanese authorities had pledged themselves to respect foreign rights and interests in Shanghai. Thus when hostilities ceased in this vicinity, it was expected that the Japanese, in fulfillment of these pledges, would allow the return of foreign and Chinese residents and the reopening of commercial enterprises in Hongkew and Yangtzepoo, the areas under Japanese control. Although these parts of the Settlement which lie north of Soochow Creek contained important Japanese industrial and shipping concerns, they were equally the center of British and other foreign interests, since almost all of the larger foreign manufacturing firms had their factories and godowns in this area. Hongkew and Yangtzepoo were also the sites of public utility installations, including the Shanghai Power Company (American) and the Shanghai Waterworks Company (British). This area, moreover, contained the chief municipal refrigerators and food storage depots. In addition, nine-tenths of the Settlement's developed water frontage on the Whangpoo lay north of Soochow Creek, and British-owned wharves and docks in the area represented a financial investment greater than did the Japanese. Outside this area there was no wharfage accommodation for vessels of any size in the Settlement proper. Moreover, the industrial and commercial life of the Settlement could not revive until Chinese laborers were allowed to return to their homes and occupations in Hongkew and Yangtzepoo. The Japanese, however, refused to open these areas, maintaining that it would result in guerrilla activities. On December 15 foreign residents together with their Chinese servants were permitted to return to certain portions of the Settlement north of the Creek, but numerous restrictions made the permission almost valueless.

The Japanese also gave indication that the unoccupied parts of the Settlement might come under Japanese influence or domination. General Matsui, the Japanese commander in Shanghai, on November 11, 1937, told foreign correspondents that it was extremely difficult to maintain peace and order in Shanghai in co-operation with the foreign powers. The future, he said, would decide whether the Japanese would have to take over the sections defended by the powers. The Foreign Office spokesman in Tokyo was quick to give a categorical assurance that this did not mean that Japan had any intentions of occupying the Settlement. Nevertheless, the Japanese consul-general in Shanghai did make a number of requests to the authorities in the International Settlement and the French Concession, compliance in which was reported to have been promised as far as was possible. These requests included suppression of all anti-Japanese activities, especially on the part of branches of the Kuomintang, and the removal of the Chinese Government offices and central and local government representatives. General Matsui was understood to have informed the secretary-general of the Municipal Council that if the steps taken did not produce the desired results, the Japanese Army reserved the right to take independent steps in that direction. Furthermore, *Asahi,* on November 26, reported that the Japanese prime minister had told the press on the previous day that "as regards the Shanghai International Settlement issue, Japan may find it necessary to resort to force." These threats to the International Settlement, the foundation of Britain's position in central China, seemingly aroused no great concern in the home government. Lord Cranborne on November 26, in reply to questions in Parliament, evaded the issue of the International Settlement, claiming that the Government had not been consulted about the course pursued by the British members of the Shanghai Municipal Council. Nevertheless, on later occasions, when the British Government wished to act on this question, it did not leave the initiative for action up to the Council.

Attitude of the Shanghai Press

The home government's do-nothing policy was in accord with the accommodating attitude of the British press in Shanghai during this period. The Japanese views on the International Settlement were accepted without challenge and the "realities" of the situation were stressed. On November 24, 1937, *Finance and Commerce* wrote:

> Broadly speaking, Japan considers that she has taken the place of China in this area, and, consequently, is entitled to have her wishes respected in connection with all such activities as were formerly directed, influenced or controlled by the Chinese, as distinct from the Council authorities. If this is the correct interpretation of the situation and, on the basis of information so far available, there seems to be no other, there would be no more interference with the Council's authority or administrative duties than there was previously from China herself. In effect, Japan has intimated that everything associated with foreign interests within the Settlement limits should proceed as before, but reserves to herself the right, "in principle," to supersede the Chinese in the conduct of Chinese Government institutions, the extent to which that right will be exercised depending, presumably, upon a variety of considerations, which have not been specifically enumerated, but which will naturally include satisfaction of the Japanese command that nothing in any way disadvantageous to Japan will be attempted by those now in control.
>
> Japan justifies this stand upon the argument that the Council's jurisdiction is limited by the Land Regulations, which is certainly true, and apparently is satisfied that no international complications will arise if nothing is done to interfere with the authority which such Regulations give. There is no doubt her officials believe that they are treading a strictly legal path and from the foreigners' point of view and even from the point of view of China, if the Chinese leaders have any regard for their civilian population, it would seem that a way out of an impasse is being provided which, in all the circumstances, should be welcomed.

The justification for this attitude was found in the "basic" weakness of the British position in Shanghai:

> Let us endeavour to look at the realities of the situation and describe them in a light most favorable to foreign and Chinese interests. If it were assumed that the Municipal Council could oppose Japan and categorically reject any suggestion of Japanese influence in Settlement activities, whatever the nature of these activities might be, and further, that Japan was willing to accept the rebuff, the prospect of any improvement in conditions here would not be improved in the slightest degree. If the war is going to be a protracted one, Japan would not need to take any further drastic action in this area in order to bring Shanghai into line with her wishes. She might adopt a passive attitude, ignore the Settlement entirely, but keep a cordon of troops in the outlying districts, and before twelve months had passed

the city would be dying of inaction. At any rate half of the foreign community would be leaving. There would be no purpose in their staying, for it must be recognized that the congested population of the International Settlement and the French Concession depends upon trade, and trade is now completely under the control of the Japanese forces.

Writing the following week in a similar vein, *Finance and Commerce* stated that

developments, as far as they have gone, do not appear to provide ground for the alarmist reports that the status of the Municipal Council is endangered and that Shanghai will, in the future, be a Japanese preserve and no place in which other foreigners may expect a fair deal. . . . No one seems to know what precisely are the legal rights of an army, which has obtained possession of terrain by force without a declaration of war, but obviously the Council, as the administrators of a small piece of neutral territory in the middle of a battlefield, are not in a position to argue over legal technicalities. Nor, in one sense, can such legalities be regarded as of vital concern either to them or to the ratepayers whom they represent. Broadly speaking, the ground landlord has been changed for the time being, and, viewing the matter from a strictly business point of view, unclouded by sympathies or predilections, that is a matter of indifference to the leaseholders, providing the conditions of the lease are respected.

The position may become a difficult and delicate one. . . . It behooves the Council to act upon their own initiative, and to discuss with the new and possibly temporary, ground landlord, questions of detail concerning the estate in as reasonable a manner as possible. According to official statements made, that is being done.[1]

This make-shift and opportunist policy did not mean, however, a general condoning of Japanese actions. For example, the "victory parade" through the International Settlement staged on December 3 by the Japanese troops as a warning against anti-Japanese activities among the Chinese population aroused marked antagonism among British residents. Informal efforts to persuade the Japanese military authorities not to carry out the demonstration were not successful and about 3,000 men marched through the Settlement. When the demonstration was nearly over, a Chinese threw a small bomb which slightly wounded two Japanese soldiers, one civilian and a British police inspector. The Japanese troops deployed and occupied the area in which the incident occurred. Representations made to the Japanese commander by the British commissioner of the Settlement police succeeded in having the Japanese troops withdrawn.

[1] *Finance and Commerce,* December 1, 1937. See also *North-China Herald,* November 24, 1937, "The Mood Subfusc," for expression of a similar opinion.

The opposition to the parade in Shanghai was supported by the home government. Mr. Eden stated to the House of Commons on December 6 that the British ambassador in Tokyo, on hearing of the projected march, at once made representations to the Japanese Foreign Office pointing out that the march appeared to be both provocative and uncalled for, and that the Japanese military authorities had to take full responsibility for any trouble that might arise. Nevertheless, the government's basic attitude toward the whole situation in China was reflected by Mr. Eden's refusal to accept a suggestion that British possessions in the Far East were "in imminent danger."

Attack on the Customs Administration

The unwillingness of the British Government to take a firm stand against direct or indirect attacks on British interests was in evidence in the discussions which took place on the Customs issue. The Japanese demand for the withdrawal of all Chinese governmental agencies from Shanghai, if carried to its logical conclusion, would mean that the regular Customs Administration would no longer collect the revenue at this most important port. Moreover, the Japanese spokesman intimated on November 24 that his government was prepared to support General Matsui in whatever action he took as to the Customs and Postal Administrations in Shanghai. The Japanese, he said, considered it proper that the Customs should be under Japanese military control in view of their close connection with the Nanking Government. The British Government, in response to these threats to the Customs, sent instructions to its ambassador in Tokyo to make clear to the Japanese Government that the British claimed the right to be consulted on any arrangements concerning the Customs. The Japanese Foreign Office replied on November 29 that the Japanese forces considered it necessary to take control of the Shanghai Customs as a means of attacking the Chinese military power, but added that the interests of foreign powers would be respected.

Mr. Eden outlined the position of his Government in the House of Commons on December 1.

> During the course of last week, publicity was given to a number of utterances attributed to the Japanese military authorities in Shanghai which appeared to His Majesty's Government to constitute a serious threat to the proper functioning of the Chinese Maritime Customs, and to the service

of the foreign loans secured on the Customs revenues. His Majesty's Government accordingly entered into consultation on the subject with the United States and French Governments. His Majesty's Government have reminded the Japanese Government that the Chinese Maritime Customs have at all times been an international interest, and that they expect to be fully consulted in regard to any arrangement which may be reached for the carrying on of the Customs service during the present hostilities. Similar representations have been made by the United States and French Governments. Discussions on the subject are still proceeding.[2]

Discussions did not restrain the Japanese from shelling the Chinese Customs cruiser *Cha Hsing* in Hongkong waters or prevent the Provisional Government in Peking from taking over the Maritime Customs offices at Tientsin and Chinwangtao. The Japanese had promised that loans secured on the Customs were to be dealt with "in a fair and just manner" and the principle of the open door and equal opportunity was to be maintained, but the Domei Agency in Shanghai stated that now that so many Japanese had been appointed to high posts, Great Britain would no longer be able to take the "former highhanded measures, thus ending the deep-rooted evils surrounding the Chinese Maritime Customs."

The "Ladybird" Incident

At this time the spectacular *Ladybird* and *Panay* incidents drew attention from the Customs issue, as well as all other less colorful questions. After the taking of Shanghai, the Japanese troops had begun a drive up the Yangtze toward Nanking, and on December 1 foreign vessels were warned to move upstream as the Yangtze was to be blocked just below Nanking. The attacks on the *Panay* and *Ladybird* received the greatest attention and publicity, but were really the climax of a series of similar incidents. On December 5, 1937, several British ships lying off the port of Wuhu, which is above Nanking, were attacked by Japanese aircraft. The steamer *Tuckwo* and a hulk belonging to Jardine, Matheson and Company were destroyed, while the *Tatung* (Butterfield & Swire) was damaged. At the same time, H.M.S. *Ladybird* was struck by splinters and her captain wounded. The Japanese Admiral commanding at Shanghai expressed his regret to the British commander-in-chief, and Tokyo informed the British ambassador that they were prepared to consider compensation for damage. This readi-

[2] *Parliamentary Debates,* House of Commons, Vol. 329, col. 2047.

ness to apologize did not prevent the occurrence of a more serious incident exactly one week later. On December 12 a concentration of British shipping accompanied by H.M.S. *Cricket* and *Scarab* was bombed thrice in succession at a point on the river between Nanking and Wuhu. No hits were registered and no results of the return fire were reported. At Wuhu H.M.S. *Ladybird,* while moving to the support of a British tug which had been attacked by machine-gun fire, was fired on and hit by field guns, and one of her crew was killed. The flag captain was wounded. One, at least, of the British merchant ships was hit and H.M.S. *Bee,* which arrived on the scene later, was also fired upon. The British consul-general and the British military *attaché,* who were on board the *Ladybird,* went ashore and protested to the senior Japanese officer in the Wuhu area, Colonel Hashimoto. He said that he had orders to fire at every ship in the river, and at the same time offered the feeble excuse that his troops were incapable of recognizing foreign flags. Rear Admiral Holt, on H.M.S. *Bee,* also landed and protested.

The British Ambassador in Tokyo immediately lodged a strong protest and the Japanese promised to make immediate inquiry. Investigation showed that the attacked vessels had been in an area designated as a safety zone by the Japanese commander-in-chief, and that Colonel Hashimoto had been officially informed of the arrangements for the concentration of British vessels. Moreover, this officer in his interview with a British senior naval officer had stated unequivocally that if any ships moved on the river they would be fired upon, and he had kept the British gunboats covered by the guns of his battery at a point blank range.

This inexcusable attack was glossed over by the British Government. Although Mr. Eden, addressing the House of Commons on December 13, spoke of the "grave issues" and "the seriousness of these incidents," the government declared the Japanese apology satisfactory. It was made with the banal assurance that the necessary measures to prevent the recurrence of incidents of this nature had been taken, that those responsible would be dealt with upon investigation, and that compensation would be paid.

The Japanese in a more formal and comprehensive reply on December 28 completely evaded their obvious responsibility for the attacks. Tokyo maintained that the incidents occurred because of the assumption that all foreign warships and vessels had sought refuge from the vicinity of warfare and that, therefore, the vessels remaining were enemies. This, combined with poor visibility, was given as reason for the affirmation that "there is no room for doubt that they did not intentionally attack the vessels knowing them to be British." The note assured the British Government that those responsible for the incidents had been dealt with properly for failing to take the fullest measures of precaution. In addition, strict orders had been issued against attacks on vessels not clearly identified as being used for military purposes by the Chinese. The naval authorities had also enjoined the greatest caution in areas where foreign vessels were to be found. The hope was expressed that the British Government would appreciate the measures taken in the "sincere desire to render more effective and valid their guarantee of the rights and interests of Great Britain and other Third Powers."[3] A British note of December 31, 1937, expressed satisfaction with the declarations by Tokyo, and asked to be informed of the details of the measures to be taken and their effective application, thus ending the diplomatic exchanges arising out of the *Ladybird* incident.[4] Thus the British Government allowed this, like the other flagrant violations of British rights, to be settled by the repetition of apologies, assurances and monetary indemnifications.[5]

[3] London *Times*, December 3, 1937.

[4] The *Panay* incident, which took place simultaneously with the *Ladybird* incident, received more popular attention both in Great Britain and in the United States.

[5] An important example of this was the bombing of Nanking and Canton. On November 19 the raids upon Nanking were resumed. On the same day Vice-Admiral Hasegawa notified the consular body that "the Chinese forces and establishments pertaining to military activities in and around Nanking" would be bombed. "Full consideration will be given to the safety of the lives and property of the nationals of friendly Powers but in view of the possibility of such becoming dangerously involved in spite of precautions, the Commander-in-Chief of the Third Fleet is constrained earnestly to advise such officials and residents, also the warships now in Nanking, voluntarily to move to greater safety farther up the Yangtze River." The interested foreign powers were quick to reply. Oral representations were made by the British, American and French ambassadors in Tokyo, in which the bombing of other than military objectives and the suggestion that foreigners should be withdrawn were protested. The Japanese Government would be held responsible for any loss of the lives or the property of the nationals concerned. Mr. Hirota replied to the British and American protests by giving a guarantee that non-combatants would not be attacked and that foreign rights would be respected. Admiral Hasegawa's warning had only intended to ensure the safety of foreigners and to avoid causing incidental damage

The British Government not only practiced this policy of retreat, but even openly stated its inability to check Japan's aggression. Mr. Eden, speaking to the House of Commons on December 21, 1937, said:

> We are told that in the Far East today we ought to be upholding the rule of law. . . . If hon. Members opposite are advocating sanctions . . . I would remind them that there are two possible forms of sanctions—the ineffective, which are not worth putting on, and the effective, which means the risk, if not the certainty of war. I say deliberately that nobody can contemplate any action of that kind in the Far East unless they are convinced that they have overwhelming force to back their policy.
>
> Do right hon. Gentlemen opposite really think that the League of Nations today, with only two great naval Powers in it, ourselves and France, has got that overwhelming force? It must be perfectly clear to everyone that that overwhelming force does not exist.

The *North-China Herald* wholeheartedly supported the "calm manner" in which the British Cabinet was handling the Far Eastern situation. It also expressed satisfaction with Japan's apology and offer of indemnities for the *Ladybird* and *Panay* incidents.

> It would be unjust to ascribe to them motives which few thinking people will believe. The world at large will be ready to give them the benefit of the doubt.[6]

This readiness to mollify the Japanese contrasted sharply with the attitude toward the Chinese. By the first week in December 1937, the fall of Nanking appeared inevitable. Again, as earlier in the war, the Chinese were called upon to surrender.

---

to foreign residents. The United States, not satisfied with this reply, sent a note strongly condemning the proposed attacks. The British Foreign Office, although expressing satisfaction with the action taken by the United States, chose to make only oral representations through the British ambassador in Tokyo. Attacks on Nanking followed. These, coupled with an attack on Canton on September 23, evoked representations from six foreign powers; Great Britain, the United States, France, Germany, Italy and the U.S.S.R. The Japanese saw fit to draw back, and assurances were given that fresh and strict orders had been sent to the Japanese commanders in China to safeguard the lives and property of non-combatants, especially those of neutral countries. On September 29 the Japanese replied in identical notes to the British, French and American representations of September 23. No pledge to refrain from bombing was given, but the assertion was made that the aerial operations were not directed at non-combatants. The suggestion that foreigners should evacuate areas subject to Japanese air attack was repeated. Nanking was spared direct assaults on the civilian population but in Canton residential districts were raided. The Japanese promises about non-combatants and foreign residents and property were broken again and again during 1938 and 1939.

[6] *North-China Herald,* December 22, 1937. See also issue for December 9.

The Government has shown itself courageous in steeling the nation's resistance. It can show itself infinitely more courageous if it acts in full recognition of the fact that the possibility of continuing that resistance is beyond human competence.[7]

Finance and Commerce wrote:

The hope may be expressed that the capture of Nanking by the Japanese will see the beginning of the end of the war in China, and that differences will permit of a return to more normal conditions at the beginning of the New Year.

It may be true that certain sections of the Chinese army could carry on the fight, but their resistance would not be that of the country as a whole, and while it might delay, it is doubtful whether it would prove any serious permanent obstacle to the development of plans which Japan would inevitably put into effect for the administration of the territory now under military control. . . . In her drive upon Nanking, Japan has bombed and fired upon British ships and has sunk an American gunboat, and there are those who contend that these attacks were planned in full realization of the consequences that might follow. We do not subscribe to that view because, although the Japanese military command may seem to be running amuck, it is inconceivable that it has so completely lost all sense of responsibility as to provoke deliberately a war with Great Britain and America combined. At the same time, it must be recognized that while this undeclared war in China continues, there is the ever-present danger of more widespread catastrophe. For the sake of China and for the sake of the world, we trust that Nanking will see the finish of the conflict.[8]

But the fall of Nanking on December 13 did not see the end of hostilities and the "unfortunate fact" had "to be faced that the prolongation of hostilities for an indefinite time is the only remaining probability." The indication that the conflict would continue was described as "the most tragic development since that fatal day in July when the crisis arose." Attempts were made to convince the Chinese that their decision to continue resistance was not wise.

China may be better situated to fight a prolonged war than Japan, but it is only the confirmed optimist who will believe that she has any real chance of expelling the enemy from her shores. Her industrial schemes have now been completely wrecked by Japanese action, and when peace does come it will be years before that damage can be repaired. In the meantime foreign interests are suffering badly and may be expected to continue to do so. For many concerns in China the outlook is black indeed, and the possibility of ruination without any prospect of ultimate recovery is something which many firms are already obliged to contemplate. And so from every point of view it is desirable that the question of coming to terms

[7] *North-China Herald,* December 9, 1937.
[8] *Finance and Commerce,* December 15, 1937.

should still receive earnest consideration. The war-mongering pacifists who shout encouragement to China to fight to the last man, may be paying adequate tribute to the sacredness of principles, but such advice given from the safety of the foreign areas of Shanghai savours too much of unreality.[9]

The concern expressed over the future of British interests in China was well justified by the actual situation. Shanghai was facing an acute economic crisis, business in Tsingtao was at a complete standstill, while Hankow was suffering from the disruption of its normal relations with Shanghai.

The conciliatory attitude adopted by the British was not reciprocated by the Japanese during this period. The Japanese policy of attempting to keep Great Britain and the United States apart by attacking the former and mollifying the latter now began in earnest. Thus *Yomiuri* published an article on November 11 declaring that Japan's ultimate enemy was Great Britain and interpreting the Brussels Conference as a British maneuver against Japan. Admiral Nobumasa Suetsugu, Japanese home minister, in an interview granted to the Tokyo correspondent of the *Paris Soir*, clearly indicated the Japanese line of attack, divide and rule. Overtures were made to France to draw her away from co-operation with Great Britain since friction between Japan and France "could only arise from too close a cooperation between France and Great Britain." The *North-China Herald* commented that this statement

must be taken to mean exactly what it implies, namely that Japanese policy is aimed at isolating Britain from states with whom she is in the friendliest contact and to weaken the relation of the nations whose interests in the Far East are being imperiled by Japanese action.[10]

[9] *North-China Herald,* December 29, 1937. See also *Finance and Commerce,* December 22 and 29, 1937.
[10] *North-China Herald,* December 29, 1937.

CHAPTER VII

FROM NANKING TO THE INVASION OF
SOUTH CHINA—I

Concern over Japanese policy increased during the period from the capture of Nanking to the taking of Canton, but the dominant characteristics of British policy remained neutrality, impartiality and diplomatic friendliness to both sides. In practice this meant increased conciliation toward the Japanese, at times even capitulation. The significance of this attitude on the part of Britain was heightened by the already abundant evidence that the Japanese actions were a challenge to Western interests as well as an attack on China. The primary concern in Great Britain at the outbreak of hostilities in North China had been with their effect upon the international system. Later Japanese bombing drew attention to the horrors of air warfare and the plight of civilian non-combatants. But with the attacks on foreign nationals and property, culminating in the *Panay* and *Ladybird* incidents, the threat to foreign rights and interests in China came to the center of the stage.

The succession of events after the fall of Nanking proved the futility of the British policy of conciliation and concession to aggression—more popularly known as "appeasement." The only instance in which an Anglo-Japanese agreement was reached was at the expense of Great Britain. In the other conflicts between Japan and Great Britain, no agreement could be reached, and major British interests suffered.

Agreement on Customs Administration

The agreement on the Customs Administration came after many months of negotiation. The British ambassador at Tokyo had impressed upon the Japanese Government the importance which his government attached to the maintenance and protection of their interest in the revenue of the Chinese Maritime Customs. The Japanese gave assurance that they had no intention of taking over the Shanghai Customs but were merely placing the customs revenue in the Yokohama Specie Bank for "safekeeping." In March 1938 they promised to maintain the service of foreign debts secured on the Chinese Maritime Customs. An agreement to this effect was reached between the British ambassador and the Japanese foreign minister in April and published simultaneously in London and Tokyo on May 3. The text of the *communiqué* was as follows:

Unofficial conversations have been taking place since February last, between the British Ambassador and the Vice-Minister of Foreign Affairs regarding the servicing of Foreign obligations secured on the Chinese Maritime Customs, and other relevant matters.

As a result of this exchange of views, the Japanese Government has notified the British Government in the United Kingdom, of the temporary measures it proposes to take, during the period of hostilities, to regulate these matters.

In reply, the Japanese Government has received assurances that the British Government will, for its part, offer no objection to the application of these measures for the period mentioned.

It is further understood that the Governments of the United States and France do not propose to raise any objections to the temporary application of these arrangements, which will be subject to reconsideration in the event of a radical change occurring in economic conditions.

All revenues collected by the Customs at each port within areas under Japanese occupation are to be deposited with the Yokohama Specie Bank.

From the revenues thus deposited, Foreign loan quotas will be remitted to the Inspector-General of Customs to meet in full the servicing of foreign loans and indemnities secured on the Customs revenue.

The servicing of such foreign loans and indemnities will be treated as the first charge on the Revenue, after deducting the maintenance expenses of the Customs Administration and certain Customs payments and grants.

Foreign loan quotas for each port will be determined monthly in proportion to the share of that port in the total gross collections for all ports during the preceding month.

Arrangements will be made for payment to the Japanese Government of the arrears of the Japanese portion of the Boxer Indemnity held at the Hong Kong and Shanghai Bank since last September.

Arrangements will also be made:

For meeting future payments in respect of the Japanese portion of Boxer Indemnity and the Japanese share of the reorganization loan of 1913;

For repayment of the overdraft incurred by the Inspector-General of Customs since January in relation to the Shanghai share of the Foreign loan which has been accumulating in the Hong Kong and Shanghai Bank, at Shanghai;

For the transfer to the Yokohama Specie Bank of the balance of the Customs accounts with the Hong Kong and Shanghai Bank in each port under Japanese occupation, and its utilization for the future servicing of foreign obligations.

The arrangements, having regard to the military situation in the Far East, appear to the British Government to offer the best guarantee obtainable for safeguarding the interests of the holders of China's Foreign obligations secured on the Customs Revenues and, by this, assist in maintaining China's credit.[1]

The agreement received a half-hearted reception in England. The London *Times* regretted that no assurance had been offered on the preservation of an element of international control over the Customs Administration. The *Manchester Guardian* drew attention to the difficulty of knowing when the hostilities were over and to the fact that the quota of the Manchukuo Customs for loan service was obtainable only on condition that China recognize Manchukuo. "Might not a similar situation result in North China?" it inquired. "The people of this country should remember these facts before congratulating the British Government on rescuing their money." The *North-China Herald* of May 11, 1938, described the arrangement "as the only effective means of making the best out of a bad business," and accepted it "as one which may tend towards the fuller execution of the Japanese assurance regarding the intention scrupulously to respect the interests of foreign neutral Powers in China, which if amplified in other directions would also serve greatly to restore some of the confidence which is at present lacking." On May 11 *Finance and Commerce* asked whose credit was meant when the British Government agreed to continue to help maintain China's credit. Did it refer to the "Provisional Government" in Peiping, to the "Reformed Government" in Nanking which had come into existence under the Japanese protection, or to the "National Government" which the Japanese had sworn to destroy?

The Chinese Government, aggrieved by the entire matter, declared in a note to the British Government that it was in no way bound by the Customs arrangement and that China reserved her full rights and freedom of action in matters pertaining to the Customs.[2]

This Customs Agreement was a turning-point in British influence in China, for it ended a period of eighty years during

[1] *British Chamber of Commerce Journal*, Shanghai, May 1938.
[2] In Shanghai the Chinese staff of the customs service struck in protest against the provisions of the agreement and the appointment of a representative of the Japanese-sponsored Nanking Government to a high executive post in the customs service.

which the predominant interest of Britain in the Chinese Customs Administration had been undisputed. Although the Japanese, by their seizure of the treaty ports of Shanghai, Tientsin and Tsingtao, controlled, on the basis of 1937, about sixty per cent of the total Customs revenue of China, the revenue derived by the Nationalist Government from the trade of Hankow, Canton and Kowloon, plus the returns from the interport duty, would have sufficed to cover all of the current service on China's Customs-secured foreign indebtedness, amounting to roughly Ch.$ 75,000,000 annually.[3] The British Government, however, chose to play safe and concluded the Agreement.

The provisions did seem to provide additional security for China's creditors, but on the debit side the right of the Japanese-controlled autonomous regional governments in China to take over the Customs was conceded. In addition, the custody of the Customs funds was transferred from the Hongkong and Shanghai Banking Corporation to the Yokohama Specie Bank —an action not contributing to British prestige in the Far East.

The Customs Agreement proved to be a blunder of the first magnitude, for while Britain's predominant position in the administration was transferred to the Japanese, the creditors of China were not safeguarded and attacks on the Customs Administration outside of the occupied territory continued.[4] As seen by the authoritative *Oriental Economist* (Japanese edition),

> The present agreement ... is ... an elegy telling of the decline of British influence in the Orient. By this agreement, the British have consented to retreat from the scene and to remain content with only the assured position of creditor to China, the same position held by other countries.[5]

By July 1 the Japanese had defaulted on the monthly installments due on the foreign loans.

The apprehension caused by the Customs Agreement was increased as a result of various other measures which were being taken by the Japanese themselves or by the Japanese-supported Governments, and which were greatly injuring British interests. The most important of these were tariff revisions, closure of the

[3] At the rate of 1s. 2½d. per Chinese dollar.
[4] On August 2, 1938, a Chinese Maritime Customs cruiser was bombed by Japanese seaplanes 36 miles below Hankow and the British commander was killed.
[5] "Significance and Effect of the Anglo-Japanese Customs Agreement on the Chinese Maritime Customs Administration," *Oriental Economist*, Japanese Edition, Tokyo, No. 1812, May 14, 1938, p. 23.

Yangtze, pressure on the International Settlement, failure to prevent smuggling and neglect of conservancy work in the Whangpoo River.

On January 21, 1938, the Peking Provisional Government announced a series of reductions in the North China Customs tariff.[6] The Customs surtax was abolished, and a five per cent duty imposed for the benefit of the war-ravaged areas. There were substantial reductions in the duties on cotton and woolen piece goods, cotton yarn, artificial silk, petrol, metalware, etc., and the export of cotton seed and linseed was to be free, while duties on raw cotton, iron, wool and ores were quadrupled.[7] The Provisional Government stressed "that the revision of the tariff rates is based solely on the desire to aid the populace of the distressed areas, and is not in any way intended as discriminatory treatment against other nations," but, as stated by the *British Chamber of Commerce Journal,* "this spontaneous solicitude for the welfare of the people of the North will in effect be very beneficial to trade between Japan and North China, though it is hardly calculated to have equal beneficial effect on trade between North China and other Foreign Countries."[8] The British were reported to have made representations to the Japanese Foreign Office on the matter, pointing out that the revision was contrary to treaties establishing a unified customs tariff throughout China. The Japanese took the position that the issue of customs tariff did not concern them and that any representations on it must be lodged with the local authorities.[9]

The Customs Agreement of May 1938 did not restrain the Nanking Reformed Government from announcing on May 31 that, as from June 1, 1938, the new tariffs in force in North China would be applied throughout the territory controlled by the Nanking and Peking Governments. The revision was announced as being only temporary and further amendments were to be made when the two governments were merged.

The significance of these changes was evident to the British community. Although foreign business would not be much affected immediately, because of the almost "dead" market at this time, it was understood that a so-called "economic bloc" of

[6] East Hopei was brought within the scope of the new schedules.
[7] For the schedule of revised tariff rates, see *British Chamber of Commerce Journal,* February 1938.
[8] *British Chamber of Commerce Journal,* February 1938.
[9] *North-China Herald,* February 9, 1938.

Japan, Manchukuo and China was planned. The one point which was regarded with satisfaction was the promise that Japanese goods would be subject to the rates, for this would end the increasing amount of smuggling at Shanghai. Comment in foreign business circles was cautious for the most part, and the inspector-general of Customs was advised to recognize the accomplished fact. The *North-China Herald* spoke in guarded and at times apologetic tones.

> This journal is still inclined to believe in the validity of the many promises which have been given and prefers to think that the wide divergences between the import figures of Japanese and other goods is the result of those eccentricities for which the Tokyo Government cannot entirely be held responsible.[10]

The Yangtze River Closed

Japan's intention of dominating not only northern China but also the Yangtze region was indicated in the tariff changes adopted by the Nanking Government, but an even more serious threat to Britain's predominant position in the Yangtze valley was Japan's refusal to open this river to Western commerce. British trade on the Yangtze, the most important trade artery of China, had suffered severely as the result of hostilities. The Chinese had placed a boom at Kiangyin[11] to impede the Japanese advance, making detours around it necessary in order to reach ports upstream. Until after the fall of Nanking the two major British shipping companies concerned—the Indo-China Steam Navigation Company (Jardine, Matheson & Co.) and the China Navigation Company (Butterfield and Swire)—were content to maintain regular services between Shanghai and Nantungchow, situated just below the Kiangyin boom. Early in 1938, however, the companies endeavored to extend the service to Kuan, which is above the boom and about a mile from Chunkiang (156 miles from Shanghai). The Japanese naval authorities opposed this plan on the ground that the river was still heavily mined. It was undesirable, they said, for merchant ships to proceed above the boom without a proper convoy, and they did not favor requests for naval convoys for

---

[10] *North-China Herald*, June 8, 1938. This conciliatory attitude was not in accord with the general editorial policy of the time and was perhaps a result of the overtures of friendship being made by the Japanese to the British at this time.

[11] Kiangyin is about 95 miles upstream from Shanghai, but it is the first place where the Yangtze narrows enough to make a boom effective.

merchant ships. In this way British shipping was kept from going up the river. Furthermore, official British objections to interference with freedom of navigation on the Yangtze were discounted by the Japanese as invalid because the Yangtze was "open." Thus on the one hand it was maintained that the river was not closed to non-Japanese shipping and, on the other, military necessity was pleaded as the excuse for closing the river.[12]

However, by March 1938 the Japanese were ready to "admit" that the Yangtze River was closed to foreign shipping. The excuse was still given "that the Yangtze is not yet safe for the navigation of foreign vessels." The argument of military exigencies, which could be used with some logic before the fall of Nanking, had less value after the fall of Hsuchow in May 1938. The British authorities then again proposed that the Yangtze be opened to merchant shipping. Mr. R. A. Butler, Under-Secretary of State for Foreign Affairs, revealed to the House of Commons on June 20, 1938, that Vice-Admiral Sir Percy Noble, commander-in-chief of the British China Squadron, had pressed the Japanese military and naval authorities in Shanghai to allow freedom of transit on the Yangtze. The Japanese had replied that they regretted their "inability to concede this request, on the ground of military necessity." The British

---

[12] "As is known, a part of the booms on the Yangtze River which were originally constructed by the Chinese for their military purposes has recently been forced through by the Imperial Japanese Navy with a view to utilizing the opening only for military navigation.

"Since the Channel forces through the booms cannot be opened for free navigation without causing, in the present circumstances, no small obstacle to the military operations of the Japanese Forces, any vessel whether it be government-owned or private-owned, other than those of Japanese nationality, which has the desire of passing through the channel, is hereby cordially requested to get in touch with the Japanese Navy and secure beforehand their understanding for its prospective navigation through the booms.

"Needless to add, the Japanese Navy are always ready to give sympathetic understanding to the navigation of foreign vessels so far as is permissible from the military point of view and to offer facilities for the passage of such vessels by supplying a convoy.

"It is, therefore, the earnest desire of the Imperial Japanese Navy that the vessels of the interested powers, taking full cognizance and appreciation of the above-mentioned circumstances, will scrupulously refrain from attempting to navigate through the forces channel freely or in such a way as may invite misunderstanding with the Japanese Navy."

Note of January 10, 1938, handed to Mr. N. Hall, the senior consul at Shanghai, by Mr. Suemasa Okamoto, Japanese consul-general, to be circulated to the other members of the consular body.

Government, Mr. Butler went on to say, while feeling that there might be some ground for a refusal based on this reason, providing that no discrimination was practiced, were "dissatisfied with the position" and were considering whether any further steps could be taken in the matter. This was the situation in the summer of 1938.

Meanwhile, Shanghai could not recover its pre-war importance if it continued to remain divorced from its hinterland, the Yangtze region. Thus the closure of the Yangtze was in effect an attack on Shanghai itself, as well as on British shipping and trade on the river. Nor was this the only Japanese action which obstructed the recovery of Shanghai. Other acts were interference with shipping, smuggling, censorship of the foreign press, termination of the Whangpoo conservancy works and restrictions in the areas of Shanghai and the International Settlement occupied by the Japanese.

On March 22, 1938, regulations for inland water navigation were issued by the Japanese authorities. They required that all vessels obtain permits from the Japanese authorities under penalty of the seizure of both ships and cargo. The British Government was quick to deny the right of Japan to apply such regulations to British ships, but, like many other British protests, this one also went unheeded.

Smuggling

Japanese smuggling at Shanghai reached serious proportions, hampering all non-Japanese foreign trade. The right to import military supplies free of duty, which was accorded to Japan by the Treaty of 1930 with China, was used to cover evasion of duty on ordinary merchandise. All steamers were designated "transports," though they carried cargo for both Japanese and foreign shippers. The goods which were being brought into Shanghai without the payment of customs dues included artificial silk, sugar, beans, piece goods, bean oil, cigarette paper and sea products.

On reply to a question in the House of Commons on May 4, Mr. Butler said that the Japanese Government had repeatedly been urged to put a stop to this abuse. He expressed the hope of the Government that more effective action would be taken as a result of the Customs Agreement. The situation again came up on May 11. Mr. Hannah, National Conservative, asked if the Japanese Government, in notifying Great Britain of arrangements relating to the disposal of Chinese Customs revenue, had given assurance or made any statement regarding repeated complaints that Japanese goods were being admitted to Shanghai without payment of duty. Mr. Butler replied that in recent discussions Japan had assured the British Government that normal conditions would be restored and payment of duty by all Japanese importers would begin at the earliest possible date.

Similar assurances had been given in Shanghai on May 9 by a Japanese Embassy spokesman: "The Chinese Maritime Customs in Shanghai and the Japanese-occupied area in Central China will begin to function normally in the near future." The Customs, he added, were not yet collecting duty on goods destined for the use of the Japanese community in Shanghai, but goods now entering free of duty (with the exception of those destined for the armed forces) would in the future pay the required duty. The Japanese authorities thus admitted the existence of legalized smuggling.

This smuggling continued in spite of Japanese assurances, even after the Japanese took over control of the Customs Administration. Smuggling had been a chronic problem in China for many years. Now, with the Shanghai Customs under the supervision of the Japanese, the situation was somewhat similar to that which existed in the "East Hopei Autonomous Region" before the war, where the responsibility of the Japanese officials had been apparent. Only one of many Japanese policies injurious to British interests, the Shanghai smuggling was now regarded as part of a general, deliberate policy of embarrassing and squeezing British interests out of Shanghai and Central China.

Conservancy Work in the Whangpoo River

The failure of the Japanese to resume conservancy work in the Whangpoo River, on which the port of Shanghai is situated, was another indication of Japan's anti-British aims. When hostilities broke out in Shanghai in August 1937, conservancy work was naturally suspended. With the capture of Shanghai, the Japanese fell heir to the material belonging to the Whangpoo Conservancy Board.[13] There was no criticism of this step, the British accepting it as an inevitable result of the war. However, the dredging apparatus, which in peacetime was continuously active for the maintenance of the port of Shanghai, was allowed to remain idle. By April 1938 it was seen that the Whangpoo, with its rapid, silt-laden current, was effecting big changes in the port. Wharves were in some cases imperiled by the fast-moving waters while continual deposit of water-borne earth was quickly making others inaccessible. Cases were reported in which wharves could only be reached at high tide, where previously they were available at the lowest water. The normal risks attendant upon bringing large, ocean-going vessels up to their berths in the harbor were being increased, and fear was expressed that the dangers would increase to such an extent that shipping companies would not dare to risk their craft by coming up the river.[14]

Upon the state of the Shanghai harbor largely depended the commerce, industry and economic well-being of the city. The responsibility for the harbor's deterioration obviously lay with the Japanese. All the apparatus for the maintenance of the

[13] While the Whangpoo Conservancy Board was an organ of the Chinese Government, the foreign interests involved bestowed upon it an international status. On April 9, 1912, an agreement was reached between the Peking Government and the ministers of the Treaty Powers providing for the formation of the Whangpoo Conservancy Board of Administration and also a Consultative Board. The Board of Administration was to consist of three members—the Kiangsu Commissioner for Foreign Affairs, the Shanghai commissioner of customs and the Shanghai harbor master. The Consultative Board was to be comprised of the following:

(a) Five members appointed as follows: the several ministers at Peking of the five nations having the largest tonnage entering and clearing at Shanghai shall each determine at their discretion the means by which one member of their nationality shall be selected, and the consuls-general at Shanghai shall notify the Conservancy Board of the selection made and of any subsequent changes.

(b) One member appointed by the Chinese Chamber of Commerce. Toward the financing of the scheme the "several Chambers of Commerce and Associations representing the Commercial interests of Shanghai" agreed for conservancy purposes to levy a tax of 3 per cent on the prevailing Customs duties and a new .15 per cent tax on duty-free goods. There was also provision for a governmental grant, but actually about 80 per cent of the board's income was contributed by foreign-flagged shipping.

[14] *British Chamber of Commerce Journal,* May 1938. In addition to those caused by the discontinuance of the dredging, serious difficulties had resulted from the seizure by Japanese of a number of small Chinese wharves around the Point. These had been handed over to the Mitsubishi Steamship Company for its own exclusive use. Foreign shipping companies formerly using the wharves were considerably inconvenienced by being shut out from these berthing accommodations, which had proved useful in the existing serious shortage of such accommodations.

port had been taken over by the Japanese authorities and allowed to remain idle, and with no military or naval justification. Dredging operations would not have impeded the passage of Japanese ships supplying the armies in the fields, nor would they have interfered with the movements of the Japanese navy. Although no accident had occurred, it was recognized by the spring of 1938 that the danger was increasing each month.

The Joint Committee of the British Chamber of Commerce (Shanghai) and the China Association (Shanghai Branch) brought the matter to the attention of the British authorities. However, all that Mr. Butler could say to the House of Commons on May 24, 1938, was that "negotiations are now proceeding between a committee of the Consular Body, supported by His Majesty's Ambassador, and the Japanese authorities for the resumption of dredging by the Conservancy Board and for the return of their vessels and other property."[15] In June 1938, Japanese authorities announced that arrangements were in progress to resume dredging of the Whangpoo River channel,[16] but work was not resumed and the deterioration continued. Again British representations had met with meaningless promises or frank rejections. British opinion in China, conciliatory and accommodating during the first year of the war, was becoming exasperated and aggrieved with Japan's policies.[17]

The Shanghai Municipal Council

In addition to the damage to British interests arising from the closing of the Yangtze, smuggling, and the discontinuance of conservancy work, there was diplomatic pressure brought to bear during this period against the position of the Municipal Council of the International Settlement. The Japanese threats to the International Settlement began with the fall of Shanghai. After the capture of Nanking they increased. A delegation headed by Mr. Suemasa Okamoto, Japanese consul-general in Shanghai, told Mr. Franklin, chairman of the Shanghai Municipal Council, that the Japanese authorities regarded the recurrence of anti-Japanese incidents as the result of the inefficiency of the Council's efforts to suppress anti-Japanese elements.

[15] *Parliamentary Debates*, House of Commons, Vol. 336, col. 1055.
[16] United States Department of Commerce, Bureau of Foreign and Domestic Commerce, *Commerce Reports*, June 11, 1938, p. 524.
[17] *North-China Herald*, April 13 and May 4, 1938.

Therefore, the Japanese might be forced "to extirpate the anti-Japanese groups from the Settlement, thus making it a safer place to live in." The Municipal Council was requested to take appropriate measures to eradicate anti-Japanese elements and to exercise rigid control of anti-Japanese newspapers. To achieve this the Council should increase the number of Japanese members of the Shanghai Municipal Police and raise their status and authority, and place Japanese in controlling positions in all the important organs of the Municipal Council. Mr. Franklin made no immediate reply, promising to make a thorough study of the matter.

The situation was unique in Shanghai's history and complicated by the peculiar basis on which the Shanghai Municipal Council was founded. The Land Regulations, which formed the basis for the Council's authority, had not been formally signed by any of the foreign powers participating in the formation of the International Settlement, although these powers had adhered to them over a long period of years. If any power should suddenly decide to flout the Land Regulations and no longer recognize them, a political situation would be created which could only be settled among the interested powers, as there was no law applicable to such a situation. Up to this incident there had been no serious differences among the powers with regard to matters relating to the administration of the Settlement. The Japanese by presenting these demands directly to the Council, instead of presenting the proposals at a Council meeting, had placed the Council in an awkward position, as it could not come to a decision upon a matter of such great importance without referring it to the Consular Body.

The Japanese did not follow up these demands with any concrete action and the situation eased. However, a statement issued by General Matsui on January 29, 1938, helped to continue the state of anxiety. General Matsui felt that "if Great Britain goes beyond her policy of simply defending her interests in China and makes a determined stand to maintain her political and economic relations with the Kuomintang, a conflict of very serious nature may arise between our country and our former ally."[18] Rumors followed that the Japanese were preparing to occupy both the International Settlement and the French Concession.

[18] London *Times,* January 31, 1938.

Nevertheless, the Japanese took no direct action against the authority of the Municipal Council and the latter, by March 1938, felt able to reject the Japanese demands. The Council denied that it had shown inefficiency, which was the basis of the Japanese position, but made a small concession toward giving the Japanese community a larger share in the administration. Changes in the Secretariat, it stated, were difficult and it pointed out that the Japanese deputy-secretary already had direct access to all senior officials. The Council even took the opportunity to urge that the Japanese authorities should assist the return to normal conditions by taking steps to restore full Council control in the area north of the Soochow Creek.

The Japanese consular authorities in Shanghai on April 6, 1938, rejected the Council's position in a letter handed personally to Mr. C. S. Franklin by Mr. Shinrokuro Hidaka, the new Japanese consul-general. The letter asked the Council to reconsider its position and to meet the Japanese demand fully "when the present tense situation is mitigated and the Council's financial condition is improved." Appended to the letter was a list of requests for changes in the municipal police force. They asked the immediate appointment of a Japanese officer as a special deputy commissioner, next in rank and status to the commissioner of police, who would have authority to command the whole Japanese staff and would participate in the general administration of the Municipal Council as the representative of Japanese interests. The memorandum took especial note of the Council's expressed intention to afford the Japanese deputy-secretary extended facilities, including the privilege of attendance at important conferences at which matters affecting the Japanese community were discussed. In announcing Mr. Hidaka's letter, a spokesman for the Japanese Embassy said that the return of northern areas to municipal control was not considered by the Japanese authorities as a *sine qua non* of the Council's acceptance of the Japanese requests.

The attitude of the British community in China on the Japanese position, which was a mixture of a desire to placate the Japanese and a decided unwillingness to make any real concession, was well reflected in a leading article of the *North-China Herald*. While on the one hand it described the Japanese and the Municipal Council as being "really not so far apart as it would be seen at first blush," on the other, it said that, the Council's proposals of March 18 went a very long way towards meeting Japanese aspirations. . . . In some directions the Council was unable to go the whole way with the Japanese and in this they have the hearty support of this journal. . . . There can be no agreement with the contention that because of the presence of large numbers of Japanese residents in certain districts the police administration shall be in any way—save, perhaps, for modification in the nationality of the personnel—different from that in other areas where the same conditions do not apply. To accept any such contention would be to pave the way for an ultimate betrayal of the internationality of the whole body, and . . . bring about conditions which could do nothing but contribute towards disunion and consequently inefficiency. . . . There is no reason to believe that the Japanese authorities desire to do anything which might disrupt the efficiency of an excellent service, but there is always that grave danger if, in circumstances such as prevail here, changes too sudden and too drastic are made.[19]

The Japanese chose not to press the demand for changes in the administration of the International Settlement, and during June a marked improvement in the relations between the Japanese Army and the foreign communities in Shanghai was reported.[20] This did not mean, however, any change in the restrictions which the Japanese had placed on Hongkew and Yangtzepoo.[21]

The Hongkew barriers had been lifted on February 19, 1938, and restrictions on foreigners and Chinese relaxed, but on March 22, 1938, martial law was suddenly clamped down on all districts north of the Soochow Creek for the first time since the cessation of hostilities in the Shanghai area. The occasion was the assassination of a Japanese in North Szechwan Road by an unknown assailant.[22]

This situation aroused considerable interest in London. Mr. Chamberlain was queried in the House of Commons on May 9 as to what steps he had taken to prevent the continuance of such conditions. Mr. Butler, replying for Mr. Chamberlain,

[19] In the House of Commons on May 6 Commander Marsden asked the prime minister whether he would call a conference of the powers enjoying treaty rights in the International Settlement of Shanghai with a view to issuing a joint demand to the Japanese Government to withdraw from the area of the International Settlement all Japanese naval and military forces, save such as might reasonably be required in accordance with treaty rights for the protection of the lives and property of Japanese nationals in the area of the Settlement. Mr. Butler: "I fear that my hon. and gallant friend's suggestion presents many difficulties and would not be likely to lead to any practical results."
[20] *North-China Herald,* June 22, 1938.
[21] For details of regulations, see *North-China Herald,* February 23, 1938.
[22] See *North-China Herald,* March 30, 1938.

assured the House that representations were continually being made on this subject both in Tokyo and Shanghai and that individual cases were being taken up with the local Japanese authorities by the British consul-general in Shanghai.

The futility of the British protests was admitted in the House of Commons on May 30, 1938. In reply to Mr. A. C. Moreing, Conservative, who asserted that the Japanese military authorities were refusing to allow the free passage of British-owned trams in the Hongkew and Yangtzepoo district, thereby preventing a resumption of work in British and other factories, Mr. Butler replied that, despite British representations, the position remained substantially as described. Replying to another question, Mr. Butler said that, since the cessation of fighting in Shanghai last November, the British Government had lost no opportunity of representing to the Japanese authorities the desirability of the Shanghai Municipal Council being permitted to resume normal control of the Settlement area. He also indicated that the Government had not yet received a reply.

The situation remained the same throughout the summer of 1938 and when on July 20, 1938, it was brought up again in the House of Commons, all Mr. Butler could say was that further representations in the matter had been made in Tokyo on July 13, but that no date had yet been fixed for the restoration of the Hongkew and Yangtzepoo districts to the Shanghai Municipal Council.

CHAPTER VIII

FROM NANKING TO THE INVASION OF SOUTH CHINA—II

British Impatience with Japan's Attitude

These continued attacks on British interests lessened the willingness of the British in China to accommodate themselves to the new situation resulting from the Japanese invasion. They began to waver in their policy of advocating conciliation and co-operation with the Japanese, and an uncertain and vacillating attitude was the result.

The shift in the British attitude toward the Japanese was in evidence at the meeting held on April 7, 1938, of the British Chamber of Commerce of Shanghai, an outstanding organ of British interests in China. Mr. R. Calder Marshall, chairman, indicated the growing distrust of Japanese intentions:

> Though the Japanese Government has given repeated assurances regarding the maintenance of the territorial and administrative integrity of China and though her spokesmen have been equally emphatic regarding non-interference with foreign rights and interests, it is difficult to reconcile such statements with the events of the past eight months.[1]

These views were echoed by *Finance and Commerce*, which clearly indicated that its main grievance against the Japanese was not the invasion of China, but interference with British interests.

> For eight months there has been practically no new business, and except for the time occupied in looking after deviated cargo and obtaining delivery from congested godowns, the period has been one mainly of waiting upon the future, and hoping against hope that peace would not be too long delayed. . . . But peace seems to be as far off as ever and, meanwhile, political movements are on foot affecting wide areas which, if developed in the lines now apparently favoured, suggest that even when the period of waiting is over there will be small prospect of the foreign merchant obtaining again any fair share of the trade to be done. . . . Many merchants are anxiously enquiring what are the Japanese intentions with respect to

[1] British Chamber of Commerce, Shanghai, Twenty-Third Annual General Meeting, *British Chamber of Commerce Journal*, April 1938.

trade, when trade is once more a practical proposition, and it would add immeasurably to confidence if a satisfactory answer could be given to these queries.

Commenting on the Japanese puppet governments and their liberality in giving monopolistic franchises to Japanese corporations, *Finance and Commerce* indicated the well-springs of its attitude on the situation in China.

It is impossible to foretell how long hostilities will continue, when ambitions will be satisfied or powers of resistance exhausted, but there is no doubt that the Japanese plan is to introduce some semblance of law and order in the territories under their control through the operation of local Chinese administrative bodies, and then gradually to merge these administrations into one unit, which may claim to be the Government of China. It may be admitted that some attempt in this direction is essential if whole tracts of land are not to remain waste, and the peasants are to be induced to return to their homes and to resume labor on the farms. Indeed, unless the plan is temporarily successful, there is grave danger that the occupied territory will be swept by a devastating famine within a comparatively few months, when harvest time comes round and there are no crops to gather. Local administrations, therefore, even under Japanese direction, should be welcomed and there is little sense in characterizing as traitors those Chinese who, during this great emergency, are willing to help in establishing them. As to whether the plan will be a permanent success depends, naturally, upon the outcome of the war; if the Japanese are not completely victorious in their military campaign it must fail.

But as regards foreign prospects, the point at issue is not the success or failure of these forms of administrative control or whether they will be temporary or permanent, but whether the Japanese, in endeavoring to re-establish some semblance of order out of the chaos which has been created, are building for their own exclusive benefit or whether they will honor these principles of the "open door" and "equal opportunities" which they have repeatedly proclaimed. Though Japanese spokesmen have emphasized that the "open door" policy will be maintained, Mr. Calder Marshall declared it to be evident from the statements emanating from Tokyo that it was not intended that other nations should enjoy "equal opportunity" in major development work or industry or even in commerce.

This view, coming from the chairman of the British Chamber of Commerce, must be respected. By no stretch of imagination can it be termed encouraging, but if truth is to be told, it is probably shared by the majority of foreign merchants engaged in the import and export trade, and accounts for the feeling of pessimism with which in some quarters the future is anticipated. There is certainly nothing to be hoped for from Japanese success and domination if the "military necessities" which are now preventing the quick reopening of normal trade channels, are to be replaced in peace-time, by monopolies and tariff manipulations entirely favoring one nation.[2]

[2] *Finance and Commerce*, April 13, 1938.

The belief that the Japanese were determined to destroy British interests became so strong that conciliatory Japanese statements were now rejected. When Mr. Masaji Yoshida, president of the Shanghai Chamber of Commerce and Industry, at that body's annual meeting on April 19, 1938, speaking for the Japanese community in Shanghai declared that the Japanese intended to "carry on enterprises with fair play based on an equal footing," skepticism was openly expressed by the British.

> These, like so many promises given in the very recent past, sound very well and look even better on paper, but judged in view of all that has happened, and is happening, they have to be very considerably discounted, if not completely abandoned. They simply do not coincide with the facts as foreign interests find them in these particularly trying times. . . . There can never be any misunderstanding as to what the Open Door policy means, no doubt as to whether its terms are being faithfully observed, and all the eloquence in the world will fail to convince the foreigners that what they see before their eyes is not really happening. Indeed this is very much of an instance in which soft words butter no parsnips.[3]

This reaction was easy to understand, since, on the very day that Mr. Yoshida's address was published, there appeared in the local press in Shanghai a dispatch from Peiping announcing plans for the formation of a Japanese, Manchurian and Korean combine with a capital of twenty million yen to take control of oil marketing in North China, while another report from Dairen told of a Japanese scheme for controlling railways, harbors, and bus-services in North China.

> These plans certainly suggest that the "open door" is to be made more convenient for egress than entrance, and similar schemes are being formulated for that part of Central China which is now under Japanese military occupation.[4]

Such Japanese activities brought to the fore the question of the open door. The Japanese argument that changed conditions justified a change in the interpretation of the open-door doctrine was flatly rejected by the British in China. They said that as long as China retained her sovereign independence and territorial integrity, which Japan had undertaken to respect when signing the Nine Power Treaty at Washington, and as long as China remained a national entity recognized by the seven other signatory powers, who, together with Japan, had agreed to assist

[3] *North-China Herald*, April 27, 1938.
[4] *Finance and Commerce*, April 27, 1938.

Chinese efforts at political and economic advancement, it was not for Japan to say how widely China's door should be opened, and who might enter thereby. That was a matter which had to rest with an independent China.[5]

This growing impatience with Japanese tactics in China did not, however, mean a complete and clean break with the former attitude of co-operation. Two weeks following the above-quoted *Finance and Commerce* issue, this same publication restated its hopes for co-operation. Recognizing that the Japanese pledge to make conditions in Shanghai less oppressive for the British had not been honored, it felt that "just where to place the responsibility is exceedingly difficult." The average Japanese business man in Shanghai was pictured as being no more satisfied with the existing situation than the average foreigner, "and both are equally anxious to see an early lifting of all restraints which can be removed without detriment to the military situation." It applauded a suggestion put forward by Lord Elibank, former president of the Federation of Chambers of Commerce of the British Empire, in a letter to the *Times* of April 23, 1938, that since in recent weeks it had been made clear that the Japanese Government was anxious to be on good terms with Great Britain, one way of doing so would be for Japan to put an end to her intolerable military intrusion at Shanghai, and give that important center some chance of retrieving its fortunes, shattered by no fault of its own.

> That is a view we most warmly endorse, and commend it to the attention of the Japanese authorities both in Shanghai and in Tokyo as representing the general opinion of British and other Western businessmen in this city. Meanwhile, what do Japanese merchants in Shanghai think about the situation? Are they perfectly satisfied with the way things have been going, or are they in favor of a policy which would restore to Shanghai something of that "equal opportunity" which was formerly offered to all business men, irrespective of nationality? On this point it is possible to quote some authoritative opinions which should encourage the optimists in their faith as to an eventual resuscitation of foreign activities which for so many months have been in a state of suspended animation.

The opinions quoted are indicative of what the British considered a possible basis for co-operation. Mr. Masusaburo Amano, president of the Japanese Shanghai Residents' Association, had said that rehabilitation of the city would be a task of immense difficulty "which seems to be well-nigh impossible

[5] *Ibid.*

without outside assistance." Discussing where such assistance might be found, Mr. Ryusuke Miyazaki, director of the Shanghai Office of the Hsingchung Kungsu (China Development Company), had said:

> In the work of rehabilitating Shanghai, the question is whether to seek British, American, French and Chinese co-operation or to reject it. Rejection of foreign co-operation is not advisable. Business circles wish to secure foreign co-operation. Big investments are needed for the economic development of Shanghai and South China. Japan alone cannot make the investments and we hope to obtain low interest capital from Britain, America and France. We believe private foreign bankers will willingly make such investments. Some oppose foreign investments for the reason that investors would have their own way, but when foreign investors have their own way to too great an extent, we may consider means of remedying the situation.

Mr. Gengo Yasui, a former president of the Shanghai Japanese Residents' Association, was quoted as having said that in developing trade with Central and South China, "Japanese should co-operate more closely with foreign traders." Mr. Tozo Hirano, director of the Shanghai office of the Bank of Taiwan, had said that Japan should be careful not to impair the interests of the Western powers in Shanghai. Mr. Masaji Yoshida, president of the Japanese Chamber of Commerce in Shanghai, had said that Japanese should "co-operate with dependable Chinese and foreign business men." Mr. Kanji Tanaka, manager of the Shanghai office of the Mitsubishi Shoji Kaisha, had said that he did "not believe the idea of creating a new Japanese colony, irrespective of the International Settlement and the French Concession, can be carried out. Without foreign settlements, Shanghai would be reduced to a fishing-village."

Finance and Commerce took an optimistic view.

> These are opinions of Japanese residents in Shanghai who are not only familiar with business conditions as they were, but are qualified to intimate as accurately as anyone the future possibilities. We most sincerely hope their views can be effectively presented in Tokyo, where it is possible Lord Elibank's opinions would not be given the same consideration. Since Japanese business men in Shanghai recognize the importance of co-operation with the Chinese and foreign merchants around them, there is no reason for action or inaction by the Japanese military authorities which makes such co-operation either difficult or quite impossible.[6]

This vacillation between severe criticism and denunciation

[6] *Finance and Commerce,* May 4, 1938.

of Japanese policies and willingness to co-operate was also evident in the columns of the *North-China Herald*. Mr. Koki Hirota, the Japanese foreign minister, in an interview with the Reuters correspondent in Tokyo had said: "Other Powers will continue to enjoy an equal right to trade in and develop the natural resources of the occupied territory, for the economic development of which the investment of foreign capital is desirable." The *North-China Herald* caustically pointed out that if Mr. Hirota was sincere, then he was surely "grievously misinformed." As for his "hoary old assurance that Japan will continue to protect Third Power commercial interests in this country," "the time has long passed when a few concrete proofs of the good intentions, which the Japanese Government are said to have, would do more to restore foreign confidence in the *bona fides* of Japan than a dozen such declarations."

This newspaper, however, took the opportunity to make clear that there was no fundamental obstacle to Anglo-Japanese co-operation and to indicate how it could be achieved.

> Foreign sentiment is not so anti-Japanese as some people seem to think. There is disapproval of the policy followed by Japan in China and a great deal of criticism to be heard of recent developments: there is definitely nothing in the shape of hatred which would make conditions here unbearable. But a large number of foreigners have seen their businesses damaged by the outbreak of the hostilities, and the chance of their rehabilitation daily lessened by the delay in permitting Shanghai to get back to work. These are matters which affect their personal fortunes, and it is but natural that resentment should be felt owing to the conviction formed by all that has happened that, no matter what Mr. Hirota may say, there are Japanese authorities who are deliberately frustrating the declared policy of the Japanese Government. That is a matter which closely concerns Tokyo, but no less closely affects foreign outlook upon developments in this country, and any indication that the declared policy of the Japanese Government was being implemented would do more to restore neutral confidence than is, perhaps, at the moment believed amongst the Japanese themselves. Mr. Hirota provides an instance of what could be done speedily in this direction. He is reported to have expressed the hopes that Japanese imports into China would shortly pay the normal Customs dues. The day when this happens will see the commencement of the reorientation of foreign ideas on Japanese methods which prevail at the moment. The very real fact that Japanese importers in this country were again paying the same Customs dues as other foreigners would do much to allay present discontent and anxiety. It is not unreasonable to suggest that if foreign opinion is unfavorable to Japan it is Japan's own fault. The remedy is in her own hands, and,

if she fails to apply it, she has only herself to blame for the sentiment which must necessarily continue to be felt.[7]

British Support of China

As the British in China steadily lost faith, though not hope, in the possibilities of co-operating with the Japanese, more and more support was voiced for the cause of Nationalist China. When the Japanese forces were on the verge of capturing Nanking, the Chinese had been advised to surrender. But the Chinese continued to fight. This refusal to capitulate made a deep impression on the attitude of the British in China. Not only did advocacy of surrender become a meaningless policy, but the prestige of the National Government was greatly heightened and doubts arose about Japan's ability to carry her plans to a successful conclusion.

After a lull of some months the Japanese forces began a campaign in February 1938 to take Hsuchow and thereby secure domination of the whole of the Tientsin-Pukow railway and its junction with the Lunghai Railway. The *North-China Herald*, commenting on the significance of the coming battles, noted that the Nationalist authorities realized that the Japanese might succeed, yet declared that "The prospects of severe fighting and, perhaps, the fall of Hankow itself, will not necessarily dampen the ardor of the resistance which China is presenting to the Japanese invasion." In its analysis of the possible effects of the fighting, a new respect for Nationalist China was clearly evident.

> They have accepted the idea of a long-drawn-out struggle with the possibility of repeated military defeats in the field, believing that an intolerable strain will be placed upon Japan's resources, such as to bring ultimate victory to themselves. There are many who believe that this is not only possible but probable. . . . Despite claims to the contrary there is very little real evidence that in the defeats which the Chinese troops have sustained in the field they have suffered any material diminution in morale, and though the

[7] *North-China Herald*, May 25, 1938. The comment by *Finance and Commerce* on Mr. Hirota's statement was even more skeptical: "The open door will give everybody equal opportunity providing (1) Japanese military operations are not interfered with and (2) providing Japan can keep the door open without trespassing upon the rights and privileges vested (by Japan) in the new administrative regime. Looking through Mr. Hirota's long statement, we cannot find many crumbs of comfort. No doubt the Foreign Minister means what he says, but he and others in civil authority have said the same things so many times before, without results strangely in conflict with their assurances, that this latest pledge will not convince the chairmen of Foreign Chambers of Commerce in Shanghai, Hankow, and Tientsin that in reviewing the situation their facts have been faulty or their fears unfounded." *Finance and Commerce*, May 25, 1938, pp. 401-2.

impending battle for the Lunghai Railway may prove a distinctly fateful one to either side, its loss need have no greater effect upon Chinese determination than the fall of Shanghai or the capture of Nanking.[8]

This emphasis on the drawn-out nature of the war and on the difficulties facing the Japanese was reiterated during the following months. Thus, commenting on Chinese claims to substantial victories over the Japanese forces operating along the Tientsin-Pukow Railway (before the fall of Hsuchow):

> The Chinese are giving the Japanese command a particularly hard nut to crack, and it is more than likely that the latter will require considerable reinforcement in men and material before they will be able to bring about the downfall of Hsuchowfu and thus secure union between the troops operating in the North and those in Central China. Whether eventually the Japanese succeed in doing this or not the fact emerges that they have undertaken a task which is proving not so easy of fulfillment as it was anticipated in those months before they embarked upon this adventure in China. It leads to the conclusion that the end of hostilities is, from a military point of view, still very far away, and it is this, and not military reverses which may be tending . . . to sober the Japanese nation.

Since the British in China were at this time still advocating a policy of co-operation with the Japanese, such statements might indicate not only a change in attitude toward the Chinese, but also the hope that if the difficulties of invasion were emphasized, the Japanese might become more amenable to the mediation which Great Britain was repeatedly offering.

This supposition is further borne out by other statements made by the *North-China Herald*. Thus, in discussing the fight for Hsuchow which was developing with increased tempo during the second week of May 1938 and the Japanese claims that the downfall of Hsuchow would bring the downfall of the Chinese Government, it wrote:

> In this the wish may be father to the thought. There are at present no indications of anything of the nature occurring, and, indeed, the utterances of the Generalissimo and his supporters indicate that the determination to resist the Japanese aggression is just as strong as ever it was, and even the possible loss of Hsuchowfu, which has long been contemplated by the Chinese command, is unlikely to have any great effect in reducing it.

For Chiang Kai-shek had said that, if necessary, he would retreat into the mountains of West China whence he would continually harrass the Japanese forces, putting Japan to continual and great expense and bring about that financial attrition

[8] *North-China Herald*, February 16, 1938, pp. 235-6.

which the Chinese leaders regarded as one means of ultimately winning the war.

Pursuit of such a policy might, it is true, not lead to the driving out of the invaders, but it may eventually induce them to come to terms which at present they so steadfastly refuse to do.[9]

Chinese Overtures for Financial Credit

The combined effect of the Japanese attack on British interests and the growing belief that the protection of these interests demanded increased support for Nationalist China led to increased dissatisfaction with the ineffective policy of the home government. This was seen in the unfavorable response to Great Britain's refusal to extend financial aid to the Kuomintang Government. In March 1938 Reuters reported that certain Chinese interests had approached a group of London banks asking for twelve or twenty-four months' credit. It was believed that the object in seeking these credits was to guarantee China's payments on foreign loans.[10] Mr. Sun Fo, president of the Legislative Yuan, who was in London in April 1938 endeavoring to raise a loan for China, admitted that he had been informed that the chances of raising a loan, whether for China or any country, were "at present hopeless in view of the general confusion of world conditions." Commercial credits for China, however, were considered feasible, he said.[11]

The British Government, which was a party to the League resolutions of October 1937 and January 1938 pledging to give every possible assistance to China, straddled the issue of financial aid. Sir John Simon, replying to Mr. Arthur Henderson on April 14, stated that if the Chinese Government found it possible to obtain a loan from British financial institutions, any request for government approval would be sympathetically considered. This passive attitude ended the Chinese attempts to raise a loan in London for the time being since no proposal for a loan could succeed unless the British Government took the initiative in guaranteeing it.

The Chinese showed diplomatic finesse in refusing to become outwardly nettled with the British attitude. Mr. Sun Fo ended his previously quoted interview with words of high praise for

---

[9] *North-China Herald*, May 18, 1938, pp. 265-6.
[10] *North-China Herald*, March 9, 1938, p. 362.
[11] *North-China Herald*, April 20, 1938, p. 90.

the prime minister. When Sir Archibald John Clark Kerr, British Ambassador to China, arrived at Chungking on April 9, 1938, to present his credentials, he was given a warm and elaborate welcome by the Kuomintang authorities. Such demonstrations of friendship for the British were especially effective at this time since they came during a period when the Japanese were becoming increasingly unfriendly.

Although these early Chinese overtures for financial credit received comparatively little attention from the British in China, when the next opportunity was offered to them for indicating their approval of such aid, they did so. The occasion came soon as the result of events in Geneva.

On May 10, 1938, Mr. Wellington Koo made a statement to the Council of the League of Nations, protesting that the resolutions of the Assembly and the Council of October 6, 1937, and February 2, 1938, remained unfulfilled, and that nothing had been done to help China. China, he said, was quite prepared for further sacrifices, but she did expect the members of the League to come forward with material aid. He appealed to the Council to apply the measures of the Covenant and to implement the two resolutions. At a meeting of the Council on May 13th, Mr. Koo demanded strong League action against Japanese aggression, and suggested the possibility of sanctions. The members declined to contemplate sanctions but, instead, assured the Chinese delegate of their determination to put no obstacle in the way of continued Chinese defense. On the following day (May 14) the Council adopted a resolution urging League members to do their utmost to give effect to earlier resolutions of the Assembly and Council regarding the needs of China's defense and to take into consideration any request she might make in accordance with them. Lord Halifax declared that the British Government had done its best "within the limits which the situation in the United Kingdom imposes upon them" to implement its obligations to China under the resolutions previously adopted, and that it would continue to give serious and sympathetic consideration to requests for material and financial aid.

The British in China were quick to indicate that they favored not merely "consideration," however serious and sympathetic, but the actual granting of British aid to China. For example, *Finance and Commerce* gave much prominence to the League resolution and to a letter to the London *Times* of May 21, 1938, written by Mr. F. L. Kerran who had visited China during the hostilities. In this "a definite move to help China thoroughly to defeat Japan" was strongly advocated as a "gesture which would substantially improve the future of Great Britain on the Continent of China as well as in India; moreover, it would considerably weaken the effectiveness of the Berlin-Tokyo axis." This letter did not suggest credits for China but rather equipment, munitions and expert advice. It did, moreover, offer an explanation of Britain's policy which is not significant for its novelty, but rather because *Finance and Commerce* conspicuously reprinted this type of analysis.

The explanation offered in informed circles of the British Government's passive and timid policy in the Far East is that, if Japan wins the war, she will be compelled to come to London for credits and loans for the purpose of exploiting her victory, and for capital development in China. When this position is reached, it is argued, Britain will be able to determine the terms on which they will be prepared to lend their money to Japan and to safeguard their present investment in China.

Mr. Kerran was willing to concede that

This may have seemed a plausible policy at the early stages of the Sino-Japanese conflict, in view of past conflicts and their outcomes between Japan and China, but not in the present struggle.

Finance and Commerce printed this strong request for British aid to China next to a letter written by Mr. R. A. Butler, Under-Secretary for Foreign Affairs, defining the Government's attitude in response to an inquiry from Mr. R. H. Morgan, M. P., as to whether His Majesty's Government had taken any action in conformity with the League resolutions. Mr. Butler's vague and evasive reply contrasted sharply with Mr. Kerran's letter, and their juxtaposition tended to emphasize the obscurity of the Government's position. The Under-Secretary wrote:

Dear Morgan,
I am sorry there has been so much delay in replying to the letter which you wrote to the Secretary of State on April 14 on the subject of the action taken by His Majesty's Government in conformity with the League's Resolution recommending Members to give what assistance they could to China in the conflict with Japan.
We recognize that the Members of Parliament may have considerable difficulty in dealing with the questions put to them on this subject by their constituents, and we have been considering what is the most helpful advice we can give. In the first place, we feel that it is essential that the precise

terms of these Resolutions should be borne in mind. You will recall that both the Resolution of October 6, 1937, and that of February 2nd, recommended that Member States should consider "how far they could individually extend aid to China," and should "lose no opportunity of examining, in consultation with similarly interested Powers, the feasibility of any further steps which may contribute to a just settlement of the conflict in the Far East."

You would be perfectly safe in assuring constituents that His Majesty's Government have already taken practically all the steps that are open to them as a Government to implement their undertakings to give assistance to China, such as, for example, keeping Hongkong open. The needs of our own rearmament programme preclude us from permitting the export of munitions on a large scale to any foreign country, but we have placed no obstacles in the way of British armament firms executing any orders for China which did not interfere with Government work. The Chinese Government are aware of the difficulties with which we are confronted in various respects, but they are equally aware that we are always prepared to consider any further suggestions that they may put to us. The Chinese Government, moreover, know that if they attempt to obtain help from non-Governmental sources, His Majesty's Government will do whatever they can to assist.

As regards consultation with similarly interested powers, His Majesty's Government have made it clear to all concerned, including the Chinese and the Japanese Governments, that they are prepared to lend their good offices in any endeavour to reach a settlement, provided that these good offices are desired by and are acceptable to both sides.

In general, it would be correct for you to say that His Majesty's Government are not in the least losing sight of the League Resolutions in question and are constantly reviewing all possible ways and means of assisting China in some way and of helping to promote a fair and reasonable settlement of the dispute.

Yours sincerely,

R. A. Butler.[12]

In brief, nothing positive about credits to China and merely a reiteration of Britain's policy of keeping Hongkong open and offering to act as a mediator. This was little or no advance over the policy which was causing discontent among the British in China.

By July 1938 the campaign for British credits to China had reached a more definitive stage, and sharp disagreement with the policy of the British Government was expressed in Great Britain and China. Lord Lytton in a letter to the London *Times* on July 5, 1938, urged serious consideration of steps to help China maintain a stable currency. Britain's most material interests, he maintained, apart from considerations of justice and human-

[12] *Finance and Commerce,* June 8, 1938, p. 454.

ity, dictated that she should help prevent China's monetary system from collapsing under the strain of the hostilities with Japan.

If such projects are to be abandoned at a time when the value of the dollar is falling purely on account of foreign invasion, not only shall we be open to the charge of placing in quarantine the victim of aggression instead of the aggressor, but we shall also be neglecting our own manifest interests.

Lord Lytton also urged that the British Government give careful consideration to every possibility of economic co-operation with China, especially in the undeveloped areas of the southwest.

This lead was followed on July 14 by several members of the House of Commons who pressed the Government for a declaration of its attitude on the question of extending financial aid to China. Mr. Arthur Greenwood, Labor, asked Sir John Simon, chancellor of the exchequer, "whether the Chinese Government has applied to the British Government for a loan and, if so, has the application been agreed to?" Sir John replied that various proposals had been made by the Chinese Government for a loan in Great Britain. He referred to his statement of April 14, 1938, to the effect that "if in present circumstances the Chinese Government found it possible to obtain a loan from British financial institutions, any request for Government approval would be sympathetically considered."[13] The government, Sir John added, had no power itself to grant or guarantee a loan without special legislation, which in the present circumstances it was unable to introduce.

Sir John Wardlaw-Milne, Conservative, asked if the Chancellor realized "the immense importance for all British interests and for peace in China of this possibility of a loan being guaranteed to the Chinese Government in some form or another at the present time." Sir John Simon's reply was: "My honorable friend can be assured that the Government have had very closely and carefully under review the considerations which he has raised."

Mr. Arthur Henderson, Labor, then asked if Sir John would assure the House that the obligation undertaken by the British Government, when it subscribed to the League resolutions

---

[13] *Parliamentary Debates*, House of Commons, Vol. 338, col. 1424.

The question of a loan to China was bound up with the negotiations which were going on at this time between Japan and Great Britain. Those who favored an agreement with Japan naturally opposed a loan to China.

pledging every possible assistance to China, would be fulfilled as far as possible by the British Government. The Chancellor of the Exchequer replied that "the terms of the League of Nations resolutions to which we are party have been very fully borne in mind." Whereupon, Mr. Geoffrey Mander, Opposition Liberal, asked if Sir John did not feel, in view of all that had happened in the Far East, that China's claim to assistance in the form of a loan was at least as great as that of Turkey.[14] "The circumstances in each case," replied Sir John Simon, "of course have to be weighed, and the circumstances in the present case are very grave and serious; but there is the consideration, which must not be overlooked, that in the case of Turkey we were dealing with a loan to a country which is not engaged in hostilities."

Thus, Sir John was evidently of the opinion, when he stressed the fact of hostilities, that any support to China other than purely commercial transactions was undesirable since it would be regarded by Japan as an unfriendly act and therefore undesirable. Although it was obvious that there was a marked difference in the circumstances in Turkey and China, it was precisely the existence of hostilities in China which had evoked the League resolutions calling for aid to China. Notwithstanding Sir John's statement that the League Resolutions "have been very fully borne in mind," nothing had been done to carry these resolutions into effect.

Finance and Commerce described the Chancellor's statements as being "a carefully phrased and extremely frigid reply to Lord Lytton's letter in the *Times*." This journal then quoted the "semi-official" *Japan Times* as saying that the powers would do well not to give aid to Chiang Kai-shek.

> Chiang has not a hope. Therefore, any Great Power who encourages him in this is inflicting a great wrong on China. Moreover, it is inflicting a great wrong on itself. For what use can China ever be now to the Democracy bloc? In fact, the longer the struggle continues, the greater the damage to the Powers' interest in China.

Finance and Commerce then asked,

> Is it possible that arguments of this character have been urged upon and aroused sympathetic response from Sir John Simon? His reluctance (as Foreign Minister) to support the United States Government in February 1932, in making a *démarche* to Tokyo under the Nine Power Treaty—a note

---

[14] Turkey had recently been granted credits, mainly in the form of guarantees up to £10,000,000, by the Export Credits Guarantee Department.

most carefully worded in order not to prejudge the question of responsibility for the Sino-Japanese clash in Manchuria—has led to consequences which, perhaps, Sir John thought possible, but were the inevitable sequel to his disastrous hesitation to face realities. Crying over spilt milk is useless, but equally futile is it to pass resolutions at Geneva pledging help for China if these expressions of sympathy do not mean anything more than a desire to carry on "business as usual." . . . There is no sentiment in business, and if Britain's relations with China are to be guided solely and exclusively by business considerations, then the pledges made at Geneva should never have been given. Kinder to have said nothing about helping China in her desperate struggle than to pledge support and not give it. . . . Looked at as a purely business proposition, it certainly does seem a little queer to talk of lending money to China when the potential lender already has £130,000,000 invested in Chinese territory which has been taken by Japan—and wherein Japan is herself planning some very comprehensive development schemes. Prince Konoye recently said that when the "true intentions" of Japan are realized, the attitude of England, France and America will gradually change. The Japanese Premier's forecast seems to be in course of fulfillment, but whether due to realization of the true intentions of Japan and the possible reaction upon lawfully established foreign business interests is more than we can say.[15]

The sharp criticism of the Government's attitude was voiced on other details. What had been the result of "the strongest representations" which Mr. Butler said had been made to the Japanese Government on certain matters concerning important British interests in China was a question asked in the House of Commons on May 23. Mr. R. A. Butler had replied, "more in sorrow than in anger," as *Finance and Commerce* put it, "I regret we have not yet received a satisfactory answer."[16] To this, *Finance and Commerce* remarked sarcastically, "which is precisely what frequently happens in the House of Commons itself when an honorable member tries to get a straight answer to a straight question put to a Cabinet Minister or his representative."

Another question had been put to Mr. Butler in the House of Commons on May 23 concerning the recent appointment of a superintendent of customs at Shanghai, and Mr. Butler had replied that the appointment had been made by the Provisional Government at Nanking, which the British Government did not recognize. Therefore, it could not control the appointment.

[15] *Finance and Commerce,* July 20, 1938, pp. 41-3.
[16] The particular matter at issue was the Japanese military occupation of the Shanghai-Nanking Railway, the consequent losses falling upon British bondholders, and the repeated refusal of permission for British engineers to inspect the damaged track.

Mr. A. C. Moreing then asked: "Are we going to recognize an appointment made by an administration which we do not recognize, when services of the greatest importance to British trade are concerned?" Mr. Butler replied: "His Majesty's Government have made it clear that in the recent Customs Agreement, they have not acquiesced in any interference with the Customs services and its present international personnel."

> This reply by the Under-Secretary for Foreign Affairs [said *Finance and Commerce*] is unpleasantly like those "unsatisfactory answers" which he has been receiving from Japan in reply to his own questions. It is an evasion of Mr. Moreing's inquiry, which was designed to ascertain whether the British Government "recognized" an appointment made by an "unrecognized" administration. Mr. Butler simply says that it has been "already made clear" that Britain "did not acquiesce in any interference with Customs Service and its international personnel"—which is precisely not the point raised by his questioner. Britain does not "recognize the legitimacy" of the action taken by Japan in regard to the Customs but has "acquiesced" in an arrangement arising out of that "unrecognized" act. Mr. Moreing wanted information regarding a similar anomaly—but got an evasive and therefore unsatisfactory answer.[17]

Craigie-Ugaki Talks

The discontent, which had been engendered among the British in China, was due to the uncomfortable feeling that their interests might be sacrificed as the result of a conciliatory policy toward Japan. Therefore, the conversations held in the summer of 1938 between Sir Robert Craigie, British ambassador to Japan, and General Ugaki gave them further cause for uneasiness.

In June 1938 General Kazushige Ugaki was appointed foreign minister of Japan. It was generally felt that this meant that Japanese foreign policy would be brought more into line with the existing military situation. At his first press conference with foreign correspondents, General Ugaki declared: "We have had special relations with Great Britain of traditional friendship. I will do my best to restore them and make them even closer

---

[17] *Finance and Commerce*, June 1, 1938. This article contains the following addendum: "As we go to press, comes news from London of yet another 'unsatisfactory answer' to a question in Parliament. On May 30th, Mr. Butler said that since the cessation of fighting in Shanghai last November, the British Government has lost no opportunity of representing to the Japanese authorities the desirability of the Shanghai Municipal Council being permitted to resume normal control of the Settlement area. Sir Patrick Hannon asked whether the Government had received a reply. The Under-Secretary for Foreign Affairs tersely replied 'not yet'."

than in the past."[18] This friendly attitude toward Britain was heartily endorsed by the leading Japanese newspapers which until then had been representing Britain as the main instigator of Chinese resistance. All of these newspapers, however, held that the prerequisite for rapprochement would be the cessation of the support allegedly being given to the Chinese Nationalist Government. General Ugaki himself made clear on what basis an Anglo-Japanese understanding could be reached. He intended "to endeavor to maintain maximum harmony with those nations who correctly understand Japan's position."

However, it was not a lack of understanding but the fact that Japan's aims in China were completely understood by the neutral interests that made them critical of Japan's policy. Thus, for example, the *North-China Herald* was deeply skeptical of the General's seemingly friendly overtures. It emphasized that the Japanese military caste had been placed more firmly in control than ever before, and that a foreign policy in line with militarist desires was more possible than an adaptation of Japan's military programs to the necessities of the international political situation.[19]

Although General Ugaki in the previously quoted interview[20] seemed reluctant to consider a mediation proposal, saying that the motive for such mediation would first have to be made clear, the British Government took the opposite tack and on June 27, 1938, Mr. Butler indicated to the House of Commons that the British Government would gladly take any steps in its power, alone or in conjunction with other powers, to bring about a cessation of hostilities in China. The British Government, however, Mr. Butler stated, had no information which would lead it to suppose that any proposal involving the withdrawal of Japanese forces from China would be likely to be accepted as a basis of mediation in the hostilities. The Japanese immediately rejected this suggestion of mediation. This quick refusal of the British proposal was one of many indications that General Ugaki intended no real change in the Japanese policy toward British interests in China.

Still, the Tokyo Government did indicate a willingness to

---

[18] *Japan Weekly Chronicle,* June 23, 1938.
[19] *North-China Herald,* June 22, 1938.
[20] In this same interview, General Ugaki gave assurance that the Japanese were not contemplating any action in Hainan.

reestablish friendly relations with Great Britain. For example, General Ugaki in an interview with Sir Robert Craigie, spoke of Japan's policy as one of friendly co-operation with Britain, making special reference to Japan's regard for British rights and interests in China. The British ambassador immediately communicated the Japanese foreign minister's assurances to his government. On receipt of this report, Lord Halifax directed Sir Robert to notify General Ugaki that the British Government was highly satisfied with his affirmation of Japan's regard for British rights and interests in China and that it expected this policy to be carried out faithfully by the Japanese Government.

Thus began a series of informal conversations between Sir Robert Craigie and General Ugaki. The talks covered a large scope of interests, but were reported to be devoid of political character. Mr. Butler, in the House of Commons on July 26, 1938, and Viscount Halifax in the House of Lords on July 27, indicated the scope of the talks when they said that the questions raised in the House regarding the wool monopoly in North China, freedom of transit for British merchant-shipping on inland waterways in China, the Peiping-Mukden Railway, conservancy in the Whangpoo and other matters were to be discussed in the course of a specially arranged conversation between Sir Robert Craigie and General Ugaki. Mr. Butler said:

> We shall judge the sincerity of the Japanese assurances in these matters by the success which, we trust, will attend the course of this important conversation.

Mr. Chamberlain did his part to reassure the anxious members of Parliament and to preserve the amiable atmosphere brought about by the Japanese overtures. The Brussels Conference of November 1937, the Prime Minister maintained, had shown clearly enough that a proposal involving any intervention in the Far Eastern conflict on the part of members of the League of Nations would have no chance of acceptance, and the British Government could not undertake alone such a step as intervention in the hostilities. This meant, concretely, that no special legislation would be introduced to enable the government to guarantee a loan to China.

> We came finally to the definite conclusion that we should not be so

FROM NANKING TO THE INVASION OF SOUTH CHINA—II 151

justified in the case of a loan which would have to be based on security of hypothetical value, and as to which it was by no means certain that, if it were granted, it would achieve the objects which were intended.

This rejection of a China loan was followed by the vague assurance that there were various proposals which were not open to the objections raised to the granting of a loan, and which were under examination by the government departments concerned. Later he assured the House that Japan must recognize that "we too have our interests in China, and that we cannot stand by and see them sacrificed in the process." He made the by-now-traditional offer of Britain's services to bring about a cessation of hostilities in the Far East, "if ever and whenever we see an opportunity which presents a favourable prospect of success."[21]

Lord Halifax took a somewhat firmer position on the following day in the House of Lords. The British Government, he declared, was "already considering the possible action open to us if we do not get that consideration for our interests and rights which we have a right to expect." As for the Japanese claim that their China policy was "in defense of their interests," Lord Halifax countered that the British had every right "to expect them to recognize that if they have certain interests to protect, we have the same, and are not unmindful of our responsibilities, which we have every intention to discharge."[22] He enlarged the Prime Minister's statements of the previous day by more specific statements as to the British Government's attitude on China and what it was doing or might do. Thus, after stating that it was uncertain whether the loan would achieve its object of maintaining the Chinese currency during the war, he went on to say: "I can readily assure your Lordships that we shall be entirely ready to consider other proposals of that kind on their merits, as and when they are made to us." This firmer position was underscored by the tone of the debate in the House of Lords, especially the statements of Lord Elibank, which were uncompromisingly critical of Japanese policy.

That General Ugaki "deplored," but refused to be seriously disturbed by, the unfriendly attitude in the British Parliament was an indication of his desire to reach an understanding with

[21] *Parliamentary Debates,* House of Commons, Vol. 338, cols. 2961-2.
[22] *Parliamentary Debates,* House of Lords, Vol. 110, col. 1274.

Great Britain.[23] The first formal conversation between the Japanese foreign minister and Sir Robert Craigie took place on July 26. As reported by General Ugaki, some 150 issues were brought up by the British representative, although none was discussed in detail. In future conversations, General Ugaki said, the policy of the Japanese Government would be set forth frankly in order to deepen Britain's understanding of the situation. He expressed the conviction that once Britain understood Japan's position perfectly, the Japanese Government could and would consider all British claims within the limits consistent with the strategical and other requirements of the situation in China.

The Japanese press was more reluctant to gloss over the statements made in the British Parliament. *Nichi-Nichi* spoke of these utterances as "casting gloom" over Anglo-Japanese relations. It regretted this attitude in view of the fact that Anglo-Japanese relations had improved recently as a result of the Craigie-Ugaki talks. *Hochi* undertook to remind Lord Halifax that Japan's actions in China were not merely designed to protect Japanese interests. The interests of Japan and Britain in China were not on the same footing for "British interests in China are only the result of imperialistic desires and the exploitation of China, whereas Japanese interests in China form a life and death question for Japan." While expressing "sympathetic understanding" of the concern of Britain and France over safeguarding their interests in China, *Kokumin* asserted that the "financial assistance extended by Britain and France to the Chiang Kai-shek regime forms the fountain head of the latter's so-called protracted warfare." The question of safeguarding British interests in China or maintaining the Chinese currency "must be settled with Japan as a party to negotiations,

[23] The desire of the Japanese Government to put the best possible face on the debates in the House of Commons and the House of Lords was clearly seen in a statement of Mr. Masayuki Tani, Japanese ambassador-at-large, made in Shanghai on July 30. "Recently the question of protection for British rights and interests in China was the subject of much discussion in Parliament. This fact endorses Japan's military successes and speaks volumes for the fact that British interests must depend on us for protection. Dispatches from London say that the British Government is prepared to mediate between Japan and China if Hankow is captured and the Ugaki-Craigie conversations are successful. However, there has been no change in Japan's original policy of settling its differences with China by itself, without outside mediation. This will continue for the future." (*Trans-Pacific*, August 4, 1938, p. 26.)

and not with the Chiang Kai-shek administration, which is on the verge of collapse."

Miyako was critical of the speeches in Parliament: "If the acrimonious atmosphere continues much longer, there is danger of the Craigie-Ugaki conversations being stalemated. If things come to such a pass, Britain will be responsible for the situation arising from it." *Kokumin*, in a less sympathetic vein with regard to the remarks of the Opposition in Parliament, said of the Craigie-Ugaki talks: "These talks are not intended to bring about an Anglo-Japanese understanding with regard to China or to settle the China hostilities. . . . The cardinal aim of the Ugaki-Craigie talks is discussion of how to handle British rights and interests in the parts of China occupied by Japan. . . . To be frank, an opinion of some vigor prevails in Japan that there is not the slightest need to conduct such negotiations with Great Britain while hostilities are in progress."

Asahi, more sympathetic toward an Anglo-Japanese understanding, maintained that Mr. Chamberlain and Lord Halifax did hope for an improvement in the relations between the two countries and that Sir Robert Craigie was endeavoring to realize their hope. As for the debate in Parliament, it was "regrettable as the replies of Mr. Butler and even Mr. Chamberlain apparently imply a bluff against Japan or an intention to check Japanese influence." Britain was warned that her "diplomatic bluff failed miserably in Italy in connection with the Ethiopian campaign" and that "no better success can attend a similar British attitude against Japan." Nevertheless hope for some agreement was not abandoned. "But for the ugly atmosphere deliberately created by Britain, most of the pending questions regarding British interests in China ought to be settled amicably by local negotiation."[24]

The *North-China Herald* applauded the authoritative pronouncement of the determination of the Government to uphold British interests in China. The feeling had become common that the British Foreign Office had "not been quite so sympathetically active as could be desired, and that the Government was following a policy of caution to an almost unwarrantable degree." This, it was thought, had encouraged the idea in Tokyo that Great Britain was losing "some of her vitality" in the Far East. That this lack of an energetic policy was respon-

[24] Quoted in *North-China Herald*, August 3, 1938, p. 190.

sible for much of the damage to British interests was clearly recognized, but willingness to let bygones be bygones was expressed if the British Government would now take such steps as were "calculated to prevent the further incursion of Japanese into the rights and interests of British traders in China, and to remedy as far as possible the damage which has already been done, as well as securing reparation in those instances where such a course seems to be the most appropriate."

The strength of Great Britain in coping with the situation was stressed and the point was made that it was not in the guise of "a helpless suppliant," that Great Britain would come to a conference table with Japan. The time had passed for mere assurances and Japan now had to carry out the promises which she had already made.

> Whatever transpires in Tokyo it is clear that from now on it will be necessary to maintain an increasing vigilance over British rights and interests in China, and to take every step necessary for their adequate protection.[25]

The exasperation of the British residents in China was visible in the temporary rejection of the familiar method of excusing the actions of the Japanese in China on the ground of the division between the civilian government in Tokyo and the military in China. Now the *North-China Herald* took the London *Times* to task for contending that the Tokyo Government had only a precarious control over the Japanese commanders in China, and that the discipline of the Japanese forces on the mainland was not of a sufficiently high standard to overcome the ultra-nationalistic prejudices inflamed by anti-British propaganda. This newspaper pointed out that the key positions in the Japanese cabinet were now held by military men, and "if what is practically a military Cabinet is unable to control the policies of its commanders in the field, what sort of organization can ever be expected to?" This retort was followed by the additional argument that

> for the purpose of international negotiation it really does not matter who is actually guilty of what is going on in China so detrimental to foreign interests. The only question which arises is as to who is responsible, and that responsibility rests fairly and squarely upon the shoulders of the Tokyo Government. It, and it alone, is responsible for the acts of its agents in

[25] *Ibid.*, p. 181.

China, and if the latter are following policies calculated to embarrass it, that is no concern of the victims of their rapacious deeds.[26]

These statements, denying the existence of the oft-stated dichotomy between the military and civilian arms of the Japanese Government and rejecting the corollary that a government is not always responsible for the acts of its military forces, were indeed as exceptional as they were valid. It will be seen that on future occasions, when the military nature of the Japanese cabinet became even clearer, the *North-China Herald* reverted to the position of emphasizing the distinction between the Tokyo Government and the Army in China. That they saw fit to deny the split at this time might have indicated their unwillingness to leave the negotiators in Tokyo a line of retreat. The failure of the conversations could not then be excused on the grounds of the inability of the government in Tokyo to check the military authorities in China.

The outbreak of fighting at Changkufeng on the Korean-Soviet frontier between Soviet and Japanese troops on July 30 interrupted the Tokyo conversations, which were not resumed until September 14. In the meantime not only General Ugaki, but also other ministers, including Mr. Ikeda, minister of finance, stressed the desirability of not antagonizing the Western democracies, particularly Great Britain. But this did not mean any abatement of the infringement of foreign rights in China. There were simultaneous indications that this conciliatory policy was becoming increasingly unpopular in governmental, civilian and military circles. The large anti-British element was demanding that Britain recognize Japan's new position in the Far East, refuse aid to Chiang Kai-shek and co-operate more specifically with the new Chinese regimes in Nanking and Peiping.[27]

The renewed conversations in Tokyo failed to reach any agreement, mainly because of General Ugaki's insistence that many of the questions be referred to China for local negotiation. They were again interrupted—this time finally—by the resignation of General Ugaki on September 29. Although it was officially announced that there would be no change in the foreign policy of the Japanese Government, General Ugaki's

[26] *Ibid.,* pp. 181-2.
[27] An interesting analysis of the situation was made by the Tokyo correspondent of the London *Times,* August 27, 1938.

withdrawal from the cabinet did mark a definite turn. Not only did the position of British interests in China grow steadily worse, but, more and more, the guise of official friendship for Great Britain was dropped and instead open hostility was shown. The Japanese invasion of South China followed immediately after the resignation of General Ugaki.

CHAPTER IX

FROM CANTON TO THE NOVEMBER NOTES

The invasion of South China, which began on October 12, 1938, was a turning-point not only in the Sino-Japanese conflict, but also in Great Britain's relations with the contending parties. The Munich Agreement, the climax of Britain's appeasement policy, provided the occasion for this Japanese venture, but its causes were more deep-rooted than a mere desire to take advantage of a favorable opportunity. The Japanese had concluded that their China policy could not be carried through successfully as long as third-party interests, especially British, continued to exist. In North China and later in Central China, British interests had felt the pincers of Japanese imperialism, in the form of discriminations coupled with Japanese monopolies, and now the same process was being repeated in South China. The new threat, however, proved to be a boomerang and in the long run weakened rather than strengthened Japan's position in China.

The Japanese invasion of South China was heralded by the successful landing at Bias Bay. Its immediate purpose was to occupy the important commercial city of Canton and thus sever the main artery connecting unoccupied China and the coast. Canton owed its importance to its location as the southern terminus of the Canton-Hankow Railway, with water and rail connections to Hongkong, the main port of South China. The Canton-Hankow Railway had replaced the Yangtze River as the Chinese Government's main connection between Central and Western China and the coast, and the harbor facilities at Hongkong had accommodated the greatly increased traffic over this route occasioned by the war.

Effect of the South China Invasion upon Hongkong

Hongkong was experiencing boom conditions. Her trade had vastly increased at the expense of other ports like Shanghai, and she received an influx of wealthy refugees and business enterprises. These prosperous conditions were reflected in the Colony's fiscal position. At the end of August 1938 the Hongkong Government had an excess of assets over liabilities amounting to Hk. $15,630,000, a record in its financial history. Actual revenue on that date was Hk. $24,740,000, which was Hk. $3,000,000 more than the total for the corresponding period in 1937. As the government had budgeted for a total of Hk. $30,254,000 for the year, there was every anticipation of an excess of revenue of at least Hk. $5,000,000. Revenue from the Kowloon-Canton Railway (which connects the Colony with Canton) had increased sharply, while revenue from land sales was more than three times that for 1937. Surveying this situation, the *North-China Herald* could well write: "There is no cause for even the tiniest frown on the face of the treasurer as he surveys the Colony's ledger."[1] On the morning that this statement was published, Japanese troops began their invasion of South China, a move calculated to undermine the basis of Hongkong's position as a chief *entrepôt* for South, Central and West China.

Officials of the Japanese Foreign Office immediately visited the embassies of the foreign powers in Tokyo to define for them Japan's policy in South China. They assured the foreign representatives that during the South China drive Japan would continue to safeguard foreign interests. The powers, however, were requested to co-operate with Japan in her effort to reduce to a minimum possible losses which they might suffer, and to avoid becoming involved in the Sino-Japanese difficulties. Present operations in South China, it was pointed out, were designed to deal a death-blow to the existing Chinese regime and thus accelerate "stabilization" in the Far East.

In London, the Japanese action was connected with the resignation of General Ugaki, and it caused considerable concern. Moreover, since it had followed on the heels of the Munich Conference, it might well be a sign that Japan, too, desired to be appeased. It was authoritatively stated that Great Britain through Sir Robert Craigie had warned the Japanese Government that the latter's action would possibly imperil Anglo-Japanese relationships and reminded Japan of Britain's economic and political interests in Hongkong and South China. This warning was, indeed, restrained since the Japanese acts

[1] *North-China Herald,* October 12, 1938, p. 45.

threatened not only Hongkong, a British colony, but also the entire British position in South China. British traders and investors had long been predominant in this region, and increased interest in the possibilities for trade and investment expansion had been shown during the hostilities. Japanese occupation of Canton would mean the end of such plans.

The Japanese soon indicated that in the South China campaign, as in those in North and Central China, the interests of third powers would be subordinated to those of Japan. The Japanese Government requested all foreign powers to refrain from moving their troops, warships and aircraft in South China in the area from Swatow to Pakhoi during the continuance of Japanese military action. More important, the Pearl River was closed to all shipping. In addition, third-power nationals were warned to avoid the zones of hostilities in South China and to mark foreign property clearly so that it could be distinguished from the air. The note which contained this warning followed the model of previous similar communications concerning North and Central China and was interpreted by the British as the preliminary groundwork upon which rejection of responsibility for untoward incidents might be based. There was no reason to suppose that the treatment of the British in South China would differ from their treatment in North China or in the Yangtze Valley.

The problems which faced Hongkong as the result of the invasion were clearly seen. On the following day, October 13, Sir Geoffrey Northcote, governor of the Colony, referred to the new situation in the course of an address on the budget before the Legislative Council. He pointed out that hostilities so close to the borders of Hongkong were of grave concern to the Colony, since three-quarters of its vegetable needs and a large portion of its meat supply were drawn from the province of Kwangtung. In addition, the Colony was faced by a very serious refugee problem. This would mean heavy charges on the Colony's funds. Furthermore, the Colony's revenues were bound to be seriously affected owing to the interruption of trade and commerce. The governor concluded by expressing his confidence that the citizens of Hongkong would face the difficult situation with "sense and dignity," relying on the British Government to do everything in its power to protect their interests.[2]

By October 21, only nine days after the landing at Bias Bay,

[2] Hongkong Legislative Council, *Reports of the Meetings*, 1938, p. 128.

Canton was in Japanese hands, and on October 22 Hongkong was taking stock of its new isolation from China. This was the first time in the ninety-seven year history of the Colony that it had ever been completely cut off from China. British circles there believed that Hongkong's 13,000 British residents faced virtual ruin. The considerable amount of Chinese war materials, including airplanes, tanks, guns, munitions and trucks which were stranded in the Colony, was an indication of the future of Hongkong's trade. The possibility of traffic via Indo-China was not overlooked but its full potentiality was not yet realized.

The importance of the fall of Canton was recognized in London. Thus, the Sunday *Times* of October 23 maintained that the consequences of the capture of Canton were equally serious for China and Hongkong. Not only did it involve the future of Hongkong but also the future of British trade with China in general. For even if the British colony feared no military attack by the Japanese, British commercial interests in Hongkong and South China faced severe danger.

British Suggestions for Mediation

The British press in China took a very pessimistic view of the markedly changed situation brought about by the Japanese capture of Canton. Accepting the interpretation that the rapid fall of Canton was due to "silver bullets," they counseled the Chinese Government to make peace.

> Whatever chances China had of winning the planned long-drawn-out war must disappear in view of the patent fact that the unity which is an imperative necessity for such a scheme can no longer be depended upon.[3]

The time seemed ripe for third-power mediation. That mediation should be suggested at a time so patently unfavorable to the Chinese indicates how deeply the fall of Canton had shaken the confidence of the British in China in the continued ability of Chiang Kai-shek's government to resist. Peace at this time would have meant granting considerable concessions to the Japanese at the expense of the British as well as of the Chinese. The same circles which had first discouraged Chinese resistance, and then, impressed by the Chinese determination to continue hostilities, had encouraged the National Government to fight, now again spoke of ending the war. Peace based on compromise

[3] *North-China Herald,* October 26, 1938, p. 134.

brought about by third power mediation was now considered the best possible solution.

That this point of view proved temporary was due mainly to two factors—continued Chinese resistance and the failure of the Japanese to take advantage of the changed atmosphere and offer any real concessions to third power interests. The much-abused formula of military necessity and the well-known phrases, "as a matter of principle we intend to respect scrupulously the rights and interests of third party Powers; those interfered with will be gradually restored," were again paraded out, but these were ignored as being unworthy of serious consideration. By now the conviction was prevalent that many of the Japanese actions were dominated by the desire to obtain bargaining-points for the purpose of extracting concessions.

The Japanese press frankly spoke of the capture of Canton as an anti-British move. *Nichi-Nichi* saw in the capture of Canton a blow against Hongkong.

There is one way by which Britain can hope to save Hong Kong from being placed in a position where the Canton area will cease to be its hinterland, and that is by understanding the intentions of Japan and co-operating with it. If it refuses to co-operate, it is sure to see the city wither. The fall of Canton has created a situation which will find Britain under the necessity of revising the policy, a mistaken one, it hitherto has followed toward this country.

Asahi believed the capture of Canton would mean the cutting-off of British aid to Chiang Kai-shek.[4]

The reaction of the British in China to this outburst was highly significant, particularly in view of the impending fall of Hankow. For example, the *North-China Herald* on the one hand said, "Great Britain is being held up before the Japanese public as the wicked ogre responsible for most of Japan's troubles," and on the other hand adopted a most conciliatory and patient tone. It was

a matter for very real regret that attempts to bring about a better understanding between Great Britain in the early months of last year were brought to naught by the opening of the Sino-Japanese hostilities.

Again,

One of the main beliefs . . . is that Great Britain is following the policy she is, in the hope that Japanese national power will be spent. Nothing is

[4] Quoted in *Trans-Pacific*, Tokyo, October 27, 1938.

further from the truth. A weakened Japan, with all that might entail, might very well prove a serious unstabilizing factor in the Far East. A collapse of its national system as the result of unduly prolonged warfare in China is most certainly not to be desired either by the British or by those other nations with which Japan is at present in closer amity.

This conciliatory attitude was, however, qualified by a reminder that there were many "vulnerable spots in Japan's armour," and that the successes achieved in China were "not necessarily auguries of similar achievements against other nations."

These friendly overtures were joined with mediation proposals, although it was recognized that there was every chance of the Chinese forces retreating successfully westward from Hankow and re-forming themselves for further fighting.

> When the fall of Nanking revealed in so tragic a light the probability of what has now happened to such large areas of China, with all the misery, suffering and death it has brought in its train, this journal entered a plea for peace. Strong as the arguments then offered undoubtedly were, they have been reinforced by the tragedy of the past ten months. All that is left to China is a wild gamble that things may ultimately turn towards victory, a gamble based upon the opinions of economic experts who have proved so woefully wrong in the past when they endeavored to apply their science to the unexpected features of war. In the light of that, it is again argued that China's imperative need is the intervention of friendly Powers with the aim of putting a period to this insensate squandering of man, money and material.[5]

In London, Reuters reported that tentative movements had been made by influential Japanese quarters to induce the British Government to offer its services for the restoration of peace in the Far East. It was understood that one or two prominent British business men were supporting the movement, but that nothing of an official nature had taken place. It was suggested, however, that Great Britain might inquire of both China and Japan whether they now wanted peace, and invite them to a conference merely on that basis, making no mention of terms or stipulations. These Japanese circles affirmed that the Japanese generals were as anxious as the civilians to end the war, in

---

[5] *North-China Herald,* November 2, 1938, p. 177. It is interesting to compare this with a leading article written about a month before. In this the Chinese were warned against expecting "immediate prospects of victory," and the weakness of the Japanese position was stressed. In conclusion it had stated: "Japanese realization that the fall of Hankow will not end the war is in itself something of a moral victory, and direct encouragement to continue along the hard path of warfare until the desired end is in sight." *North-China Herald,* September 21, 1938, p. 486.

view of the enormous losses already caused to Japan in men, money and materials. Hence it was confidently expected that Japan would accept terms which would also be acceptable to China. Nothing, however, was done, although the British Government continued to maintain the position that it was prepared to offer its services as peacemaker when both sides made clear that such an offer would be welcome.

Hankow fell on October 25, and again rumors of mediation were heard. The Nationalist Government, however, repudiated the talk of peace and decided on a policy of continued resistance to Japanese invasion. Furthermore, at this critical point the United States note of October 6 was published. This very strong note from the American Government to Japan protested in great detail against Japan's closing the open door in China, demanding immediate assurances and action to protect American interests in China.[6] An early reply was requested but was not forthcoming. This was quickly followed by a message from the American Chamber of Commerce in Shanghai to Washington supporting this step. A meeting of representatives of the American and British Chambers of Commerce, together with the British and American trade officials as well as the Australian and Canadian Trade Commissioners, also took place. This not only encouraged the British in China to hope that their own government might enter into a "common front" with the United States or take perhaps an "equally determined parallel action," but also helped to encourage the wavering elements in the Chinese Nationalist ranks to continue the conflict.

That the British in China, especially in Shanghai, welcomed the prospects of Anglo-American unity in support of third-party rights was to be expected in the light of the unhappy position in which they still found themselves and the little likelihood of any basic improvement. Thus, even before the capture of Hankow, *Finance and Commerce* had called for the formation of a so-called "popular front" to defend foreign rights. Unable to rely on the oft-repeated Japanese assurances and pledges that foreign rights would be respected, and with all hopes of mediation gone, it urged a united front among foreigners in Shanghai to defend their treaty rights as the only alternative to surrendering their privileges.

[6] For complete text, see United States Department of State, *Press Releases*, October 29, 1938, pp. 283-6.

The fact that nothing has been yet achieved by protest must not be allowed to discourage further effort to defend the lawful interests of the foreign community. On the contrary, failure to secure satisfaction should serve as a stimulus to more intensive and extensive action in preparation for the occasion when further evasion of fundamental issues is impossible. Sino-Japanese hostilities must come to an end some day, and when that day comes all foreigners who have treaty-rights and wish to retain them must be prepared to state their case in defense of their interests. No more effective manner of presenting legitimate claims to those with an acknowledged right to consider them is conceivable, than by effecting close co-operation between the British, American and other organization of nationals whose Governments are in treaty-relations with the National Government of China, and a "popular front" which maintains close contact with diplomatic and consular officials in China, and with influential circles in their respective homelands, can assist very materially in effecting a just and equitable settlement of problems which are of most vital importance to every foreign resident in this country.[7]

The Capture of Hankow and British Interests

All hope that Japan would change her discriminatory policy toward third-party interests was destroyed by her refusal to open the Yangtze to foreign shipping. Just before the fall of Hankow, Vice-Admiral Oikawa had assured foreign newspapermen that the reopening of the Yangtze to foreign shipping would be considered as soon as Hankow had been taken. With the fall of Hankow and with the return of Japanese officials and civilians to the Japanese concession at Hankow, which had been abandoned in 1937, the Japanese authorities no longer had their previous reasons for delaying the reopening of the Yangtze. Although during the Japanese drive up the Yangtze the presence of booms and mines had made navigation difficult, and military operations had made use of the river highly dangerous, this situation no longer existed. General Hata admitted as much when he told foreign correspondents that "the Yangtze is quite safe," but added that it would be opened to foreign shipping when military operations permitted and he could not say when that would be.[8] In place of the desired opening of the Yangtze, third powers were requested by Japanese naval authorities to co-operate by giving notification of the movements of foreign ships on the Yangtze. Neutral vessels were asked to take refuge as far upstream as possible from Hankow in view of the extension of the zone of hostilities as far inland as Shasi and Changsha. The Japanese

[7] *Finance and Commerce*, October 19, 1938, pp. 301-2.
[8] *North-China Herald*, November 9, 1938, p. 227.

naval note ended with the cryptic statement, "and in view of the fact that there is now no section of China over which Japanese planes cannot operate, we desire to call attention to the fact that what has been desired is information of vessels in the 'whole stretch of the river above X point,' irrespective of the distance at which such vessels are located."[9] Thus the entire river became a possible zone of hostilities.

This refusal to reopen the Yangtze showed that the capture of Hankow was not going to usher in a period of improved conditions for foreigners, for if the Japanese pre-Hankow assurances on freedom to navigate the Yangtze were being violated, then there was no reason to believe that other promises would be kept. In an interview with a Reuters correspondent before the capture of Hankow, General Hata had been questioned as to whether or how soon the Imperial Japanese Army would be in a position to meet British complaints not only in regard to the Yangtze but also on the restoration of Hongkew and Yangtzepoo to the authority of the International Settlement, permission for the International Settlement police to patrol the Hungjao Road in order to protect foreign property there (which was exposed to danger on account of the withdrawal of the Japanese military posts), payment of the interest due on the railway bonds, freedom of access to the British staff, and other legal rights now denied in connection with the British-constructed railways—notably the Shanghai-Nanking and the Shanghai-Hangchow-Ningpo railways. General Hata's reply to all of these questions had been,

All measures that are being taken by our forces at the present time were adopted because of military necessity. I believe that their revision will be considered as soon as a real relaxation in conditions take place.[10]

Even if the capture of Hankow did not signify a sufficient "relaxation" in conditions on the Yangtze to warrant its reopening to foreign commerce, there was no reason to suppose that the other British grievances would receive different consideration, and they did not.

The attitude which Japan was going to adopt toward Great Britain was clearly stated in the Japanese press and by the Japa-

[9] *Ibid.* The "X point" probably referred to those places on the Yangtze which had been designated the western extremities of the Japanese zones of hostilities. At this time Shasi, 287 miles up the river from Hankow, was designated as this point.
[10] *North-China Herald,* October 26, 1938.

nese authorities. *Nichi-Nichi,* commenting on the future policy of the new foreign minister, Mr. Hachiro Arita, indicated that Mr. Arita was ready to resume conversations with Sir Robert Craigie, but only if a new basis for negotiations were adopted. Japan, it said, regarded Britain's recognition of the new situation in the Far East as a matter of course, if negotiations were to lead to an understanding. *Asahi* observed that it would be correct to say that the new minister had been appointed at the beginning of a new chapter in Japan's foreign policy toward Occidental powers.[11]

Against this background of thwarted British interests and positive manifestations of continued Japanese hostility, the optimism of the British Government stood out in bold relief. Mr. Chamberlain, referring to China on November 1, took a cheerful view of future British trade with China, and taunted Mr. R. C. Attlee for having been "too gloomy" on the subject. There could be no development in China, Mr. Chamberlain emphasized, without a great deal of capital, and for that Japan would have to go to other countries, including Great Britain.

> China cannot be developed into a real market without the influx of a great deal of capital and the fact that so much capital is being destroyed during this war means that even more capital will have to be put into China in the future, when the war is over. Who is going to supply the capital? It is quite certain that it cannot be supplied by Japan. . . . It is quite certain that when the war is over and the reconstruction of China begins she cannot possibly be reconstructed without some help from this country.[12]

This belief that in the long run Great Britain would benefit by either a Japanese or a Chinese victory was in strange contrast to the actual situation in China. That the Prime Minister should have stated it so soon after the publication of the United States note of October 6, emphasized its nature as an olive branch held out to the Japanese. It perhaps gives a clue to the impartial attitude which the British Government had consistently maintained.[13] The complacency of the Prime Minister aroused considerable criticism in British circles interested in the Far Eastern

[11] Quoted in *Trans-Pacific,* Tokyo, November 3, 1938.
[12] *Parliamentary Debates,* House of Commons, Vol. 340, col. 82.
[13] King George VI in a speech on November 4, 1938, on the occasion of the prorogation of Parliament said: "I regret that the hostilities between China and Japan still continue, with great loss of life to both combatants and with considerable damage to the rights and interests of third parties. I earnestly hope that this conflict will be brought to an early termination."

situation. For example, in London the *Financial Times* of November 3 deplored this view and pointed out that the British Government had never before made a general *démarche* of such a nature. It quoted the statement of the Japanese ambassador to Italy, Mr. Shiratori, that British pre-eminence in China had ended and that the new China created by Japan would be a second Manchukuo. The British Government, this journal maintained, should consider effective means for bringing pressure to bear on Japan rather than continue the polite exchange of opinion which had been going on for some months between Sir Robert Craigie, British Ambassador to Japan, and the Foreign Office in Tokyo.

Finance and Commerce was inspired to new heights of sarcasm by the Prime Minister's remarks.

> Possibly because distance lends enchantment to the view, Mr. Neville Chamberlain seems to regard the situation in the Far East with the same bland (or blind) optimism with which he views the European situation since the sacrifice of Czechoslovakia. Confident that Hitler and Mussolini will cooperate with him in building a new Europe, the British Prime Minister seems just as certain that Anglo-Japanese cooperation will be possible in a new China. . . . It is not to be expected that Mr. Chamberlain should have intimate knowledge of conditions and trends but he has sources of information at his command which would confirm the opinions of those on the spot if made use of. Sir Arthur Cadogan . . . now in the Foreign Office, is in a position to enlighten the Premier.[14]

Meanwhile the British Chamber of Commerce in Shanghai had cabled to London its strong exception to the Prime Minister's statement. It pointed out that even if Japan should need British capital to develop China, this anticipation did not warrant an optimistic view of the condition of British trade in China. Some financial interests in London, the Chamber of Commerce maintained, might profit by making loans to Japan, but this would not safeguard British industrial and commercial enterprises in China. The cable ended by placing the Chamber of Commerce on record as doubting whether the situation in China was, in fact, as satisfactory as Mr. Chamberlain seemed to believe.

Prince Konoye's Proclamation of the "New Order in Asia"

The validity of the complaints of the British in China was soon substantiated by the actions of the Japanese, who answered the

[14] *Finance and Commerce*, November 9, 1938, p. 368.

British overtures with demands for increased concessions. These were implicit in Prince Konoye's famous "New Order in Asia" broadcast of November 3. The Japanese Prime Minister spoke of a new order based on a "tripartite relationship of mutual aid and coordination between Japan, Manchukuo and China in the political, economic, cultural and other fields." The confidence was expressed that other powers would "correctly" appreciate Japan's aims and policy and adapt their attitude to the new conditions. Prince Konoye elaborated on this in his radio address. He declared that Japan had no intention of refusing to co-operate with foreign powers or injuring their legitimate rights and interests in China, but he also said that foreign powers should have a clear understanding of the new situation which was being unfolded, i.e., they should recognize Japanese supremacy.

The *Japan Times* of November 4 interpreted the prime minister's address as a "warning to other Powers, polite in expression but resolute in mind, that Japan will not tolerate any nation which dares hamper Japan's peaceful efforts now steadily progressing with Chinese cooperation." *Kokumin* said that the government's statement was a "declaration of independence, or a Monroe Doctrine for East Asia." Although these newspapers may have interpreted Prince Konoye's address too broadly, even in the narrowest sense it implied the unilateral abrogation of the Nine Power Treaty and was so recognized in foreign countries.

The reaction in Great Britain to Prince Konoye's address was mixed. Britain, it was said, would be compelled to consult the other signatories of the Nine Power Pact upon the line of action to be adopted, if confirmation of the Japanese position were forthcoming. Although Britain must now face the facts of the new situation in China "realistically," British interests must not be sacrificed. Great significance continued to be attached to Mr. Chamberlain's statement of November 1, and Britain's past willingness to co-operate with Japan and other powers in China on a basis of equality was noted. Nevertheless, the absence of any explicit assurance in Konoye's speech concerning the future of the open door was pointed out, and in this connection Mr. Chamberlain's optimism was severely criticized. Reuters reported that there was

ground for stating that influential persons, both in business and political circles, have, within the past few days, made very pressing representations to the chief members of the Government on the immediate danger to British interests throughout China, of which full details are supplied.

In the United States Mr. Cordell Hull reaffirmed the position outlined in the October 6 note. He said that the existing treaties and the generally accepted principles of international law and of fair play among nations would govern the United States' attitude toward the Sino-Japanese situation.

In Shanghai, the *North-China Herald* spoke of "the new challenge" to the Nine Power Pact. It encouraged Britain as well as France and Holland to follow the American lead as given in the October 6 note.

> Whether the nations concerned determine upon cooperative or parallel action does not really matter, so long as what they all do is properly timed and emphatically backed. The grave threat which is being offered to their interests in China verges upon these limits of patience, trespass beyond which not even the most forbearing of nations can afford to countenance. The swinging of the focus of international irritation between Europe and Asia must eventually be stopped, and if Japan does proceed to the lengths which rumour and the deductions to be made from recent pronouncements would appear to indicate, then the sooner a stop is put to it the better. The argument that circumstances in China would justify the action Japan is reported to contemplate is worthless. These circumstances, if they exist anywhere except in the facile brains of the Tokyo Government, have been brought about by the wrongful action of Japan taken in complete breach of solemn treaty obligation, and of those fine ideals of justice which Japan is now so earnestly and so strangely invoking.[15]

Anglo-American Co-operation

The result of Japan's enunciation of the "new order in Asia" was a reversal in Britain's diplomatic policy. The British countered this Japanese pronouncement by raising the specter of what Japan feared most—a united front of the United States and Great Britain.

The first concrete manifestation of this shift was the dispatch of parallel notes to Japan by the United States, Great Britain and France on November 7, objecting to the closure of the Yangtze to neutral trade. The United States had prepared a sharp note on this subject, but had held up its transmission until Britain and France had had a chance to consider whether they wanted to take similar action. The British note protested against allowing Japanese merchant ships to use the Yangtze, while ships of other nations, that had equal rights under treaties and by cus-

[15] *North-China Herald*, November 9, 1938.

tom, were prohibited on the ground that the river was a war zone. The British questioned the validity of this contention, and recalled the many unkept promises to reopen the river to foreign commerce.

The new emphasis in British policy was clearly seen in Mr. Butler's statements in the House of Commons on November 9. Referring to the Tokyo declaration regarding the formation of an economic and political bloc comprising Japan, Manchukuo and China, Mr. Butler declared:

> I should like to say that the position of Great Britain in this matter is governed by the Washington Treaties and other international agreements to which His Majesty's Government, in conjunction with a large number of other Governments, are parties.
>
> We could not, therefore, consider any alterations in the position, as laid down in the Treaties, which have been brought about by unilateral action.
>
> In this matter our stand is the same as that which has been so clearly laid down by the United States' Secretary of State in his statement on November 4, which would serve equally to define the attitude of His Majesty's Government in the matter of the Washington Treaties.
>
> The United States Government had previously protested in their Note of October 6 to Japan against the infringement of the policy of the Open Door in China.
>
> In this connection I wish to say that His Majesty's Government have, for their part, made formal protests in the same sense as the United States Government, to the Japanese Government in recent times and have made their position quite clear.[16]

The last reference was probably to the November 7 notes, which had not yet been made public. Although the texts have not yet been published, general acknowledgments of the sending of the notes and of their contents was made on November 12. While Secretary Hull indicated that the United States representation was not parallel to the London and Paris representations, it was reported in London that Great Britain, France and the United States would continue the three-power conversations in Tokyo which had been

> initiated just prior to the parallel protests lodged with the Japanese Government concerning closing of the Yangtze River to foreign shipping.[17]

In Japan the notes were unfavorably received. Even before issuing any formal reply, Japan indicated her rejection of the

[16] *Parliamentary Debates*, Vol. 341, col. 165.
[17] This same (United Press) report made the significant statement, if correct, that the British note had failed to mention the Nine Power Treaty, one of the strongest legal arguments in support of Britain's China position.

claim that Japanese vessels exclusively were plying the Yangtze River. It was true that Japanese vessels were using the Yangtze, but these were military boats traveling between Shanghai and up-river ports. The arguments given were that military operations were still going on along the upper Yangtze and that floating mines were still a serious menace to safe navigation on the river. Naval circles observed that when the Chinese had closed the Yangtze with booms and mines, none of these Western countries had filed any protest with the Nationalist Government.

This recalcitrant attitude characterized Japan's formal replies to Britain, France and the United States. The Yangtze was to remain closed, and the arguments put forth to support this position indicated complete rejection of the contentions in the November 7 notes. The Japanese claimed that booms constructed by Chinese troops at Kiangyin had been removed by Japanese forces only to such a degree as would permit movements of military vessels, and that the river was "fully occupied" by Japanese warships and transports. Furthermore, large-scale military operations were still going on upstream above Hankow, and the river between Shanghai and interior points formed an important avenue of communication. In addition, Chinese guerrillas were still active on both banks of the Yangtze and frequently fired on Japanese warships and transports; Chinese troops were letting loose drifting mines which endangered navigation in the Yangtze, and a Japanese transport had recently struck one of these mines and had been sunk; and finally, considerable time would be required completely to remove the mines laid by the Chinese and to replace navigation markings.[18]

The Japanese refusal received warm support and widespread endorsement in the Japanese press. *Yomiuri,* a popular Tokyo daily, in a bitter attack on Great Britain, France and the United States, made the baseless contention that Great Britain had voluntarily forfeited her right of free navigation on the Yangtze by supporting behind the scene "Chinese strategy based upon the creation of booms in the river." How Great Britain would benefit by the closure of the Yangtze was not made clear.[19] The

[18] *China Year Book,* 1939, p. 448.
[19] General von Falkenhausen, head of the former German military mission, is known to have said that the Matung boom and its defenses had been made impregnable. This supports the belief that the boom and its fortifications had been placed and constructed with German advice.

Nine Power Pact, it said, was "a dead letter"[20] and if Japan really desired the establishment of a new order in the Far East, she should take effective measures to throw off the yoke of the Nine Power Pact immediately. *Miyako* spoke of the government's action as being too reasonable to require any explanation. *Asahi* supported the government but in so doing refuted one of the Japanese arguments. It admitted that Great Britain, France and the United States had protested to the National Government against the booms and mines. It squared this admission with the official Japanese stand by adding that the representatives of these powers in submitting these protests had reassured the Chiang Kai-shek government that their protests were designed to make Japan guarantee free navigation on the Yangtze River in the future.[21]

While the Japanese were thus rejecting the three-power protests on the Yangtze, the Chinese were urging Britain to take a firm line. The *China Times*, in a leading article welcoming Sir Archibald John Clark Kerr to Chungking, declared:

> The present critical situation in the Far East does not permit of further hesitation or over-cautiousness on the part of Downing Street and Great Britain, for Sino-British interests must take immediate effective action to check Japanese aggression. . . . The successive loss of British interests in Manchuria, North China, Central China and South China has been entirely due to the failure of Britain's so-called realistic policy.

It urged Britain to carry out the promises made under the League of Nations' resolutions, "to give active and full assistance to China's resistance against Japan's invasion." Such opinions were also voiced by General Chang Chun, director of Chiang Kai-shek's headquarters in Chungking. Feeling in China was "at present a little disappointed, perhaps even sceptical, towards Britain because of the recent trend in British foreign policy" and because China had placed more hope and faith in England than in any other of the powers. "Her policy seems subject to change; she is realistic, but has not enough foresight." "Nevertheless," he concluded, "we still believe that Britain will help us the most."[22]

The British in China rejected the Japanese arguments and urged a firm policy against Japan. The *British Chamber of Com-*

[20] The *New York Post* was quoted as using this term in supporting this contention.
[21] Quoted in *North-China Herald*, November 23, 1938.
[22] *Ibid.*

merce Journal, with its usual restraint, characterized the Japanese reply as unconvincing and satisfactory to no one. The Japanese arguments of military necessity and solicitude for the safety of third-party nationals were not accepted as being the real basis for Japan's actions. Rather the conclusion was reached that Japan desired

> to conserve trading opportunities to Japanese nationals and gradually to freeze out the nationals of these powers. Solicitude for the safety and welfare of others is all very well but there are times when such solicitude can be dispensed with.[23]

Finance and Commerce was not so gentle in its comments. The world was "skeptical and suspicious of Japan's policy," it said,

> simply because so many authoritative and inspired explanations of Japan's policy fail either to fit notorious facts or agree with generally accepted principles governing international relations.

It expressed no surprise at the Japanese reply.

> Deep disappointment is reported to have been expressed abroad. . . . Just what was expected in Washington, London and Paris from Tokyo in answer to these Notes is known only to those who drafted the original protests, but it is safe to say that no American, British, or French businessman, resident in China, expected anything more helpful or hopeful than the answer Japan did give to the three Governments.

According to *Finance and Commerce,* thousands of tons of freight were passing up and down the river in Japanese steamers, and were permitted to pass the boom at Kiangyin which marked the "limit of safety" for all other vessels. Japanese shipping companies and transportation agencies were advertising regular services between Shanghai and Nanking, Chinkiang, and Wuhu in the vernacular newspapers, and it was the impression of "competent observers" that Japanese steamers were plying on the Yangtze as freely as they ever did, and were engaged in much the same trade as was handled before the outbreak of hostilities. Piece goods, cotton yarn, kerosene, gasoline, sugar, paper, cigarettes, etc., were taken up-river, while foodstuffs, hides, bristles, feathers and the other produce which had customarily been sent to Shanghai for transshipment overseas were being brought back. Moreover, the railways running out of Shanghai, the Shanghai-Nanking and the Shanghai-Hangchow-

[23] *British Chamber of Commerce Journal,* Shanghai, November 1938.

Ningpo, in which British bondholders had invested nearly £4,000,000, were running for commercial as well as military purposes. Japanese currency was being used for fares, and Japanese authorities were deciding what permits should be issued for the transportation of goods and passengers.

In short, the railway door is "open" just as the Yangtze is "open"—with the difference that the lines from Shanghai to Nanking and Hangchow are mortgaged to British bondholders, whose representatives have been denied permission even to inspect their damaged property.

This severe criticism of the Japanese showed one-half of the mental state of the British interests in China at this time. The other half was the complete disagreement with the policy of the Home Government. This is well described in the following caustic description of the prevalent attitude in London and of the policy of the Home Government:[24]

A London cable tells us that Japan's reply to the British Note "is considered detrimental to foreign trade." There must be some bright young men in London for such a shrewd conclusion to be reached so swiftly—but they go further, "It is believed here that Japan's intention is to restore traffic on the river only when Japanese traders have entirely won over the domestic market." What could have put such an idea into anyone's head? We recall most distinctly that Prince Konoye . . . last July, declared that while it was impossible just then for foreigners to move freely in North and Central China, the existing restrictions were "only temporary," and when the "proper time" arrived, third-party nationals would be able to travel about as they used to, because Japan did not intend to close the "open door" in occupied areas in China, and had no intention of ousting British influence from the country. These assurances were given by the Japanese Premier last July—the same month in which certain assurances were given in Parliament by Mr. Chamberlain and Lord Halifax about the defence of British interests in China.

[24] See also *North-China Herald* and *Finance and Commerce* for November 23, 1938. The article in the latter journal concluded that China would turn to communism for aid if the Western democracies failed her. "The grim fact is that unless substantial help is very quickly forthcoming, Chinese democrats will be compelled to turn toward communism in sheer desperation—and the democratic Powers will be left to wail exceedingly at the disaster overtaking a nation which, had it received the support that should have been quickly forthcoming at the very beginning, would have developed into a most powerful ally in the cause of peaceful political progress."

This argument indicated that at least some of the British in China had remembered Sun Yat-sen's explanations for the Kuomintang-communist alliance of 1924-7. For it was the failure of the Western democracies to come to the aid of the young Chinese republic which had brought about the tie with the communists and had thus been an important cause of the vigorous anti-British movement of 1925-7.

The London report quoted above declared that "considerable interest is attached to the attitude of the United States, whose interests are very much affected" by Japan's attitude on the Yangtze question, and it was pointed out that the United States Government was in a position "to exert considerable pressure upon Japan" which is perfectly true, as it is no less true that the British Government is in similar position, and observers in Washington might well wonder why observers in London should look so expectantly across the Atlantic for action to be taken on their behalf. American observers could quite properly point out that Lord Halifax, Foreign Secretary, announced on July 27th that the British Government was "considering possible action open to us if we do not secure (from Japan) adequate consideration for the interests we have a right to protect in China"— and the action that it is possible to take has not been taken although four months ago the British Government was planning what steps should be resorted to if Japan failed to give the protection to British interests which was demanded.[25]

In London, it was reported that the British Government was in no way inclined to accept Japan's reply as disposing of the matter. The British Government, according to Reuters, was consulting with France and the United States about the procedure to be adopted in this and other matters, although nothing was likely to be done until the nature of Japan's reply to the American protest of October 6 was known. Furthermore, there was ground for believing that the patience of the British Government was "beginning" to be severely strained by the continual failure of the Japanese in China to honor their government's repeated promises to respect foreign rights, and that means of applying pressure on Japan more effectively than by mere protests were under consideration.

In the House of Commons Mr. Butler on November 10 reiterated the intention of His Majesty's Government to follow the American lead and to adhere to the policy of non-recognition as mentioned in his statement of November 9. On November 16, in response to a question as to whether Great Britain had signified to the United States its desire to co-operate in maintaining the policy of the open door in China, Mr. Butler replied that Sir Robert Craigie had been "in constant contact" with his American colleague and that he (Mr. Butler) did not think that the American Government could be "in any doubt regarding Britain's policy in regard to the open door."[26]

[25] *Finance and Commerce*, November 23, 1938. See also *North-China Herald*, November 23, 1938.

[26] These statements on Anglo-American co-operation were given added weight by the conclusion at this time of the Anglo-American Trade Agreement.

The movement toward Anglo-American co-operation was given considerable impetus by the parallel action taken by eleven national bodies of foreigners in Shanghai. On November 24, 1938, these issued a statement regarding action of the Japanese with reference to restricting foreign rights in China.[27] The statement read:

> The immediate objectives in connection with the present situation of concern to the above mentioned Associations and Chambers of Commerce are:
> (1) Retention of all rights under the Land Regulations and prevention of encroachment on and interference with the administration of the International Settlement of Shanghai and the foreign concessions in China and the withdrawal of any encroachments already made.
> (2) Restoration of the Hongkew, Yangtzepoo and Western areas to the full authority and control of the International Settlement as formerly exercised.
> (3) Restoration of transportation facilities including railways, shipping, commercial airways and motor highways, with access to markets and mission centers in the Yangtze valley and other areas.
> (4) Prevention and abolition of all monopolies created in contravention of the Nine Power Treaty and the Open Door policy of equal opportunity.
> (5) Restoration of properties of their respective nationals to their rightful owners with full access to and use thereof.
> (6) Discontinuance of censorship sponsored by any third party or other interference with mails, telegrams, cables, radios, or other means of communication.
> (7) Immediate return of equipment and resumption of dredging operations necessary for the maintenance of Shanghai as a port for the use of international shipping.
> (8) Insistence on the right of their respective nationals to pursue their legitimate interests in China on the basis of equal opportunity with the nationals of any other foreign power.
> (9) Recognition and maintenance of the extraterritorial status of their respective nationals and their interests in accordance with treaties.

Thus, the foreign communities in Shanghai not only voiced their displeasure with the treatment which they were getting from the Japanese, but also, by their joint action, put pressure on their governments to secure some effective assistance.

[27] The organizations issuing this statement, which was transmitted in each case to their respective home governments, were: the American Association of Shanghai; the American Chamber of Commerce, Shanghai; the Belgian Chamber of Commerce; the British Chamber of Commerce and China Association, Shanghai; the British Residents' Association of China; the Canadian Club of Shanghai; the Danish Association in Shanghai; the French Chamber of Commerce; the Netherlands Chamber of Commerce; the Norwegian Chamber of Commerce; the Swedish Association in China.

CHAPTER X

FROM THE NOVEMBER NOTES TO THE EUROPEAN WAR

In less than a month the Japanese had lost much of the diplomatic advantage gained by their victories at Canton and Hankow. The rejection of British overtures in October, followed by the curt reply to the three-power notes in November, helped to pave the way for greater support of China as well as for stronger diplomatic action against Japan.[1]

The most important new aid for China was the granting of £450,000 in export credits in December 1938 by the Export Credits Guarantee Department for the purchase of motor trucks from England. This grant of credits re-emphasized the importance of a development which had already taken place but had attracted very little attention—the construction of the Yunnan-Burma highway. This road, begun before the fall of Canton and completed in July 1938, was China's least vulnerable route to the sea and a medium through which military supplies from Europe and America could flow into China in the event of the severance of the Hongkong route,[2] but not until after Nationalist China had lost Canton, its last important coastal center, was the real significance of the road generally appreciated. Moreover, the road's political significance as an indication of Britain's intention to maintain connection with Nationalist China was heightened by the diplomatic tension existing between Great Britain and Japan in December 1938.

This newly constructed motor road, which was about 800

---

[1] On November 18 the Japanese reply to the United States note of October 6 was released. It rejected the American contentions and refused to entertain any of the American demands. Although it stated that "Japan has not the slightest inclination to oppose the participation of the United States and other Powers in the great work of reconstructing East Asia along lines of industry and trade," the British press in China expressed complete disapproval and distrust of the Japanese assurances. Thus, the reply to the October 6 note reinforced the anti-Japanese feeling aroused by the reply to the November 7 notes.

[2] Hoh Chih-hsiang, "Southwest China—A Political, Social and Economic Survey," *China Quarterly*, Autumn 1938, pp. 415-30.

kilometers long and was reputed to have cost Ch.$ 2,000,000 linked Kunming, the capital of Yunnan, with the Burmese town of Lashio, whence a railroad connected with the port of Rangoon. This route offered the possibility of accomplishing the trip between Kunming and Burma in less than a week. By December 1938 trucks were reported to be running day and night on the highway.[3]

The attention now given in all quarters to this new highway soon broadened into a consideration of the possibilities which the development of West China held for the British. The occupation of Canton and Hankow had been followed by a period of comparative calm, and it soon became evident to the British that the predicted collapse of the Nationalist Government was not coming. Moreover, the Japanese had shown no particular appetite for pursuing the Generalissimo's forces into the vast interior of China, but were rather attempting to strengthen their hold over the occupied territory and to exploit it by means of controlled governments and monopolistic economic schemes. Therefore, the Chungking Government might very well succeed in its stated purpose, to develop Western China. If so, British interests would find new outlets for profitable trade and investments.[4]

British Credits to China

The political implications of increasing the British stakes in Nationalist China were obvious. It would increase the resistance capacity of the Nationalist Government, strengthen its diplomatic position and enhance the British desire that Japan should not conquer Nationalist China. Thus the granting of £450,000 export credits to China in December 1938, superficially merely a means of increasing Sino-British trade, was interpreted as British retaliation for Japan's discriminatory policy in China and as an answer to the rejection of the November 7 notes. Furthermore, coupled with the simultaneous American loan of $25,-000,000 it seemed to indicate that the parallel policy seen in the November 7 notes was to continue. As expressed by the London *Times* of December 28, "these credits may be taken as emblematic of a common determination to assert and defend, by

[3] See especially N. D. Hanwell, "China Driven to New Supply Routes," *Far Eastern Survey*, November 9, 1938.

[4] An excellent statement on the attitude of British interests toward Southwest China is to be found in the *British Chamber of Commerce Journal*, January 1939.

legitimate means against illegitimate discrimination, the rights and interests which Great Britain and America possess in China." This influential and authoritative newspaper then went on to give the United States credit for having shown the way. "The initiative was taken by the American Government, which during the past few months has pursued a more vigorous line in the Pacific than any other foreign Power." It was even willing to admit that "it is questionable whether our Far Eastern policy in the past eighteen months need have been as consistently long suffering as in fact it has been. . . . It is to the credit of America . . . that she has given the world this lead." That it was meant as a measure against Japan as well as support for China was also clearly stated, and it concluded by reminding Japan of her strained relations with Russia over the fisheries dispute and the resulting "delicacy" of her position. The political implications of the loan were not left to the imagination.

These credits, small as they were, encouraged the Chinese, gave renewed hope to British residents in China, and supplied the Japanese with new arguments for continuing pressure against British interests in China. The Chinese were extremely pleased, not only with this display of diplomatic support, but also with the positive material aid, for the credit was in the nature of a revolving fund and as soon as one loan had been paid, a new one could be granted. Moreover, once the British Government had departed from its policy of refusing financial aid, there was reason to hope it would give more. The Chinese became optimistic over the possibility of obtaining enough funds for the construction of the much-desired Yunnan-Burma Railway. Such a railway was bound to appeal to the British as its construction would not only link Nationalist China by direct rail connection with the port of Rangoon in Burma but would also strengthen the British commercial and financial position in Southwest China. On November 16, 1938, Mr. Butler had stated in the House of Commons that the practicability of constructing a railway was being examined by financial interests, and in December authoritative reports in London and Chungking indicated that Britain and China had already reached an agreement in principle upon the grant of a £10,000,000 loan to the Chinese Government for the construction of a 500 kilometer railway between Hsiangkwei and the Burmese border. This railway project, it was stated, would be financed exclusively by British interests with the assistance of the Export Credits Guarantee Department. A total of £6,000,000 would be devoted to the actual construction of the railroad, while the other £4,000,000 would permit the Chinese Government to purchase extra railway material and motor lorries. Although there is no evidence that these credits were actually given, work did begin on the Yunnan-Burma Railway in February 1939.[5] A railway line was being added to the functioning highway as another link connecting Rangoon with Southwest China. This seaport in Burma promised to become a new gateway to China's interior, replacing the isolated coastal centers.

The grant of export credits and the American loan were, of course, heartily applauded by the British in China. They interpreted them as a welcome stiffening in the attitude of Great Britain and the United States, "for while there is every sympathy with the perplexities which confront the two Governments, there has been in the Far East a growing anxiety lest there should be a general failure to realize the growing seriousness of the situation here."

That the loans had definite political as well as commercial purposes was clearly recognized, and the expected complaints of the Japanese were rejected in advance.

It is possible that as a result Tokyo may decide upon retaliatory methods even though the Japanese would be put still further in the wrong by doing so. That contingency must be met if and when it arises. Retaliation is a game at which more than one can play, and if that does come into being the ability of Great Britain and the United States to reply, and reply effectively, is very much greater than that of Japan.[6]

[5] The arrangements made for the financing of this enterprise are still unknown, although probably China was to supply the land and labor while British interests furnished the capital. Mr. D. G. M. Bernard, chairman of the British and Chinese Corporation, the main organization for British participation in Chinese railway projects, reported the following at the forty-first general meeting held on May 24, 1939: "Another railway which the Chinese are anxious to build is from Szechuan to Burma via Yunnanfu. This line, about 1,200 miles long, is intended to connect the provinces of Yunnan and Szechuan with the railway from Yunnanfu to Haiphong in French Indo-China and the Burma railway at Lashio. This corporation, together with a French financial group and the China Development Finance Corporation, have been interested in the project and early this year despatched representatives to Chungking to discuss the matter with the Chinese Government and endeavour to evolve a scheme by which the finance could be provided to construct the railway."

[6] *North-China Herald*, December 21, 1938.

Japanese Reaction to Anglo-American Co-operation

The Japanese reaction was as anticipated. Mr. Arita, in an interview with foreign correspondents on December 19, categorically voiced his displeasure over the British and American loans. At the same time he gave an official explanation of Japan's relations with the Western powers. Japan, he said, still believed in the principle of equality of commercial opportunity and did not mean to exclude European and American economic activities from East Asia. However, the all-qualifying statement was added, that these powers would be subjected to "certain restrictions dictated by the requirements of the national defense and economic security of the countries grouped under the new order."[7] Thus, the British and American action had obviously not forced the Japanese Government to make any real retreat from its discriminatory policy in China.

Asahi was less restrained than the Tokyo Government in its denunciation of the British and American actions. This newspaper felt that they were "reprisals" against Japan. Great Britain was, of course, accused of being the instigator of this international aid.

> It remains to be seen whether America will elect to pull the British chestnuts out of the fire. But there is no doubt of the vicious motive of Britain and America in giving a new impetus to the long-term resistance of the Chiang régime against Japan in their extension of credits which will have the effect of giving more moral support than material to that régime, whose days are numbered.[8]

The possibilities of an Anglo-American front were heightened by repeated official assurances in the House of Commons that Britain was maintaining close connections with the United States and by reports that reprisals against Japan were being seriously considered in London and Washington.[9] These reports were given additional weight by the British support of the American note of December 31, 1938, which firmly rejected the Japanese "new order" and reserved "all rights of the United States as they exist," with refusal to "give assent to any impair-

---

[7] *Trans-Pacific*, Tokyo, December 29, 1938.

[8] Quoted in *Trans-Pacific*, Tokyo, December 29, 1938.

[9] It was at this time (January 2, 1939) that Senator Key Pittman, chairman of the Senate Foreign Relations Committee, made a declaration advocating an embargo upon Japanese products.

ment of any of these rights" in the Far East.[10] On January 14, 1939, Sir Robert Craigie presented to Mr. Arita a note which duplicated the American stand. The note expressed Britain's "grave anxiety" regarding Japan's policy in China which had not been removed by conversations between the British ambassador in Tokyo and the Japanese foreign minister from time to time, or by the recent pronouncements of the Japanese Government on the establishment of Japanese domination over China.

His Majesty's Government are at a loss to understand how Prince Konoye's assurance that Japan seeks no territory and respects the sovereignty of China can be reconciled with the declared intention of the Japanese Government to compel the Chinese people, by force of arms, to accept conditions involving the surrender of their political, economic and cultural life, to Japanese control, the indefinite maintenance in China of considerable Japanese garrisons and the virtual detachment from China of the territory of Inner Mongolia.

This interpretation of the latest Japanese declarations was followed by a statement upholding the Nine Power Treaty and applying the doctrine of non-recognition to any unilateral changes brought about contrary to its provisions.

For their part, His Majesty's Government desire to make it clear that they are not prepared to accept or to recognize the activities of the nature indicated which are brought about by force. They intend to adhere to the principles of the Nine-Power Treaty and cannot agree to any unilateral modification of its terms. . . . His Majesty's Government cannot agree, as is suggested in Japan, that the treaty is obsolete or that its provisions no longer meet the situation, except insofar as the situation has been altered by Japan in contravention of its terms.

This strong line was, however, weakened by suggesting the possibility of revising the Nine Power Treaty.[11]

While, however, His Majesty's Government maintain that a modification cannot be effected unilaterally and must be by negotiation between all signatories, they do not contend that treaties are eternal.

If, therefore, the Japanese Government have any constructive suggestions to make regarding the modification of any multilateral agreement relating to China, His Majesty's Government, for their part, will be ready to consider them. In the meantime, His Majesty's Government reserve all their rights under the existing treaties.[12]

[10] For complete text of the note of December 31, 1938, see United States Department of State, *Press Releases*, December 31, 1938, pp. 490-3.

[11] The American note of December 31, 1938 also contained this suggestion but was clearer on the necessity of including representatives of China.

[12] *Asahi* had an interesting comment to make on the difference between the British and American notes. "It is not true, however, to say that Britain and

This British note was followed by a similar French note on January 19, 1939. The American, British and French notes indicated that these powers rejected Japan's claim that she could unilaterally change the existing treaty structure on the basis that it was outworn and no longer suited to conditions in China. Nevertheless, they also indicated that these powers were ready to enter into negotiations for a multilateral readjustment of the situation in China.

The Japanese, either convinced that the United States and Britain were bluffing,[13] or desirous of strengthening their hand in anticipation of further joint action, replied with increased pressure against foreign interests in China.[14] The new Premier, Baron Hiranuma, told the Diet that the Government would take "suitable measures" to deal with any attempts to hamper the execution of Japanese policy toward China, while Mr. Arita indicated that Japan was firmly determined to consider counter-measures against any pressure which might be exerted by Britain and America.[15] The nature of these counter-measures was indicated in Japan's actions in China at this time. For example, the opening of the Yangtze and the Pearl Rivers in the near future was rendered unlikely by a declaration directing the Japanese naval authorities on the spot to act on their own discretion in this matter and, in Tientsin, strict searching regulations for

---

America are opposing Japanese policy for disposal of the China incident for the same reasons. The opposition of the United States is on grounds of theories and treaties. The British Government does not consider treaties unalterable. Believing in realistic policies, it is ready to consider any modification of treaties, but it insists that any modification must come through negotiations among the signatories. . . . The communication has left no doubt that it believes in the elasticity of international agreements." Quoted in *Trans-Pacific*, Tokyo, January 26, 1939, p. 4.

[13] The Tokyo *Nichi-Nichi* wrote that "Britain and the United States both know that should they resort to economic pressure against our country, Japan would resort to retaliatory measures against the British and American mainlands and their dependencies. They should be extremely cautious in realizing what retaliation could be taken against their interests throughout China." Quoted in *North-China Herald*, January 18, 1939.

[14] The Japanese Foreign Office spokesman described the British note as lacking "realization of the present trend in the Far Eastern affairs," in his personal opinion.

[15] *North-China Herald*, January 25, 1939, has the full text of Mr. Arita's statement. On January 26 Mr. Arita told the Diet that the Nine Power Treaty was out of keeping with the new situation in the Far East, but declined to disclose whether or not the Japanese Government intended to denounce it.

"anti-Japanese elements" had been promulgated on December 7 and lasted until February 7, 1939.[16]

Chinese Customs Loans

During this period of tension, the Chinese announced that the service of loans secured on the Maritime Customs had been suspended. This was a danger signal, warning against any Anglo-Japanese agreement which did not have Chinese approval, for it indicated the dismal failure of the Anglo-Japanese Customs Agreement. Not only had China's Customs revenue for 1938 fallen nearly 90,000,000 Chinese dollars below the 1937 returns, but also no loan quotas had been received from any region occupied by the Japanese military with the exception of one month's installment amounting to about one million Chinese dollars received from the Shanghai Customs in June 1938.[17] The Chinese Government, which had consistently refused to permit the implementation of the Anglo-Japanese Agreement concluded in May 1938, had maintained the service of the foreign loans and Boxer Indemnity out of its own resources. In order to make up the amount that should have been remitted from the Japanese-controlled areas, the Chinese Government had advanced about Ch.$ 175,000,000. The Central Bank of China, moreover, provided all the foreign exchange required. Under these conditions the Chinese Government came to the conclusion that the "situation had become too anomalous to be continued." Therefore, the request of Sir Frederick Maze for a further advance on the loan payments was rejected. Furthermore, the Chinese Government announced that it did not intend in the future to make full payments toward the loans secured on the Customs, but intended

---

[16] Without offering any evidence, the Japanese excused their actions on the ground that Chinese guerrilla activities were being assisted by wireless and were being financed from the shelter of the British and French Concessions. There is more reason to suppose that what actually was annoying the Japanese was the failure of the Japanese-sponsored Federal Reserve Bank's currency because of the attitude of the foreign banks which were still operating in the foreign concessions. If, by means of an economic blockade, life could be made very uncomfortable for the foreigners and the Chinese dependent on them, they might agree to the Japanese demands for currency exchange control and the policing of the concessions.

[17] China Maritime Customs, *The Trade of China, 1938*, Vol. 1

MARITIME CUSTOMS REVENUE, 1936–38

(in Chinese dollars)

Year	Amount
1936	324,633,291
1937	342,899,739
1938	254,565,469

to limit its payments to a proportion of the whole debt, in ratio to the receipt from Customs revenues in the areas under their control and to the total Customs receipts. On this basis the Chinese Government was prepared to set aside special amounts in the Central Bank of China as its share of the debt service. The hope was expressed that remittance of the share from the areas under Japanese occupation might be similarly forthcoming, and that interference with the Chinese currency would cease. This measure, the statement concluded, was a temporary arrangement in view of the existing abnormal conditions. It amounted to a temporary and partial moratorium on foreign loans secured on the Chinese Customs, amounting to £24,611,-367 and U.S. $25,546,000.[18]

The Japanese reply was that they were prepared to carry out the terms of the Anglo-Japanese agreement if the Chungking Government would implement this agreement. They claimed that according to the May Agreement Japanese contributions from the customs collections made in Chinese ports and remitted to the Yokohama Specie Bank for the service of Chinese foreign loans had been made conditional upon a transfer to the Yokohama Specie Bank of an amount of about two million pounds sterling, held for the Chinese Government by the Hongkong and Shanghai Bank.[19] The Chinese had refused to sanction this transfer of funds and had declined to recognize the validity of the agreement on the grounds that this would imply a recognition of Japan's activities in China. The funds collected in Japanese-controlled ports (which collected about 80 per cent of Chinese Customs revenue) were being held by the Yokohama Specie Bank.[20]

[18] The original Chinese statement of January 15 did not make clear whether domestic loans secured on the Customs were also included in the moratorium, but the Chungking Government in its formal notification to the British Embassy on January 16 indicated that only foreign loans were meant. According to the loan contracts, the foreign loans were to be serviced prior to the domestic loans.

[19] The balances lying in the Hongkong and Shanghai Banking Corporation to which the Japanese laid claim consisted of £400,000 on account of the Boxer Indemnity, which were arrears on the Japanese portion, and of Ch.$ 25,000,000— Shanghai Customs Revenue which had accumulated during the period January-May 1938, and had not been remitted to the inspector-general of Customs.

[20] It has been suggested that "since at least part of the customs has probably been paid in foreign exchange, or in Chinese national currency which is convertible into foreign exchange, this arrangement would go far to explain how the Federal Reserve Bank of Peking was able to distribute foreign exchange to importers favoring its administration. For while the Yokohama Specie Bank

The default on the loans came as a surprise to unofficial London which had been assured that the Anglo-Japanese Customs Agreement guaranteed the interests of foreign bondholders. With more than £25 million of Chinese Government-secured bonds outstanding in Britain, the news was a shock to the British financial markets. The dilemma facing the Chinese Government was, however, generally recognized in London and the impression was widespread that China would find a formula enabling her to recognize the Anglo-Japanese Agreement of May 3, 1938, in view of the importance of not allowing her credit to be damaged at the very moment when Anglo-American diplomacy seemed to be turning in her favor. Similar views were expressed by the British in China who urged that China maintain her credit and who said that to assent to any such arrangement would not infringe upon the sovereign dignity of China. The Chinese Government, however, refused to accept the British arguments and made no attempt to alter its original statement.

The Customs loans situation remained deadlocked. Nevertheless, Chinese credit did not suffer as a result of this action, and the upshot was that the onus of responsibility was shifted onto the Japanese because they refused to make any payments although they continued to collect the Customs revenues. This interpretation became more widely accepted as Japan continued to attack British interests in China both directly and indirectly.

Increased Pressure Against Western Interests

The Japanese invasion of Hainan Island on February 10, 1939, shifted interest to this new Japanese threat to Britain. The Japanese claimed that the landing of Japanese forces was a temporary move designed to strengthen the blockade against Chinese shipping and provide a firm base for Japanese operations in South China. Nevertheless, the importance of this move placing Japan astride the essential Hongkong-Singapore line was lost neither upon the British nor the Japanese. *Nichi-Nichi* in moderate tones spoke of the incident as a "heavy blow" to Great Britain and France and as a warning that "if they do not modify their attitudes in time, they will find themselves reduced to a

---

might retain the funds collected for the bondholders, it is not likely it would refrain from converting whatever foreign exchange resources it could get into Japanese yen or affiliated currencies as speedily as possible." Kurt Bloch, "Chinese Default on Customs Loans Brings Issue to Head," *Far Eastern Survey*, February 15, 1939.

position where they will suffer a blow from which they cannot recover." *Kokumin* spoke more succinctly.

> In the face of diplomatic difficulties, Japan has taken the bull by the horns. In this lies the real significance of the occupation of Hainan. One result will be complete loss of Hongkong's military value. Hongkong is a symbol of the British imperialism that led China into the dream of thinking it could rely on Great Britain. The British China Squadron based there is not very strong, but is backed by the Singapore base. Hongkong, so to speak, is the advance guard of Singapore. What the Hainan occupation has done is to cut the Hongkong-Singapore line, with the result that Hongkong's existence as a naval base had lost all its meaning.[21]

The British and French Ambassadors were immediately instructed to approach the Japanese Government to ask for the reasons, character and duration of the occupation. Mr. Arita replied that the duration of the occupation would not exceed that of military necessity and that Japan had no territorial design on the island. Similar assurances were given to the United States. With this the matter was allowed to rest.[22]

The Japanese, greatly heartened by the absence of effective foreign opposition, were encouraged to increase their pressure on Western interests elsewhere. Thus, the International Settlement at Shanghai again became the object of Japanese demands.

Early in February 1939 there had been an outburst of terrorism in the International Settlement resulting in the death of several Chinese officials of the "Reformed Government" of Greater Shanghai. The Japanese through their consul-general in Shanghai sent a note protesting against these occurrences. It asked that special precautions be taken to prevent any untoward occurrences during the coming Chinese New Year festival. Mr. C. S. Franklin assured the Japanese that all precautions would be taken. The terrorism, however, continued and the Japanese

[21] Quoted in *Trans-Pacific*, Tokyo, February 16, 1939.
[22] The *North-China Herald* comment on the incident was nearly indifferent. After a categorical rejection of the Japanese claims and assurances, it went on to say that it did not look as though Great Britain and France, "with their preoccupations closer home, will be able to do much about it in the comparatively near future. But it is a comforting thought that British and French policies are long-sighted, that ultimately there will have to be a settlement of all the questions which are being raised by Japan's behaviour, and that when that time comes they will be speaking with that authority in the Far East of which they are at present temporarily deprived." *North-China Herald*, February 15, 1939.
The London *Times* also did not consider the Hainan incident alarming, and merely expressed mild concern over the breaking of Japanese pledges to France. (February 11, 1939.)

protested again, this time emphasizing the view that the Shanghai Municipal Council had to bear full responsibility for these events.[23] Japanese officials, with the full support of the Japanese press, began openly to assail the position and, in some cases, the existence of the International Settlement. They claimed that the failure of authorities of the International Settlement to maintain peace and order was due to lack of sincerity, rather than to any inability to do so. Both Mr. Arita and Baron Hiranuma spoke of taking "fundamental means" to remedy the situation if no improvement came. The Japanese Government, however, decided to negotiate the matter with the Shanghai Municipal Council, but at the same time various Japanese authorities continued to make threats.

The now irreconcilable attitude of the Japanese was seen in their reaction to the barbed-wire barricades thrown up by the Council authorities to facilitate the suppression of terrorism. Instead of welcoming this, the Japanese interpreted it as a cunning anti-Japanese measure, for by inconveniencing the Chinese it would increase anti-Japanese feeling. Even co-operation between the British, Italian and Japanese military forces and the Shanghai municipal police was declared insufficient by the Japanese press, and voices were heard demanding the abolition of the Settlement.

The Japanese Government, however, surprised the residents of the Settlement by its willingness to accept the terms of the agreement which was reached with the Shanghai Municipal Council on March 4. The Shanghai municipal police and the Japanese consular police were to co-operate in the suppression of terrorism, but the Council retained its full policing rights. Therefore, any co-operation had to be with the consent of and under arrangement with the commissioner of police. The agreement was greeted with warm approval by the British in Shanghai who had feared that the existence of terrorism would give the Japanese an excuse to violate seriously the neutrality of the Settlement. The firmness of the Shanghai Municipal Council in refusing to accept the Japanese suggestion for independent action by the Japanese consular police in the International Settlement and the support given to the Council by the British

[23] The outstanding case was the assassination of Mr. Chen Loh, minister of the "Reformed Government," on February 19, 1939.

authorities help explain the Japanese setback. Again the Japanese had pressed forward too rapidly and too boldly.

British Assistance in Stabilizing Chinese Currency

The Japanese aims in China suffered another serious blow with the announcement of the British grant of £5,000,000 for Chinese currency stabilization. This was the British reply to Japan's use of exchange control as one of her most potent weapons in forcing out third-party interests from occupied China. The Federal Reserve Bank at Peking, controlled by the Japanese-sponsored Provisional Government of North China, had just banned the notes issued by the government-controlled Chinese banks and was trying to establish rigid exchange control over all foreign trade in that area. Normal foreign trade in this area would have been eliminated. Moreover, the new Japanese actions put trade between Shanghai (where China's national currency was and is still being used) and North China on the same footing as foreign trade. This meant cutting the normal trade channel linking North China with the commerce of the Western world.

The British Government had previously expressed its displeasure with the initial moves in Japan's North China currency program. When mere protests proved insufficient, the Chancellor of the Exchequer, Sir John Simon, announced on March 8 in the House of Commons the intention of creating a £10,000,000 exchange equalization fund. He indicated that two British banks, the Hongkong and Shanghai Banking Corporation and the Chartered Bank of India, Australia and China, would together subscribe £5,000,000 to the fund, while the remaining £5,000,000 would be granted by two Chinese state banks. The British Treasury undertook to make good any losses that might be incurred by the British banks. The fund would be operated, he said, for twelve months, with the possibilities of renewal for six-month periods. The management of the stabilization fund would be in the hands of a special committee and on this committee there would be members responsible to the British Government. Such action would render "material assistance to British trade and enterprise in China."

This step found widespread favor in Britain and China. The *Times* on March 9, 1939, said that it would be most welcomed in the City, especially in quarters interested in Chinese trade.

It denied that the loan had any political purpose but, at the same time, made clear that it was a response to the Japanese currency exchange policies. It concluded with the interesting suggestion that it was now permissible to hope that in view of the changed circumstances, the Chinese authorities would offer something better on the Customs-secured foreign loans. The *Financial Times* of London was more open in its discussion of the political significance of the British move. Although it maintained that it would be incorrect to regard the action as in any way directed against Japan, it went on to say:

> This does not mean that Japan is likely to rejoice at it. Henceforth, China will be almost a member of the Sterling bloc and any threat from the establishment of the Yuan can now have little importance. But the Japanese have no legitimate cause for complaint. One could wish that the opposite were true. Not merely our own interests, but common decency also demands that we should support China against wanton and brutal Japanese aggression. Yet hitherto only America has given any real assistance: our own contribution has been limited to a few hundred thousand pounds for the purchase of lorries. Yesterday's move was the first constructive step which the Government has seen fit to take. We should not be allowed to rest until this country has done its utmost to help China defend herself against Japanese domination.

The British newspapers in China were loud in their praise of the new measure. Here, too, the point was made that the scheme was

> not to be taken as being in the nature of a retaliatory measure, in reply to the discrimination in which Japan has been indulging against Great Britain, but a perfectly legitimate move for the protection of interests which Great Britain has every right to protect.

However, in spite of such assertions, the political significance of the British action was recognized. The *North-China Herald* wrote in a leading article,

> this new development . . . will undoubtedly be welcomed by Britons in China, as indicating a stiffening of the British attitude with regard to developments in East Asia.

The loan might not, as they insisted, have been directed against Japan, but that it would hinder Japan's currency schemes was clearly perceived.

> The loan will stabilize the value of the large quantities of Chinese banknotes which are still to be found in North China, even though they have been driven underground by the action of the Peiping government. . . .

To that extent the scheme may serve as something in the nature of an offset to the discriminatory exchange control regulations which are to come into force in the North on Saturday . . . it should serve to minimize the difficulties which China might otherwise have experienced in purchasing supplies from abroad. It is plain, therefore, that the mutuality of interests between China and Great Britain is to receive that protection against Japanese attacks which it is only common prudence to provide, and if only for that reason alone the proposal is to be most warmly commended.

The loan, it also pointed out, would strengthen the position of the Chinese Government and its determination to continue resistance. It concluded by expressing the hope that it was only the forerunner of other steps which could and ought to be taken,

if only for the purpose of impressing upon the Japanese Government the determination of the nations concerned not to yield their trading positions in China simply because Japan conceives it her duty to bring about what she chooses to call a new order.[24]

The Japanese Government officially minimized the importance of the new credits for China. The action of the British Government was "most welcome to the Chiang Kai-shek regime as a glass of water would be to one dying of thirst," but the currency of the Kuomintang Government was nevertheless doomed to collapse, said a spokesman of the Foreign Office. The British, he counseled, would do better to give up the policy of supporting the "old" Chinese national currency and support instead the "new" currency.[25] The Japanese press, however, indicated that their Government was more perturbed by the British move than the official statements indicated. *Asahi* reported that a meeting of Foreign Office officials had decided that there was need to "serve a warning upon Great Britain" and that counter-measures were discussed. (This journal suggested, as a possible counter-measure, the postponement of the settlement of the Yangtze navigation problem.) Moreover, the Cabinet held an emergency session at which the Government's attitude toward the new credits was discussed, and it was understood that it had been concluded that a "strong protest" should be made against this "unfriendly action" and that positive counter-measures should be taken.[26]

---

[24] *North-China Herald*, March 15, 1939, pp. 445-6.
[25] *North-China Herald*, March 15, 1939, p. 454. *Trans-Pacific*, Tokyo, March 16, 1939.
[26] Quoted in *North-China Herald*, March 15, 1939.

The Japanese press demanded vigorous action against the British step. *Chugai Shogyo* contended that Great Britain had "joined with the National Government in taking steps to cope with the anticipated currency operations in Central and South China." *Kokumin* professed to see nothing remarkable in the British action, but rather emphasized the fact that it indicated that Britain realized that the "China incident" had entered its "final stage wherein it is necessary for Britain to play its trump card." This action was similar to "the oil embargo against Italy during the Abyssinian conflict and the firm stand against Germany and Italy during a part of the Spanish Civil War." Therefore, this journal maintained, the course to be followed by Japan was clear.

> We have only to examine the trump card. If we do that, measures for counter-acting the British move will suggest themselves. If a mistake is not committed in dealing with the situation, it is certain that Britain will come in time to adopt the same attitude toward Japan as it adopted toward Italy in the latter stages of the Abyssinian Campaign and toward Germany and Italy in the final phase of the Spanish war. . . . We must go ahead in our plan to settle the incident without the assistance of others and to create a situation wherein Britain and other powers with interests in China will have no alternative but to cooperate with us. . . . We hope that the next move on the part of the spokesman (of the Foreign Office) will be to make clear to the British the effects of the act on relations with Japan and to point out the position in which a Britain befriending the Chiang Kai-shek regime will find itself when the new order in East Asia is finally established.[27]

The British proposal for the establishment of a stabilization fund became an actuality with the final passage of the China Currency Bill on March 24, 1939. In addition, this move in support of Nationalist China was accompanied by renewed diplomatic protests against Japanese activities in China.[28] Great Britain and the United States, as announced on March 14, protested in parallel action against the Japanese currency regulations in North China. Furthermore, as Mr. Butler declared to the House of Commons on March 14, the bombing of hospitals and the situation in Tientsin had also been vigorously protested.

[27] Quoted in *Trans-Pacific*, Tokyo, March 16, 1939, pp. 6-7. *Asahi* attacked the British loan because it bolstered the resistance power of the National Government. "Britain and the Soviet Union are leaders in the international attempt to aid the Chiang regime in the struggle against this country."

[28] The Chinese naturally applauded British aid for their currency. They saw in it not only evidence of British support for Nationalist China but also an important method of maintaining China's foreign and domestic trade, which was an important factor in maintaining the stability of China's currency.

This aid for China, coupled with pressure on the Japanese, acted as a catalytic agent in Anglo-Japanese relations. Their relations rapidly became more strained. Moves and counter-moves were made in rapid succession, culminating in the Tientsin Blockade and the Anglo-Japanese Agreement of July 1939.

The British continued to give support to the Nationalist Government. In April 1939 export credits amounting to £3,000,000 were granted by the Export Credits Guarantee Department. These were given mainly to guarantee British manufacturers the payment of orders from China on machinery and war material. The British Government's guarantee was to apply to 75 per cent of the invoice totals.

The expected increase in trade necessitated increased facilities for handling Sino-British economic and financial relations. These were established in June 1939 with the creation in London of the Chinese Government Trading Commission. Several well-known Chinese and British were connected with the concern. The chairman was Mr. Quo Tai-chi, the Chinese ambassador, and the vice-chairman was Mr. D. G. M. Bernard, a director of the Bank of England and chairman of the British and Chinese Corporation. The commission acted as a sort of clearing house for Chinese purchases in Britain.

Such economic actions were almost completely overshadowed by the crisis in Europe. Anglo-Soviet negotiations for the formation of a "peace front" took place during the spring of 1939. The implications for Japan were so obvious that indications that the Far East was excluded from any possible agreement did not suffice to calm the fears of the Japanese. The Japanese were faced with the prospect of Great Britain, freed from constant pressure in Europe and thus more capable of dealing with the Far Eastern situation, and with the Soviet Union in a similar position. There were, moreover, many indications that Germany was beginning to place little stock in the value of Japan as an ally because of Japan's heavy commitments in China and her defeat at Changkufeng in 1938. Japan, confronted with the possibility of a strengthened Russia and Britain, and a weakened Anti-Comintern Pact, adopted a threefold policy. She attempted to minimize her conflict with the Western powers, to bring pressure to bear upon Great Britain in order to prevent the conclusion of an Anglo-Soviet pact, and to cause disturbances on the Mongolian frontier in an effort to demonstrate the value of

Japanese support to Germany. Thus the Japanese were careful to point out repeatedly that the Anti-Comintern Pact was not aimed at the Western powers. Although large sections of the Japanese press demanded that Japan join the Rome-Berlin military alliance, the government debated, procrastinated and did nothing. The Japanese knew that their adherence would be regarded as an unfriendly gesture by Great Britain and, besides, the British might well be willing to pay for non-adherence.[29]

[29] The *North-China Herald*, March 29, 1939, gave an excellent statement of the British reaction to and the argument against Japan's adherence to a tripartite military alliance.

"The signing of the Anti-Comintern Pact is one thing, the definite commitment to go to the assistance of two European Powers in the event of war, two Powers who have nothing in common with Japan except their dislike of Communism, is something entirely different. . . .

"There are amongst the leaders in Japan, men who believe that the best means for a satisfactory escape for Japan from her present difficulties would be found by cooperation with Great Britain, and the United States, even though at the moment there is nothing to suggest that such cooperation is possible. . . . Great Britain and the United States have much more to offer Japan than either of the dictator states. The rapidly-increasing need for financial assistance is one of the major factors in the situation. It is likely in the long run to prove the most decisive, and is becoming clearer daily that the accumulation of bargaining points in China has been effected for the purpose of having something with which to go to Britain and the United States in the hope of securing that financial assistance without which any profit from the expensive Chinese venture must be indefinitely delayed. The proposal to enter into this alliance with Germany and Italy is just such another. It is not by itself a very potent one; nor are the others if they are thrown in, for if in the event of a European war, Japan did decide to throw her lot in with Germany and Italy, the economic effect of her action upon herself might very well prove disastrous. . . .

"From a military point of view, it has to be admitted that such an alliance would embarrass the western democracies, but it has to be remembered that the strength of the Japanese navy is very much in where it happens to be situated. In its own waters . . . the Japanese navy is unquestionably strong, but the further it goes afield, the weaker it becomes. . . . There is the further possibility to be considered, that in the event of the British scheme for securing a Four Power mutual defense arrangement succeeding, the inclusion of Russia would also necessitate the retention of a substantial portion of the Japanese fleet in the Pacific Ocean. It is true that the present strength of the Russian naval forces in this part of the world is not very imposing. Nevertheless the need for Japan to maintain her lines of communication open with the mainland would oblige her to keep considerable strength in these waters. It is difficult to avoid the conclusion that the advantages to the Rome-Berlin-Tokyo axis deriving from such an alliance as that proposed are more fancied than real. . . . Such an alliance could without a doubt cause the democracies some inconvenience but there is little reason to believe that it would make any very real change in the European situation. Further, in the event of the axis being defeated, and this is by no means improbable, Japan, as also her allies, would have to face the ultimate settlement. She very obviously cannot afford to be on the losing side, and that some of her leaders are reported to realize."

Japan's policy was also seen in her actions toward the Soviet Union and Great Britain during this period. On May 11, 1939, fighting began on the Outer Mongolian frontier. At about the same time pressure was brought upon Great Britain by the landing of Japanese troops at Kulangsu, the increased demands on the International Settlement, the sponsoring of an anti-British movement in China as well as in Japan, the blockade of additional China ports, the threats against Hongkong and the blockade of the British Concession at Tientsin. These acts demonstrated what the Japanese could do to embarrass the British even without becoming a military ally of Germany. However, it should be noted that these actions were not merely the result of the European situation, but were also in the nature of Japanese reprisals for British financial aid to Nationalist China.

The Threat to Foreign Concessions

On May 12, the day after fighting began on the Outer Mongolian frontier, Japanese landing forces entered the International Settlement on the island of Kulangsu opposite Amoy. The reason given was that the alleged assassin of Mr. Hung, pro-Japanese president of the Amoy Chamber of Commerce, was not being sought with sufficient "sincerity" by the Concession authorities. The implications of this action for Tientsin and Shanghai, where similar acts of terrorism might be used to justify invasion of foreign concessions and settlements, gave the Kulangsu incident far more publicity than the relative unimportance of the settlement warranted. The Japanese indicated the true aim of the landing when they submitted a five-point proposal for the reorganization of the Kulangsu Municipal Council which would have reduced it to a Japanese organ.[30] The Kulangsu Municipal Council through its Dutch chairman, Mr. J. M. Morhaus, protested against the Japanese action and rejected the proposals.

This firm stand received diplomatic and military support. As stated by Mr. Butler in the House of Commons on May 15, the

[30] The five proposals set forth were: (1) The exercise of strict control over anti-Japanese activities should be enforced in the settlement; (2) Japanese nationals should be appointed to the posts of chief secretary of the Municipal Council and police commissioner; (3) Suffrage and membership in the Municipal Council should be given to Formosan residents; (4) Representatives of the Chinese taxpayers should be appointed as soon as possible to fill vacancies in the Council; (5) Japanese consular police should be permitted to co-operate with municipal police in the campaign against terroristic elements in the settlement.

British Ambassador at Tokyo had been instructed to protest against forcible interference with the municipal administration at Kulangsu, "which was established by an agreement with the Chinese Government and the foreign treaty Powers, including Great Britain and Japan." The Foreign Under-Secretary then went on to reassure the anxious House that,

> As regards Shanghai, the Japanese Government can be under no misapprehension as to the unfortunate results on Anglo-Japanese relations which would be produced, were similar action taken by the Japanese in the International Settlement there.

That this was not merely another protest was dramatically indicated by the unexpected and sudden landing of British, French and American bluejackets at Kulangsu on May 17.

The Japanese retorted that the joint American-British-French action was "unfriendly" and that it had "plunged the situation on the island into chaos."[31] Although a majority of the Japanese troops had been withdrawn, those remaining, the Japanese asserted, would stay at Kulangsu until demands for the addition of three Japanese to the Municipal Council were met. The situation was thus stalemated. Soon, however, it became part of the larger question of the Japanese attack on the entire foreign concession and settlement system, especially the International Settlement at Shanghai.

On May 3, Mr. Sawada, Japan's vice-minister of foreign affairs, had made formal oral representations to the American and British Ambassadors about the Japanese view regarding the reorganization of the Municipal Council of the International Settlement. The Municipal Council, in which the British were "too dominant," had to be reorganized, "to conform to the requirements of the new age," and "to see that the voice of the nationals of the interested countries is fairly reflected in the administration." This would mean, in effect, that Japanese would be given more seats on the Municipal Council and more power in the policing and administration of the Settlement. Moreover, the Settlement authorities should act in close co-operation with the new Municipal Government of Shanghai.[32] The represen-

[31] *The Japan Chronicle,* June 1, 1939.
[32] The suggestion which was of particular interest, since the legal basis of the International Settlement is the Land Regulations, was that the land ledger of the old municipal government which was in the custody of the Municipal Council should be turned over to the Shanghai Municipal Administration, which was under Japanese control.

tations concluded with a complaint against the terroristic and anti-Japanese activities within the International Settlement and with a warning that the Japanese Government regarded this situation "with the gravest concern."[33]

This communication was rather restrained both in the nature of the demands and in the comparative lack of threats. The Japanese press, however, did not act similarly. For example, *Asahi* referred to the International Settlement as

a vicious cancer to the Japanese and to the Renovation Government of Nanking in the matter of maintaining peace and order in Shanghai since the city was occupied by the Japanese forces.

Therefore, if the Municipal Council rejected the Japanese proposals,

and if they continue to allow conditions that suggest that the foreign area is an extension of the Japan-resisting Chiang regime, a situation may arise which will require this country to demand that the administration of the Settlement be turned over to it for a certain period.[34]

The alarm aroused in Shanghai over the future of the Settlement grew so widespread that some foreigners were said to be preparing to leave, expecting that Japan intended to occupy the Settlement by armed force. However, Japan did insist, as Mr. Miura, the Japanese consul-general in Shanghai, explained, that the Land Regulations be revised and that a "fundamental solution" of the situation be achieved.[35] Such statements coming together with the Japanese occupation of Kulangsu failed to reassure the British in Shanghai. The authorities of the Shanghai Municipal Council indicated their willingness to meet those of the Japanese demands which did not infringe upon their political independence. Thus a joint declaration was issued by the authorities of the International Settlement and the French Concession proclaiming the strict neutrality of these areas and prohibiting in them all political activities of any sort. The demand for revision of the Land Regulations was, however, not met. The American and British Governments, in their replies to the Japanese oral representations, clearly stated that the time was not suitable for a discussion of such a move and the Japanese

[33] *The Japan Chronicle,* May 11, 1939, contains the complete résumé of the communication issued by the Japanese Foreign Office.
[34] Quoted in *Trans-Pacific,* Tokyo, May 11, 1939.
[35] *The Japan Chronicle,* May 18, 1939.

demands for the reorganization of the administration of the International Settlement were flatly rejected.

The Japanese, balked by the parallel action of Britain and the United States which had now developed to the point of joint military action at Kulangsu, did not desist from their verbal and written attacks on the Settlement. They professed to see in the American and British replies indications that these nations took "the position that there will be nothing wrong about the settlement continuing as a base of activities of the Chiang regime."[36] Even the Japanese officials began to speak of Japan's right to take over the concessions. Mr. Kawai, director of the Intelligence Bureau of the Foreign Office, stated this position on May 24. The international settlements and foreign concessions in China, he said, were not foreign territory, but merely areas over which the foreign countries exercised administrative powers. Therefore, since the Settlement and concessions had no sovereign rights, they could not have the status of neutrality. Having thus demolished to his own satisfaction the legal basis for neutrality of these areas, Mr. Kawai could easily justify the use of military force against them. Granted that Japan had the right to establish her control over the whole or any part of Chinese territory, it followed that she could use her armed force to crush all Chinese military action, wherever based. Since the anti-Japanese activities in Shanghai and Kulangsu were being engineered by the Chungking Government, they might

well be regarded as part of China's military action. Such being the case, Japan is fully entitled to send her military force into the Settlements and concessions to clear them of these hostile elements.[37]

The Tientsin Blockade

The incident at Kulangsu and the threatening statements which followed were disturbing enough, but with the blockade of the important British Concession at Tientsin, the Japanese attack on foreign concessions became really serious. This was an action which threatened the very existence of the Concession. Tientsin became the focal point and the symbol of Anglo-Japanese conflict in occupied China.

The dispute had a dramatic, if humble, origin. On April 9, 1939, Mr. Cheng Shi-kang, Commissioner of Customs at Tien-

[36] *Asahi* as quoted in *Trans-Pacific,* Tokyo, May 25, 1939.
[37] *The Japan Chronicle,* June 1, 1939.

tsin, was assassinated in a cinema in the British Concession. The assassin was arrested immediately after the murder, but succeeded in making good his escape. Four suspects were then placed in custody, although only one of them could possibly have been guilty. The local Japanese authorities requested the extradition of the four suspects from the British Concession. After months of obscure negotiations, the British were still unwilling to surrender the alleged assassins. For not only was there the question of actual guilt of the men, but such action was being vigorously opposed by the Chinese Government as amounting to *de facto* recognition of the "provisional Government." The Japanese in line with their actions at Kulangsu and Shanghai decided to bring the matter to a head and, on May 31, 1939, an ultimatum was reported to have been sent to the British consul-general at Tientsin, Mr. E. G. Jamieson, requesting him to deliver the persons in question to the Japanese authorities not later than noon on June 7. The British rejected these demands and requested more evidence of the guilt of the suspects. The Japanese let it be known that non-compliance would result in a blockade of the Concession, and Japanese firms began to withdraw from the British and French Concessions in Tientsin. It was generally assumed that on or about June 14 the blockade would begin. Even before the actual imposition of the blockade, the Japanese announced the form it would take. Investigation stations were to be set up at seven places along the boundaries of the two Concessions, and all persons passing those points were to be halted, searched and questioned.

For the British in China the implications of such action were clear. On June 10 the Tientsin China Association held an extraordinary meeting, at which it was decided to send a cable to the British Foreign Office, stressing the urgency of the situation. The British authorities in Tientsin attempted to meet the impending crisis by proposing that a commission of three—one British, one Japanese and a neutral chairman—mediate the dispute. The Japanese rejected the proposal and on June 14 the blockade began.

The British Government in London had not yet taken any decisive step. The Government's position was stated by Lord Halifax in the House of Lords on June 12, in response to criticism of its inactive policy. Lord Elibank had given a detailed analysis of Japanese restrictions on British interests in China and had followed this with the suggestion that Japan should be informed immediately that in reprisal for the blockade of Tientsin, Japanese ships would be denied the use of Singapore and Penang for goods in transit. Lord Davies, who was closely associated with the New Commonwealth Institute, had attacked the Government for not having given more aid to China. "The present British policy," he said, "has destroyed the reputation of the British Empire for justice and fair play." In reply to such criticism, Lord Halifax appealed to the record. The Government, he claimed, had done what it could, especially in regard to the Chinese currency.

> But those who know best the problem of China would not have been unwilling to say that no form of help, valuable as it was for British interests, could also have been more helpful to China than that which enabled the Chinese to maintain at reasonable equilibrium that on which depended their economic strength.

He admitted Lord Elibank's contentions on the treatment received by the British in China and asserted that they had been the subject of repeated representations. Moreover, the Government would "continue to exert their full efforts and influence to secure the maintenance of the right of British subjects to live and trade peacefully in China."[38]

The British press in China felt that in spite of these assurances British policy was proving ineffective in preserving British interests in China. Effective retaliation was now advocated to meet the threat to Tientsin. Measures short of war, like those suggested by Lord Elibank, and clear indications that the Government actually contemplated action in certain events beyond the mere registration of protests were demanded.

> A review of all that has happened during the past twenty-three months does nothing to remove the impression that Great Britain in common with all the other Powers interested in China, have failed to take that positive action, which is better understood by the Japanese than all the formal representations in the world. The enormous patience which has been displayed—enormous even when European difficulties are being taken into account—has created amongst the Japanese an idea of weakness which it will be very hard indeed to dispel. It is in these continual endeavours on the part of Japan to see how far she can go without inviting some sort of retaliatory action, that a continual whittling away of British rights—and other foreign rights as well, it must be remembered—is in process.

[38] *Parliamentary Debates,* House of Lords, Vol. 113, cols. 409-34.

Effective retaliatory measures should be taken to meet the threat to Tientsin.

There may be some reluctance against using them for fear of further worsening relations between the two countries, but owing to the actions of Japan alone, it is contended that the situation is now so bad that a little more worsening cannot materially affect conditions.[39]

That the British Government was still not prepared for such measures was indicated on June 14 in Mr. Butler's reply to questions in Parliament. He said that the question of what measures would be appropriate regarding the Tientsin blockade was under examination and had to depend to some degree on the nature of the action taken by the Japanese. (He also assured the House that close touch was being maintained with the French and the United States Governments.) The only important diplomatic step taken, as pointed out by Mr. Chamberlain to the House of Commons on the following day, was the representation made by Sir Robert Craigie on June 14 to the Japanese Government in which he had pointed out the danger of provocative action by local Japanese which might lead to regrettable incidents. Such diplomatic measures could hardly have been considered adequate to meet the critical situation.

If the British Government was in doubt concerning the real purpose and nature of the blockade, the Japanese lost no time in clarifying these issues. Thus Mr. Kawai on June 15 repeated the arguments for a fundamental revision of the concessions and settlements, and the Japanese press re-echoed these demands. The blockade was tightened and the isolation of the British and French Concessions was completed.

Mr. Jamieson, British consul-general at Tientsin, acted vigorously but any effective action would have had to come from the Home Government. On June 16 the British Foreign Office issued a statement defining the Government's position on Tientsin. In this it was clearly recognized that the surrender of the four accused men was not the reason for the blockade. What was being demanded was British co-operation in the construction of a "New Order" in the East. This co-operation would mean, according to the Japanese, Britain's abandoning its "pro-Chiang Kai-shek" policies, including protection of anti-Japanese and communist elements; the support of Chinese dollars at the sacrifice of Federal Reserve Bank notes; the cornering of commodi-

[39] *North-China Herald,* June 21, 1939, p. 489.

ties; connivance at the use of wireless by lawless elements and permission to use anti-Japanese schoolbooks. Acquiescence in the Japanese demands, the British Foreign Office maintained,

> would mean the abandonment under threats of force of the policy which His Majesty's Government has followed in the past, which is the same as that of other Great Powers with interests in the Far East.

The Foreign Office statement concluded by expressing the hope

> that the Japanese authorities may not maintain their refusal to give further consideration to the proposals which have been made in order to localize the incident. But if, unhappily, the new demands foreshadowed from official Japanese sources in North China should be persisted in, then it must be said at once that an extremely serious situation will arise, and that the British Government will have to consider what immediate and active steps it can take for the protection of British interests in China.[40]

These thinly veiled threats were not taken very seriously by the Japanese. The blockade continued, interference with British shipping increased, and British subjects were subjected to further indignities including searching and stripping. Nevertheless, the British Government did nothing to retaliate against these war-like acts. Instead, Lord Halifax informed the Japanese Ambassador in London that the British Government

> trusted that the Japanese Government would not desire any more than the British Government did to widen the area of disagreement or to complicate a situation that was already extremely difficult.

This conciliatory attitude was well shown in a speech made in London by the Foreign Secretary on June 21.

> I hesitate to believe that the Government of Tokyo would wish deliberately to challenge the whole tradition and policy of Britain. I believe rather that a situation has developed out of some misunderstanding, in part perhaps due to a difference of conception. We were asked to take action which on the evidence then before us we felt we could not take.
> If placed in similar circumstances the Japanese Government might have felt able to act as they wished us to act. And they are, therefore, at a loss to understand why we refuse, and attribute our refusal to a desire to harm their interests.
> I need hardly say that whatever may have been the general British judgment about events in China, it has never been any part of our policy to allow the concession of Tientsin to be used as a place for activities prejudicial to local Japanese military interests. And if they can be brought to believe that, and would give proof of their repeated declarations that

---

[40] See *Bulletin of International News*, July 1, 1939, pp. 9-11, for complete text.

they did not aim at the destruction of British interests in the Far East, I should hope that the matter may be capable of settlement.[41]

The Japanese, who in their previous actions on British interests in China had not answered kind words with compromise but rather with increased attacks, now did likewise. The wires around the French and British Concessions were electrified and the stripping of British subjects continued. The British Government now felt called upon to renew verbal protests and on June 24 Lord Halifax strongly protested to the Japanese Ambassador against the "outrageous behaviour" of the Japanese army and warned that the continuation of such humiliating and degrading activities would make an amicable settlement of the crisis there more difficult.

There was, however, no fundamental change in the British Government's position, although its language became less restrained. Mr. Chamberlain, who answered questions in the House of Commons on June 15, 19, 22 and 23, did speak of "indignities and intolerable insults." In a speech at Cardiff on June 24, Mr. Chamberlain went further. Referring to the "high-handed and insulting treatment of British subjects by Japanese soldiers," he declared that

no British Government can tolerate that its nationals be subjected to such treatment as we have heard of in Tientsin, and no British Government could submit to dictation from another Power as to its foreign policy.

But he added that he trusted that Japan had no intention of condoning the brutal acts of her soldiers or of challenging the rights and interests of British people in China. A reason for the Government's cautious and conciliatory attitude was indicated on June 26 when Mr. Chamberlain prefaced his replies to a series of questions on the Tientsin situation by saying,

while insisting that this treatment of British nationals by local Japanese soldiers to which I have referred must cease, I do not want to say anything today which would prejudice the prospect of a satisfactory issue to the conversations with the Japanese Government.

The proper atmosphere for the commencement of negotiations was achieved when General Homma, Commander-in-Chief of the Japanese garrison in Tientsin, issued orders on June 27 to Japanese searchers to cease inflicting indignities on British subjects. On the following day Japan indicated its acceptance of the

[41] *Bulletin of International News*, July 1, 1939, pp. 13-14.

British proposal that the Tientsin affair be solved through diplomatic negotiations at Tokyo. As expressed by *Asahi*, the Japanese had consented to negotiate because the "British at present are showing a sincere desire for a peaceful outcome."[42]

In London the *Times* of June 29 greeted the agreement to negotiate as a success for the diplomacy of Sir Robert Craigie. In Tokyo it was taken to indicate the realization on the part of Britain that Japan could not be intimidated into making concessions.[43] Japanese official statements maintained that any change of *venue* from Tientsin to Tokyo was not dictated by Japanese weakness. A War Office spokesman indicated that the Tientsin issue would never be settled, either on the spot or at Tokyo, unless Britain changed her alleged antagonistic policy toward Japan and supported Japan's aims in China. He warned that the Tientsin situation might be repeated in other parts of China if a settlement satisfactory to the Japanese were not reached. In Tientsin the Japanese military authorities ordered the tightening of the blockade.

Negotiations for a settlement were not scheduled to open until about July 6, but there were advance reports of their probable content and form. Local Tientsin issues of a military, political and economic nature were to be the subject of negotiation between the Japanese consul in Tientsin, Mr. Tanaka, a Japanese military representative and the British superintending-consul in Tientsin, Major G. A. Herbert, while Sir Robert Craigie and Mr. S. Kato, Japanese minister-at-large representing Mr. Arita, would take up the basic issues which had markedly affected Anglo-Japanese relations. Sir Robert Craigie himself was quoted as saying that the proposed conversations on Tientsin might possibly include related issues.[44] This, if true, would have meant an important diplomatic victory for the Japanese as the British Government had been insisting that Tientsin be settled as a local issue. Sir Robert, however, on July 5 declared that it was definitely understood that the forthcoming Anglo-Japanese conversations would relate to local issues connected with existing conditions in Tientsin. It is impossible to determine the absolute validity of the earlier statements on the subject matter of the conversations, but the actual result indicated that at some

---

[42] Quoted in *North-China Herald*, July 5, 1939.
[43] For Japanese press news, see *Trans-Pacific*, Tokyo, July 6, 1939.
[44] Domei news dispatch dated July 2 and published in *North-China Herald*.

stage in the preliminary or formal negotiations the decision was made to widen the scope of the discussions. The formal conversations began on July 17.

The nature of these negotiations and the noted Craigie-Arita Agreement which resulted from them cannot be understood in terms of the Tientsin crisis alone. For, although the spectacular character of Japanese activities here overshadowed all else, other serious attacks on the British position in China were taking place simultaneously. Newspapers might find it more sensational to stress the stripping of British citizens, but, from the point of view of British interests in China, the blockade of Kulangsu, the occupation of Swatow, the blockade of the Chekiang ports of Wenchow and Foochow, and the anti-British movement in occupied China, were major threats which could not be ignored. When the conversations opened in Tokyo, these events were an integral part of the China picture. The blockade at Tientsin was the most publicized but by no means the only anti-British move made by the Japanese during this period.

On June 14, the blockade of the British and French Concessions at Tientsin began. On June 15 the move was repeated at Kulangsu. All supplies from the mainland were stopped, leaving the 50,000 inhabitants of the International Settlement in a precarious position. According to Mr. Uchida, Japanese consul-general, Japan was seeking to make the Kulangsu Settlement authorities and the foreign powers realize that Japan could not tolerate the international area as an obstacle to the creation of a new order in East Asia. The state of isolation continued and the blockade was tightened as the American, British and French consuls refused to accede to the demands of the Japanese.

The blockades of Tientsin and Kulangsu were direct attacks on British rights in China. The seizure in turn of Swatow, Wenchow and Foochow were indirect but important attacks on Britain's interests and position. Swatow, which fell on June 21, had since the fall of Canton been one of the few remaining ports through which British trade with Nationalist China had flowed. Moreover, its proximity to Hongkong and its potential use as a naval and air base constituted a threat to Hongkong, and to communications between Hongkong and Manila. Its capture was, moreover, immediately followed by a blockade, which the British refused to recognize. However, when British ships attempted to use the port, barbed wire barricades were placed around the British wharves and the blockade was maintained in spite of British threats to convoy merchantmen desiring to enter the port. The Japanese relented early in July to the extent of allowing one vessel of each foreign power to enter each week.

The action at Swatow was followed by a blockade of Wenchow, the coastal port of Chekiang, which had been the most important pivot of cargo transportation between Shanghai and Chekiang and thus the most important coastal connection of Nationalist China. Here, too, British trade and shipping suffered considerable losses as a result of the Japanese blockade. This situation was aggravated by the closure of Ningpo, the other important port of Chekiang, and by the blockade of Foochow, an important coastal port of Fukien. By these acts, the Japanese had completely severed the coastal centers from the hinterland of Central China, the chief sphere of British trade.

The Japanese explained that the closure of these ports was not intended as a measure against Great Britain, but the Japanese sponsored anti-British campaign in China was an open attack on the British in China. The anti-British campaign began in April and May 1939, but it did not reach serious proportions until June. Superficially the movement was somewhat similar to the anti-British movement of 1925-7 but in origin and significance it was entirely different. The earlier outbreak had been an expression of the anti-imperialist phase of the Chinese nationalist movement; the latter was the artificially stimulated move of the Japanese to drive British interests out of China. Nationalistic Chinese were fully conscious of the fact that the Japanese attacks on the Western powers in China were part of the Japanese plan to secure a "new order" in China and thus gave no voluntary countenance and support to the Japanese-incited anti-British campaign. Nevertheless, by appealing to the poverty-stricken and the less politically alert Chinese and by giving the movement organization and protection, the Japanese were able to develop a serious threat to the British in China.

In the earlier stages the movement took the form of anti-British parades and the display of anti-British posters. Thus early in June, Japanese-controlled Pootung was the scene of an anti-British parade which carried such slogans as "The British have ill-treated Chinese workers and therefore they are the public enemies of the Chinese," and "British capitalists are ghosts who absorb our blood and sweat." These slogans, reminiscent of

1925-7, were inspired by the Japanese who loudly heralded their anti-communist feelings.

These supposedly spontaneous outbursts of anti-British feeling were soon accompanied by official attacks by the authorities of the Japanese-sponsored regimes in China. For example, Mr. Lien Yu, foreign minister of the Nanking Reformed Government, attacked the British for supporting Chiang Kai-shek and encouraging the Chinese Communists and threatened the British with dire consequences unless they voluntarily carried out "a thorough-going reform of the concession system."[45] In this manner Mr. Lien clearly indicated the connection between the anti-British attacks and the Japanese blockade at Tientsin.

By the second week in June, the campaign was in full blast from Peking to Canton. British diplomatic protests were of no avail. Instead the movement spread to Shansi and even to Formosa. When diplomatic negotiations opened in Tokyo between Craigie and Arita, the anti-British campaign in China was being steadily intensified.

Anglo-Japanese "Conversations"

The Japanese, determined to put as much pressure as possible on Great Britain, also fostered an anti-British movement in Japan. Thus on the eve of the Anglo-Japanese negotiations anti-British rallies were held throughout Japan under such slogans as "Crush the false diplomacy of cunning Britain," "Let the foreign concession areas, the cancers of East Asia, be abolished," and "Down with the admirers of Britain who are enemies of our people." In this atmosphere the Anglo-Japanese negotiations began in Tokyo.

On July 17 Prime Minister Chamberlain told the House of Commons the results of the first conference between Sir Robert Craigie and Mr. Arita. They had "held a friendly discussion on the general question forming the background of the situation which has arisen in Tientsin." Mr. Chamberlain emphasized that Great Britain "would not, and could not," fundamentally reverse her Far Eastern policy at the demand of Japan. Moreover, the Japanese Government had not demanded any such step. The Japanese official attitude, he said, could be more accurately described (and for this he cited Sir Robert as his authority),

[45] *North-China Herald,* June 21, 1939.

as a desire that Great Britain should endeavour to regard the Sino-Japanese hostilities with more understanding of Japanese difficulties and Japan's side of the case.

Mr. Chamberlain agreed with His Majesty's Ambassador in Tokyo

that to attribute to the Japanese Government intentions which may be found to have no basis in fact, would only be calculated to prejudice the success of the forthcoming negotiations.

The negotiations proceeded and long discussions between the Japanese Foreign Minister and the British Ambassador took place. As reported by Domei, Sir Robert indicated a "manifest desire for conciliation," while the Japanese Foreign Office stated

that Japan did not wish to interfere in British policy but that it was undeniable that the situation had now changed radically and that these changes could not be ignored in considering the background of the Tientsin affair.

On July 22 the London *Times* in a leading article indicated the way the wind was blowing. "It is necessary," it said, "to recognize the hard facts of the situation in North China," including the enormous preponderance of Japanese in North China, their *de facto* military occupation of the chief cities in that territory and their claim that the existence of foreign areas in that region should not militate against the security of their forces or their Chinese allies. The British Government, the journal asserted, could, without loss of dignity, give an assurance that the concessions would remain neutral, and could investigate the possibility of a *modus vivendi* between the Japanese forces in the occupied portion of China and the authorities in their neutral areas.

On the same day the Japanese Foreign Office issued a statement that an agreement had been reached on general questions forming the background in Tientsin. Although the terms of the agreement were not formally announced as such until July 24, on July 22 Tokyo knew and rejoiced in the content of the agreement. The Prime Minister announced that Britain had agreed to a formula applicable to the whole of China rather than one limited to Tientsin. It was this aspect of the agreement, rather than the terms themselves, which aroused jubilation in Japan, for hitherto the British had consistently refused to expand the

FROM THE NOVEMBER NOTES TO THE EUROPEAN WAR 209

Tientsin negotiations into a consideration of the entire China question.

The exact terms of the formula were stated by Mr. Chamberlain in the House of Commons and by Lord Halifax in the House of Lords on July 24:

> His Majesty's Government in the United Kingdom fully recognizes the actual situation in China, where hostilities on a large scale are in progress, and note that as long as that state of affairs continues to exist, the Japanese forces in China have special requirements for the purpose of safeguarding their own security and maintaining public order in the regions under their control, and that they have to suppress or remove any such acts or causes as will obstruct them or benefit their enemy.
>
> His Majesty's Government have no intention of countenancing any acts or measures prejudicial to the attainment of the above-mentioned objects by the Japanese forces and they will take this opportunity to confirm their policy in this respect by making it plain to the British authorities and British nationals in China that they should refrain from such acts and measures.[46]

The Prime Minister then attempted to justify this position by pointing out that the Japanese Government had, at the outset of the conversations in Tokyo, expressed the view that the background of the Tientsin situation must be recognized if misunderstandings were to be removed. This, said Mr. Chamberlain, had nothing to do with Britain's China policy, but was a question of fact. The Japanese Army, he maintained, had to provide for its own security and maintain order in the occupied areas and was, therefore, obliged to take action to see that these causes were not prejudiced. The formula, he insisted, would clear the way for discussions on Tientsin.

British opinion upon the Prime Minister's views was divided. The British in China gave it a mixed reception. The British Chamber of Commerce and the China Association in Shanghai sent a categorical protest in the form of a telegram denouncing the Anglo-Japanese agreement as "likely to result in the deplorable betrayal of British rights and interests and obligations in China." The agreement, the telegram claimed, recognized by implication that the insults and indignities to Britons in Tientsin, which had been referred to by the Prime Minister as intolerable, were justified.

> Unless the agreement is limited by precise definitions, both the present and the future of British operations in China will be subject to the control

[46] *Parliamentary Debates,* House of Commons, Vol. 350, col. 994.

of the Japanese military and will be dependent on their interpretation of the extremely wide rights conceded to them.

The protest from the two Shanghai associations concluded by saying that

> The agreement is considered here to indicate that Britain is abandoning her duty, obligations and legal position in a manner as injurious to her honour and prestige as to her interests.[47]

This protest was attacked, however, by the *North-China Herald*. This journal professed to see in the agreement merely a reaffirmation of that neutrality upon which Great Britain had insisted ever since the outbreak of the "China Incident," and condemned the protest of the British Chamber of Commerce and the China Association in Shanghai as being "rash," "tortuous of reasoning" and indicating "the breadth of vision of the three tailors of Tooley Street." When the committees responsible for the action pointed out that the decision had been unanimous, the *North-China Herald* accused them of a "purely parochial outlook," and added that

> the sooner it is realized that the China situation is but one of the many important issues with which the British Government have to deal, the sooner will come a realization that the days of immediate solutions are not yet here, and that considerable more patience needs to be shown.[48]

In spite of the assurances of the British Government and of the *North-China Herald,* many of the British residents in China as well as the Chinese Nationalists were definitely anxious about the possible results of the agreement. The Japanese interpretation of the formula as a complete about-face on the part of Great Britain, coupled with plainly spoken warnings that this must be followed by acceptance of the concrete Japanese demands, boded ill for the future of British interests.

The second stage of the Tokyo conference which was to discuss the settlement of the Tientsin issue began on July 24.[49]

[47] *North-China Herald*, August 2, 1939.
[48] *North-China Herald*, August 2, 1939. See the section called "Letters to the Editor" for interesting comment on the agreement and the action of the Shanghai bodies.
[49] The demands of the Japanese were: 1. Extradition of the terrorist who assassinated Mr. Cheng Shi-kang, Tientsin Customs official and employee of the Tientsin branch of the Federal Reserve Bank; 2. Strict policing of unlawful elements within the Concession and maintenance of peace and order there; 3. Joint search for anti-Japanese elements in the Concession; 4. Discharge of anti-Japanese Chinese officials; 5. Surrender of the silver in the Concession; 6. Prohibition of

The questions which received the most attention were the disposal of the Ch.$ 48,000,000 silver stocks being held for the Chungking Government in the British Concession at Tientsin, British co-operation in the Japanese financial schemes for North China, and the problem of maintaining peace and order within the Concessions. On July 26 Mr. Arita reported that the conference was making "smooth progress," but on July 28 the conversations were adjourned. A snag had been struck over the Japanese request that the Chinese specie held in banks in the British Concessions be surrendered, and the conference was adjourned until July 31 to enable Sir Robert Craigie to refer the question to London. However, between July 26 and July 28 another important development had taken place, for on July 27 the Government of the United States announced its decision to denounce the 1911 Treaty of Commerce and Navigation with Japan. This act altered the atmosphere of the Anglo-Japanese negotiations. Rumor in London as well as in China and Japan suggested the possibility, that Great Britain might denounce the Anglo-Japanese Trade Treaty of 1911.[50]

The changed conditions were immediately reflected in a changed attitude on the part of the British Government. Mr. Chamberlain in the House of Commons on July 31 still defended the July 24 formula but stressed that the anti-British agitation in North China (which had been steadily going on) had to stop or the British Government would be obliged to take a very serious view of the situation. Its continuance, he said, would make a successful outcome of the Tokyo negotiations very difficult.

The Japanese still gave no sign of relinquishing their attacks against the British in China and, in fact, the anti-British campaign in China and Japan was intensified and the blockade of Tientsin tightened. Sir Robert Craigie pleaded lack of new instructions and the Tokyo conference came to a standstill. Japan was rapidly losing the diplomatic advantage she had gained by

circulation of the *fapi* within the Concessions; 7. British co-operation in circulating the Federal Reserve Bank Notes; 8. Permission for examination of Chinese money exchanges, banks and firms by the Japanese.

[50] Lord Halifax indicated the effect of the American move in a speech made to the House of Lords on August 3. In this he referred to the possibility of the Government eventually deciding to denounce the 1911 Treaty. He coupled this remark with a renewal of the British offer of "good offices" in arranging a settlement in China which would take third-party interests into consideration.

the July formula. Its real importance depended upon its immediate implementation and the strong British stand indicated that this was becoming less likely every day. Prime Minister Chamberlain on August 4 made his "makes my blood boil" declaration. In this he told the House of Commons that he still favored settling the British differences with the Japanese by discussion and negotiation, but that in certain circumstances the British Fleet might be sent out to the Far East. He also made the statement that it made his "blood boil to hear and read of some of the things that have been happening there." However, he still expressed great hope for the successful conclusion of the Tokyo negotiations on Tientsin.

The Japanese countered the new British stand with the threat of a military alliance with Germany and Italy. On August 4, 1939, the Japanese ambassadors to Rome and Berlin announced that they were concluding Japan's adherence to the Italo-German military alliance. The British refused to be impressed and stalled for time. Sir Robert remained without instructions, while the Japanese fussed and fumed and threatened to break off the Tokyo parleys. The situation became worse for the Japanese as France and the United States intervened in the Tientsin currency and silver stock issues as parties having common interests with Britain. The British could and did plead the impropriety for Great Britain to negotiate without the presence of French and American representatives at the conference table. Japan did not want this, but any refusal might have brought the dreaded denunciation of the Anglo-Japanese Trade Treaty, the possibility of which the British press in Britain and in China constantly emphasized.

Instead of retreating, the Japanese decided to increase the pressure on the British. Not only was the anti-British movement further intensified, but a military blockade of Hongkong was threatened. As a result of a movement by a Japanese detachment numbering 500 men on August 16, Japanese and British troops faced each other across the border at Shumchun, while Japanese spokesmen proclaimed the necessity of isolating Hongkong "so long as Great Britain assisted the Chinese Government."

Anglo-Japanese relations seemed to have reached the breaking point. This was evidenced by the formal statements on the Tokyo negotiations issued by the British and Japanese

FROM THE NOVEMBER NOTES TO THE EUROPEAN WAR 213

Foreign Offices on August 20 and August 21, respectively. The British Foreign Office statement maintained that the negotiations had broken down over the questions of currency and silver reserves. These economic issues, it said, would be discussed only if the interests of the other parties involved were safeguarded by allowing Great Britain to consult with and to have regard to the views of these third parties. It concluded by repeating the declaration made in the note of January 14, 1939, that it did not regard treaties as eternal and that it was prepared to consider any constructive proposals which the Japanese Government might have to make regarding the modification of existing treaties, but added the important qualification that it considered it

essential, however, that all parties to the Nine Power Treaty and other Treaties which govern the situation in China will be enabled at the appropriate time to express their views and make a contribution to a settlement which should be equitable for all concerned.[51]

The Japanese Foreign Office denied the British contentions, and the British were reminded not only that the negotiations had been instituted at the request of the British authorities and that the British conferees had entered the talks with a full understanding of the nature of the Japanese demands, but that they had also agreed on a formula by which the parleys were to be conducted. Therefore, the British contention of incompetence to discuss the economic issues as the subject of an Anglo-Japanese agreement was "not warrantable." The Japanese hammered on this point and pointed out that on August 1 the British representatives had agreed to a meeting of a subcommittee on economic questions and had entered into definite discussion of the economic question. The British reference to the Nine Power Treaty was rejected with a reminder that "the attitude of the Japanese Government regarding the pact has been repeatedly made clear." Moreover, the Japanese professed to be unable to comprehend how a discussion of the Nine Power Treaty could be useful in settling the Tientsin issue. As for the British statements on the third parties involved, the Japanese Foreign Office statement rejected any intervention by third powers on the ground that it "would only serve to delay and complicate the questions."[52]

[51] See the London *Times*, August 21, 1939, for the complete text.
[52] See *Trans-Pacific*, Tokyo, August 24, 1939, for complete text.

The Japanese Foreign Office did not know when it issued this statement on August 21 that by the morrow its diplomatic position would become immeasurably weakened, for on August 22 the proposed Nazi-Soviet Non-Aggression Pact was announced and on August 23 the treaty was signed. Japan had been left "badly in the lurch" and, as expressed by the *North-China Herald,* ran "the risk of being left very much alone."

The Hiranuma Government, unable to cope with the changed situation, resigned. The British Government, however, preoccupied with the immediate prospects of a war in Europe, did little in the Far East. There are even indications, that the British were desirous of reopening negotiations for an agreement with Japan. Thus the British Foreign Office announced on August 26 that the four Tientsin suspects were to be handed over to the Japanese authorities. This step was in itself of minor importance because the point had been settled during the Tokyo conversations, but coming three days after the signature of the Nazi-Soviet Pact and four days after the breakdown of the Anglo-Japanese conversations, it implied a willingness on the part of the British Government to review the situation.

The nature of any desired agreement was indicated in a series of remarkable leading articles in the *North-China Herald* of August 30. The one dated August 28 and titled *The Crossroads* contained a complete analysis of the new situation and possible outcome as seen from the British point of view. It began with a statement of Japan's new position.

> The betrayal of Japan by the conclusion of the German-Russian non-aggression pact, including as it does agreement not to join any combination of Powers directed against either of them, and thereby completely nullifying the Anti-Comintern Pact, places Japan in a position from which she may, if she chooses, reconsider the whole of her policy in the Far East, not so much with the idea of radically changing it, as with the intention of allaying much of the suspicion and anxiety, which it has created in the minds of third-party neutral powers. It should be plainly stated . . . that past Japanese policies have estranged countries which might have been her friends, while at least one of those nations upon which she has been relying has left her in the lurch, and there is little to suggest that in the very near future Japan may not find herself completely isolated. That is desirable from no point of view whatever, and the fact is becoming recognized even in Japan itself.

The journal then examined the possibilities confronting

Japan—some agreement with the Soviet Union or with Britain, France and the United States.

It has been suggested that she might be induced to enter into a non-aggression pact with the Soviet, but it is difficult to see where in Japanese circles there can be any support for so radical a change in Japanese policy. It would amount to the negation of all that Japan has stood for in the past, and would deprive her of one of her main reasons for conducting hostilities in China.

This possibility rejected, it examined the other.

It is suggested, however, that by a very slight modification of policy Japan might be able to bring about a state of affairs in the Far East not entirely at variance with the desires which so many of her spokesmen have on occasion outlined. There is reason to believe that if the Japanese Government were to explore the possibility of inviting Great Britain, France and the United States to a conference for the settlement of outstanding questions between her and those three countries, a means might be discovered of bringing an end to the present hostilities in a manner which would do credit alike to Japanese arms and statesmanship. Recent telegrams suggest that there is a section of the Japanese public which is in favor of some such step being taken, and while it is apparent that preliminary moves would have to be made very delicately, there is no reason to believe that something of this nature could not be done.

The basis for such an agreement was then given.

At the moment the issues which Japanese action in China have presented are confused. There has been no clear definition of what Japan means by the establishment of a new order in China. If it means, as so many Japanese have claimed, the total exclusion of foreign trade other than Japanese from China, it may be said straight away that that policy can never be acceptable to those nations which have established themselves as traders in this country by honourable means and prolonged industry. If, on the other hand, Japan is ready to accept British recognition, as enunciated by Mr. Chamberlain, of the fact that Japan by reason of propinquity, etc., has a just claim to a special position *vis-à-vis* China, then a basis can be found for a discussion of the whole of the Far Eastern issues by some such conference as is suggested. On the side of the Powers this would involve recognition of a *de facto* state of affairs, which need in no way prejudice the present position of the Chinese National Government, and might very well in the not too distant future lead to that peace which this portion of the world so earnestly desires. Let it be admitted that this would be going a long way to meet the Japanese, but that is necessary in order that Japan should be given an opportunity of proving to the world the truth of her repeated assurances that she has no intention of damaging the interests of third-party neutrals. The establishment of a *modus vivendi*, whereby the eminent rights of Japan are recognized in Japan, and the existing rights of other foreign nations are admitted, should not meet with any insuperable difficulties. It would entail the meeting of some of the demands which Japan has from time to time put forward, and which, in the changed circumstances which would thus be brought about, could with justice be insisted upon, and if this does indeed amount to a compromise, it is one in which Japan not only loses nothing, but actually stands to gain considerably, and that without further damage to other foreign interests in this country.

The obvious objection that the gain would be at the expense of Nationalist China was foreseen by the *North-China Herald*.

The criticism may be advanced that any such arrangement would be a departure from that neutrality which third parties have maintained, and would amount to a betrayal of the Chinese National Government. It would in fact be nothing of the sort; for it merely involves the recognition of a state of affairs, which it is doubtful whether the Chinese will be able to remedy for a very long time to come, and, therefore, constitutes a full appreciation of realities, doing no harm to anyone, and likely to be productive of much good in the elimination of the present misunderstanding between Japan and the three Great Powers most immediately concerned.

The leading article concluded with a summary of its proposals which re-emphasized their extraordinarily conciliatory nature.

In order to emphasize this point the proposition is restated: It ought to be possible by means of such a conference for all concerned to make the best out of what is, and has been nothing but a bad business, and to bring about a greater degree of stability in the Far East than has existed for all too long a time. The question is whether Japan will seize upon such an opportunity. There is every reason why she should. The estrangement which exists between Japan, on the one hand, and Great Britain, France and the United States, on the other, has arisen not from any duplicity on one side or the other, but from an honest difference of opinion as to the correctness of Japan's policy in China. At no time have the last three Powers ever led Japan to believe that they approved of what she was doing, and consequently it can never be alleged against them that they have let her down. The failure of the Anti-Comintern Pact has left Japan isolated in a manner which no Power should be today, and there appear to be only two cures for the evil—either that she should make a complete *volte face* in her policy, and follow Germany into the wilderness of inconsistency, which is unthinkable, or so to conduct her policy as to remove existing tension, and make it possible for other Powers interested in China to cooperate as far as they logically can.[53]

The Hiranuma Cabinet did not respond to these overtures and before the new cabinet of General Abe could begin to function, war had broken out in Europe and a new chapter in British policy in the Far East had begun.

[53] *North-China Herald*, August 30, 1939. See also other editorials in this issue and the issue of September 6.

CHAPTER XI

RECAPITULATION AND CONCLUSION

The outbreak of the Sino-Japanese conflict more than two years ago brought about a major shift in the center of gravity of British interests in China. Only by examining the change which has taken place during the hostilities in China—which has been lost sight of in the welter of sensational "incidents" in the last two years—can Britain's present position, and possible points of departure in the future, be properly appreciated. This major change, in a word, was the attempt to substitute Rangoon in Burma for the coastal ports in China as a center for the economic penetration of the vast interior of Nationalist China.

That Great Britain should have been the non-belligerent nation most affected by the hostilities in the Far East was only to be expected. Of all Western powers she has the largest economic stake in China. These British interests have developed in entrepôt coastal centers which have owed their importance and their existence as separate entities to the vast hinterland. Boats, automobiles, railways and airplanes have been the means of penetration; and the rivers, canals, roads and railway lines which connect the ports with their markets, the essential arteries. The Japanese by their successive military drives in three main regions of China have been cutting these vital arteries. In the early part of the war British interests in China met the problem of forming new connections with the hinterland by using already established coastal centers for new purposes, or by vitalizing formerly obscure and unimportant Chinese ports. When, however, Japan's drive in South China, followed by her blockade of China's coast, made all these expedients insufficient, Britain was forced to seek an entrance to inland China outside the country.

The transition from the traditional British position in China to the present one began with the outbreak of hostilities in North China in July 1937. The British interests in this area were the first to experience the effects of the disruption of normal relations between entrepôt and hinterland. Tientsin had become the most important trading port of North China, owing largely to the construction of railways and the conservancy work in the Hai River, which facilitated the exploitation of the coal mines in the surrounding region, and to the promotion of the wool trade with Mongolia. British interests in and around Tientsin cover many fields of activity, including coal mining, banking and manufacturing, and especially trade. The total value of British municipal and private property in Tientsin is estimated at £10 million, and another £25 million is invested in business interests in North China generally. The trading connections and business organizations built up by British firms in the eighty years since the opening of the city would alone assure the British a substantial share in the development of the Tientsin area, provided, of course, that the open door was maintained.

This last proviso is the key to the situation. The railway lines which radiate from Tientsin and Peking—the most important being the Tientsin-Pukow and Peking-Hankow lines—are the main links between Tientsin and the interior. The Japanese have been using their control over these communications as an effective weapon in squeezing British interests out of North China. The fact that British bondholders have large interests in these railways has granted the British no immunity from discriminatory steps. These acts alone would weaken the British position, but to them has been added the establishment of monopolies, export prohibitions, exchange control regulations, tariff revisions favorable to Japanese products, and inefficient telegraph service. The blockade of the concession threatens even the existence of the concession itself. In short, at the time of this writing,[1] the Japanese are at the same time attempting to monopolize Tientsin's hinterland and to undermine Britain's power in North China at its most vulnerable point.

Although available statistics indicate that the total value of trade between Tientsin and Great Britain has increased during the present hostilities, the Japanese gain has been incomparably greater. The British increase, moreover, was not absolute and must be seen in the light of the closing of other ports, rerouting of intercoastal trade, and rising prices. Tsingtao, formerly an important center for British trade in North China, is now practically closed to British trade and the important bristle exports formerly enjoyed by Tsingtao now go through Tientsin. Cotton

[1] September 1939.

exports which under ordinary circumstances would have gone down to Hankow or Shanghai have, owing to military operations in the Yangtze Valley, been finding their way north to Tientsin. The total tonnage of British shipping (entering and clearing) in the port of Tientsin during 1938 was greater than in 1937 or 1936, but the Japanese flag has displaced the British from first place.

Two of the largest British enterprises in North China, however, have escaped the fate of most British trading concerns in this area. The Kailan Mining Administration and the British-American Tobacco Company both supply commodities of which the Japanese are in need, and both have attempted to make their peace with the Japanese. The former not only decided to increase its coal output from 5,500,000 to 6,500,000 tons to meet increasing demands from the Japanese but also expanded its activities by Ch.$ 10,000,000 worth of debentures issued in London in December 1938. The *Japan Times* pointed to this as evidence of "British diplomacy based on reality."

The British-American Tobacco Company, which has extensive interests throughout North China, has also done quite well during the present hostilities, but it faces increased Japanese competition. Its profits for 1938 amounted to £5,500,886, which was £169,563 less than that earned in 1937 but somewhat more than the sum earned in 1936. The apparent decrease in 1938, moreover, was due to increased taxation. Sir Hugo Cunliffe-Owen, chairman of the company, has expressed confidence in the future provided "we enjoy only reasonable stability in world affairs and provided we also enjoy equal opportunities with our competitors." But the experiences of the B.A.T. and the Kailan Mining Administration must be regarded as exceptional; both organizations are able to profit from what is denied to the other British interests in North China—unbroken connections between the chief ports and the interior, and freedom from discriminatory activities.

The story of British interests in Tientsin and North China was repeated in Shanghai and the Yangtze Valley. Only in the latter area the stake was much larger. The Yangtze Valley has always constituted the chief sphere of British interest in all of China, and Shanghai is its chief port. British investments in this city alone were estimated at approximately £180,000,000, or about 60 per cent of total British investments in China at the beginning of the hostilities in 1937. The losses to British interests in Shanghai as a result of more than a year's isolation from the interior were computed by the British Chamber of Commerce in October 1938 to be between £5,000,000 and £6,500,000, as contrasted with an estimated decline in the value of British investments in all China of over £120,000,000. Shanghai's isolation was achieved by Japanese control of the chief arteries which connect the port and the interior—the Yangtze River and the Shanghai-Nanking and Shanghai-Hangchow-Ningpo Railways.

Yangtze shipping, which before the outbreak of hostilities had been practically a Sino-British monopoly, had carried goods as far west as Szechwan. As long as the Yangtze was the scene of large-scale hostilities, British business circles in Shanghai accepted the argument of "military necessity" as a valid reason for the closure of the river to foreign merchant vessels. But as it became increasingly evident during 1938 that Japanese merchant vessels were doing what had been forbidden to British vessels, that tens of thousands of tons of exports and imports were passing up and down the lower Yangtze under Japanese auspices and for Japanese accounts, that the cargoes were not war supplies but rather such commodities as sandalwood, silk-waste, piece goods, candles, soap and cigarettes, and that booking offices in Shanghai were soliciting passengers and freight and offering to secure military passes, then British trading circles in Shanghai became convinced that Japan intended to maintain a monopoly over the biggest domestic market in China.

Similarly the British no longer accepted the Japanese plea of military necessity in the case of Shanghai's rail connections. The Japanese have been operating the Shanghai-Nanking Railway and the Shanghai-Hangchow section of the Shanghai-Hangchow-Ningpo Railway, but they have installed a system of military passes and permit other travelers to use the line only under the closest restrictions. Moreover, it is claimed that the Japanese have persistently refused to allow the representatives of the bondholders, chiefly British, to exercise any of their legal rights in the management of the line or to inspect it; that they have continued to operate the railway in violation of the terms of the loan agreement, and have appropriated the revenue which legally belongs to the bondholders; and that they have formed a company, the Central China Railway Company, with capital said to be subscribed by the Japanese Government and Japanese interests, and the Nanking "Reformed Government," in equal shares, to operate these lines. The Chinese Government, it should be added, has declared its inability to accept responsibility for the obligations of the railways which have fallen into Japanese hands. The loan services are now in default and the Shanghai-Nanking Railway is already £1,392,000 in arrears and the Shanghai-Hangchow-Ningpo Railway £66,000.

Of course, not all British interests in Shanghai have been adversely affected by the war. A boom in local business, building construction and industrial activity arising out of currency depreciation and an influx of hundreds of thousands of refugees has somewhat mitigated the effect of the "peaceful siege." Thus many British firms, including the Hongkong and Shanghai Banking Corporation, the Ewo Cotton Mills, the largest textile factory in China, and the Shanghai Waterworks Company made considerable profits during 1938.

While the boom has succeeded in reversing the downward trend in the volume of Shanghai's trade, it has not fundamentally affected the changes in the character of the trade brought about by barring British commercial shipping from the Yangtze and by restricting the use of the railways. With access to the raw materials of Central China gone, Shanghai not only lost a profitable export trade but even had to import the same commodities from elsewhere to supply its own needs. Thus manufactured products took on a new importance in Shanghai's export trade while, conversely, raw materials took on a new importance in her import trade. For example, imports of cotton piece goods from foreign countries declined, but imports of raw cotton rose sharply. The latter trend was a direct response to the reopening of the mills in Shanghai, the large export of North China cotton to Japan, restrictions on shipments to Shanghai, and the closure of the Yangtze which has compelled the Shanghai mills to purchase foreign cotton. Shipments of vegetable oil, tallow and wax constituted in 1936 and 1937 the main group of Shanghai's exports, but during the first six months of 1939 the export of these commodities was valued at Ch.$ 2,007,136, compared with Ch.$ 3,602,243 for the corresponding period in 1938, and Ch.$ 44,306,045 for the same period in 1937. Piece goods exports, on the other hand, totaled

Ch.$ 13,862,504 for January-June 1939, compared with Ch.$ 7,067,487 for the corresponding period in 1938.

The separation of Shanghai from the interior also seriously affected the volume as well as the nature of its trade. Only 30 per cent of China's trade passed through Shanghai during 1938 in comparison with over 50 per cent under normal conditions. Shanghai's total foreign trade in 1938 (Ch.$ 491,273,386) declined by some 46 per cent as compared with 1937 or 1936. The total value of foreign imports into Shanghai decreased by more than half between 1936 and 1938, and imports from Great Britain declined about 57 per cent. Similar declines were seen in the value of exports. The downward trend was reversed, however, in 1939 as a result of the boom just mentioned. Trade with Great Britain increased markedly, although not so much as that with Japan and the United States.

The decline in Shanghai's coastwise trade even more clearly reflected the effects of Shanghai's isolation. Coastwise imports of Chinese merchandise were valued at Ch.$ 237,700,000 in 1938 as against Ch.$ 436,500,000 in 1937, and coastwise exports at Ch.$ 319,000,000 as compared with Ch.$ 434,500,000 in the preceding year. Moreover, the Japanese blockade of the coastal ports threatened what remained of the coastwise trade. Until this blockade, Shanghai had carried on a brisk trade with the Chekiang ports of Ningpo and Wenchow. Since the closure of the Yangtze both of these ports had served as centers through which considerable tonnage of export products from the Chinese-controlled areas reached Shanghai and through which products of Shanghai moved to interior China over combination highway-rail routes. This trade has now ceased.

Shanghai's shipping—overseas, coastal and inland—has reflected trade conditions. The total tonnage entered at Shanghai during the year 1938 was 9,742,768 tons—a sharp decline from the 13,254,437 tons in 1937 and 18,826,779 tons in 1936. However, while in overseas shipping the totals for 1938 of 1,150 vessels and 5,250,874 tons were only slightly less than the figures for 1937, in coastal shipping the totals for 1938 (2,712 vessels and 1,737,495 tons) came to less than half of those for 1937. British shipping showed similar changes. British entries from abroad into Shanghai in 1938 amounted to 2,429,278 tons, which compared favorably with the 1,841,249 tons in 1937 and with the 2,615,839 tons in 1936. British entries from Chinese ports, on the other hand, have steadily declined from 2,977,964 tons in 1936 to 1,443,722 tons in 1938, primarily because of the closure of the Yangtze River. By restricting the use of Chinese ports, the Japanese have attacked the last remaining important coastal centers which gave the British contact with the hinterland of Central China. At least one thing is certain: the "prosperity" which the British in Shanghai are enjoying at present is not based on durable factors such as trade with the interior or coastal shipping. Only the restoration of the former connections with the hinterland could restore the British in Shanghai and throughout Central China to their former outstanding position.

In Central China, Hankow, 600 miles up the river from Shanghai, had been the main center of British interest in the interior. This city served as the chief feeder and outpost of Shanghai until booms were laid across the Yangtze at Kiangyin in August 1937. Then recourse was had to the recently completed Canton-Hankow Railway. The extensive use of this railway for government supplies, however, limited the importation of general merchandise from the coast to comparatively minor quantities, not to speak of the risks and delays en route caused by continuous Japanese bombardments. The net result was what might have been expected. Finally, as the Japanese military forces approached the Wuhan cities, factories, shops and people began a general evacuation and since the arrival of Japanese forces on October 26, 1938, there has been a complete stagnation of business. Here, even more than in Shanghai, the *sine qua non* of a revival of British trade is the opening of the Yangtze to British shipping.

Until the completion of the Canton-Hankow Railway in 1936, the commercial hinterland of Hongkong and Canton had been limited to Kwangtung and Kwangsi. These provinces are served by rivers flowing south and east from the mountains which form the watershed between these rivers and the tributaries of the Yangtze, and provide a market of some fifty million people. The chief characteristic of Hongkong's trade has always been its entrepôt character. There was a time when Hongkong handled and financed about 40 per cent of all China's foreign trade. Since the beginning of the twentieth century Shanghai has come to the forefront, but even so Hongkong continued until 1936 to handle approximately a quarter of China's foreign trade. Not more than one tenth of her imports was consumed in the Colony, and about the same proportion of exports was of local origin.

The outbreak of hostilities brought an upturn in business to Hongkong. For the first eight months of 1938, the Colony's visible trade was 15 per cent greater than for the same period of 1937, and 58 per cent greater than for the same period of 1936. Part of this increase was due to a brisk munitions trade, but more important was the diversion of the trade which formerly used to reach the interior up the Yangtze via Shanghai but could now be transported via the Canton-Hankow Railway. Hongkong's gain, however, was only a small fraction of Shanghai's loss.

In addition to the increased business resulting from the diversion of trade, the Colony benefited considerably by an influx of well-to-do refugees and the establishment of numerous manufacturing and other activities formerly carried on in Shanghai and in other cities affected by the hostilities. For example, it was authoritatively reported in September 1938 that six big factories were to be erected in Kowloon by Shanghai Chinese industrialists—including a synthetic nitrogen products factory, an electro-chemical factory, a satin-weaving plant, and an advertising and printing establishment. Local industries like shipbuilding and ship-repairing experienced unprecedented activity.

In contrast with the general boom, Hongkong's shipping during 1938 suffered the worst setback in twenty years. The total number of ships entering and clearing was 67,007, with a total tonnage of 30,962,756, representing a decrease as contrasted with the 1937 figure of 73,257 vessels with a total tonnage of 37,830,-736. This decline was mainly in foreign shipping. Chinese shipping had completely ceased and Japanese shipping had greatly decreased. British ocean-going shipping likewise showed a decrease of 326 in numbers with a decrease of 312,456 tons. The river-steamer trade also declined, but British river steamers benefited by Hongkong's increased trade with South China ports.

The Japanese invasion of South China, which resulted in the capture of Canton on October 21, 1938, checked the Colony's business uptrend. The Pearl River, chief connection between Hongkong and Canton, was closed to British shipping and the Canton-Hankow Railway ceased to serve as a carrier of goods to and from Hongkong. Hongkong had now lost its direct contacts with South and Central China. *Finance and Commerce* gloomily commented on the new situation:

> With the keys of Canton in her hands, along with those of the Yangtze Valley and North China, Japan will be in a position to strangle or to stimulate the foreign trade upon which Hongkong, Shanghai, and Tientsin depend.

Hongkong, bolstered up by increased population and by the establishment of new, though inadequate, connections with the hinterland, was able to adjust itself to the new situation and continued to operate at capacity with the exception of insurance. The Chinese ports of Pakhoi and Kwangchowwan, the French Indo-Chinese port of Haiphong and the Portuguese colony of Macao assumed new importance, and through them Chinese products of various categories found their way to Hongkong for transshipment, despite the disruption of normal transportation routes. Goods filtered into the interior by all sorts of devious ways and means. Macao, for example, which for over ninety years had steadily declined in commercial importance, now became a busy trading center. Nevertheless, although the British in Hongkong might congratulate themselves on the ability of the Colony to "carry on reasonably well under the present conditions of restricted trade," the fundamental weakness of the present position was recognized. For as long as the Pearl River remained closed to British shipping and the Japanese controlled the termini of the Canton-Hankow Railway, Hongkong, like Shanghai and Tientsin, was largely cut off from its traditional hinterland.

In addition Hongkong's position has been changed in another direction. With the strengthening of its fortifications, it has become an important fortress. Together with Singapore it has the task of safeguarding British trade routes in the Far East and, although its economic position as the entrepôt for South China may decline, its strategic importance has become of primary consideration with the outbreak of war in Europe. Moreover, the maintenance of a large garrison and the erection of fortifications have been acting as buffers against the effects of Hongkong's growing isolation.

The British interests which could no longer penetrate China's interior from various points on her long coast began to establish a new center to accomplish this end. Rangoon, in Burma, has become the back door through which British interests have been trying not only to re-establish contact with the central and western parts of China but also to participate in the building of the new China which the Nationalist Government is creating in the Southwest. Interest in the potentialities of this region as a market for British commodities, especially for capital goods like railway supplies, and as a field for profitable investment, became keen after the fall of Canton and the capture of Hankow. The bright prospects for the British in unoccupied China contrasted sharply with the future facing the established interests in the coastal region.

Aid to the Nationalist Government has become synonymous with the strengthening of the British economic position in unoccupied China. Participation in the construction of the already completed Yunnan-Burma highway; the provision of £5,000,000 to help establish a currency stabilization fund which would bolster British trade with Nationalist China; the commencement of the Sino-British undertaking to connect Kunming capital of Yunnan and projected railway center of Southwest China, with Rangoon by rail; the £500,000 export credit loan for the guaranteeing of British exports to Southwest China by the Exports Credits Guarantee Department of the British Treasury; and the use of remitted British Boxer Indemnity funds to purchase telephone, telegraph and railway equipment—all these indicate that the British have begun to participate actively in the reconstruction of Nationalist China, whose leaders have repeatedly stated that they not only welcome investments in war time which do not infringe upon China's sovereign rights but welcome even more aid in tackling the still greater problems of economic rehabilitation that will follow in the wake of hostilities.

It remains to be seen what effect the European war will have on British interests in China, particularly as they have been affected in the last two years. The war in Europe has altered not only Britain's position in China but Japan's position vis-à-vis the West.

Although the outcome of the European War may result in marked changes in British policy in China the factors which have determined Sino-British relations since 1931 will continue to operate and all future developments will have an organic and continuous relation to those described in these pages. It is safe to assume that Britain's China policy will continue to be the result of consideration given to the problems of imperial defense and world politics mixed with a concern for the stakes held by British business and financial interests in China.

The school of thought which has favored a return to the policy of the Anglo-Japanese Alliance will probably still argue that a strong, friendly Japan is Britain's best safeguard against the possibilities of the recurrence of a general anti-imperialist movement in China or an increase in the influence and prestige of the U.S.S.R. The impossibility of relying upon a vigorous American policy in the Far East might still be put forward as a reason for Britain's inability to take action unfriendly to Japan during a period of European crisis. There will still be those in Great Britain, as well as in the foreign settlements in China, who will be psychologically incapable of envisaging a free and independent China. Many will still feel confident that even if Japan is militarily victorious in China, British capital will be needed and asked for by Japan and that Britain's *quid pro quo* will be the continuance of Britain's traditional predominance in central and south China.

On the other hand, others will continue to argue that Japanese supremacy in China and the maintenance of the British position are incompatible; that Great Britain must support and thereby gain the friendship of Nationalist China; that the U.S.S.R. is not to be feared and might even be utilized as a means of offsetting Japan's strengthened position; that the United States, to protect her own interests, will co-operate with Great Britain in supporting China's fight for independence; that to rely upon the good-will and friendship of Japan has proved to be an unwise policy; and that Great Britain must uphold her obligations under the Washington Treaties and the Covenant of the League of Nations.

All of these various arguments in the past have been used to explain and justify Britain's recent China policy. Whether or not Great Britain, in the future as in the past decade, will continue its dual policy of attempting to maintain and defend its position in China, especially in the Yangtze valley, while endeavoring to make some adjustment with Japan, it can be said that during 1931-39 her assistance to China was rewarded by a simultaneous strengthening of the British position in China, while her attempts to conciliate Japan were at great expense to British interests.

APPENDIX A

LEITH-ROSS STATEMENT OF JUNE 23, 1936[1]

His Majesty's Government in the United Kingdom sent me out to examine the financial and economic difficulties of China and the possibilities of our assisting her, in conjunction with the other Powers interested, to overcome these difficulties. I have spent nearly nine months here and have done my best to investigate conditions as I found them without prejudice or preconceptions. A large part of my time has necessarily been spent in Shanghai, but I have visited Nanking, Tientsin, Peking, Hankow, Chungking, Amoy and Canton, and have met representatives of the Government authorities and local banking and trading communities in all these centres. It had been the hope of my Government that the United States of America, Japan and France would appoint experts to collaborate with me, but this did not prove possible. However, an important Economic Mission from the United States recently visited China and I have found their Report of great interest. I have maintained contact with the Japanese Government representatives and bankers here and have paid two visits to Tokyo so as to obtain first-hand information of the views of the Japanese.

The considered report of my mission will have to be presented in due course to my Government, but it may be useful, before I leave China, to give some outline of my impressions.

The first question to which my attention was directed was naturally the position of the currency. Silver has for many centuries been the currency of China, and the sudden and sharp rise in the value of silver during 1934 caused a similar rise in the exchange value of Chinese currency. Chinese produce became too dear in relation to world prices, exports fell off, and silver had to be exported to meet the adverse balance of trade. This, in turn, caused a contraction of credit and an acute deflationary crisis; prices began to fall, debts could not be met, and the banks became more and more "frozen" particularly in Shanghai where the collapse of the real estate boom created a special problem.

By October, 1934, the situation had become so serious that the Chinese Government imposed a variable export tax on the export of silver, thereby divorcing the Shanghai dollar from the free silver standard. But this measure, while it mitigated the extreme effects

[1] London *Times*, June 23, 1936, p. 15, cols. 1-2.

of the rise in silver, did nothing to remedy the difficulties which that rise had already caused; and when I reached Shanghai last September, it was evident that further positive measures had to be evolved. China had abandoned silver without adopting any alternative currency basis. I did not bring any cut and dried scheme out with me to "put over" the Chinese Government. There were several possible alternatives, and the decision between them, depending as it did largely on Chinese psychology, could only be taken by the Chinese Government. I was examining the situation with a view to the preparation of a detailed programme with adequate safeguards and, if possible, with international support. But before any such scheme could be devised, the exchange market became dangerously weak and the Chinese Government decided to adopt an inconvertible managed currency on the basis of their own resources.

I had no responsibility for this bold step, but I have of course closely followed the situation and I have no hesitation in saying that the action taken has been fully justified by the success which it has achieved. It was accepted throughout China without any serious difficulty. The notes of the Government banks have been steadily replacing the silver dollars in circulation. Their exchange value has been fully maintained and the resources at the disposal of the Government banks for this purpose have substantially increased. The rate of exchange fixed has tended to encourage exports and the resulting increase in agricultural prices should, in due course, lead to an improvement in the purchasing power of agricultural producers. The adverse balance of trade has been greatly reduced, and it seems probable, so far as can be judged from the statements available, that the international receipts and expenditures of China on income-tax are now evenly balanced. Thus the fundamental economic conditions for a stable currency are fulfilled.

I think the Chinese Government are to be congratulated on the progress which their policy has achieved. Already much has been done to re-establish sound financial and economic conditions. Confidence in the currency is growing. But much has still to be done before it can be solidly assured as a basis for long-term trading and investment plans. The currency reform had to be put into force at short notice, and the various measures necessary to make it watertight have had to be drafted piece-meal and fitted together gradually. The unification of the note issue and the reorganization of the Central Bank as an independent Reserve Bank have not yet been carried through effectively. There have been unfortunate speculative movements of a non-commercial character which have disturbed sentiment. There is a large Budget deficit entailing constant recourse to Government borrowing. The domestic bond market is depressed and Government credit low. Though the market is now comparatively easy, many of the commercial banks are far from being liquid.

Meanwhile, both in the Southern provinces and in the North there have been political difficulties in carrying through the currency reform, as it should be done, on a national basis. Lastly, the sharp fall in the price of silver, following the suspension by the United States Treasury of silver purchases on the world market, aroused temporary misgivings. But, all things considered, there would appear to be every reason, so far as economic factors are concerned, for confidence in the present currency system, provided that the Chinese Government complete and carry through efficiently the programme of internal reforms, including especially the reorganization of the Central Bank and the reform of the Budget.

The prospects of the currency, and indeed of the whole financial situation of China for the future, will depend first on the maintenance of peace and order in the interior of China, and secondly on a settlement of the special situation in North China. In particular, Customs revenues are a vital factor in Chinese finance and every effort should be made to put an end to difficulties in the way of their collection in East Hopei. These difficulties cannot be removed without a better political understanding between China and Japan. During my last visit to Japan I was assured that the Japanese Government desire such an understanding: that they favour the maintenance of the Chinese Customs Administration and will give no support to the creation of a special tariff by any local authority in China: and that they have no wish to interfere with the internal administration of China. It is greatly to be hoped that a solution of the present difficulties will be reached that will restore general confidence and security for trade and investment.

I have dealt at length with the currency position because financial security is the basis of trade. Erratic exchanges and contraction of credit strangle enterprise. The currency reform has laid the foundation for an increase of trade activities. Exports are expanding and the adverse balance of trade has been greatly reduced. But the export trade could be still further stimulated if the burden of local taxes, inter-port duties, and export duties could be reduced and if the standards of production, manufacture, and handling could be improved. It rests with the Chinese themselves to promote exports by such means; but I would sound a note of caution in regard to the tendency to create control by monopoly or anything resembling a monopoly of natural exports of China. As regards imports, the immediate prospects may not seem encouraging. But it is no use importing goods that cannot be paid for, and the export trade of

China must improve before progress in imports can be looked for. If, however, present tendencies are maintained, there is every reason to expect a gradual and steady improvement in the import trade.

I hope that British exporters will take advantage of the turn in the tide when it comes. They must expect to face keen competition and enterprise, and expert salesmanship will be required, as well as readiness to take some risks. Needless to say, they must make a careful study of market requirements and in every field of business cooperation with China interests should be aimed at. The establishment of Sino-British Trade Councils in Shanghai and Hankow will, I hope, help in this direction.

Imports, of course, are largely affected by the tariff, and I hope that the Chinese Government will consider whether the present tariff cannot be revised in a downward direction, so far as this is possible without reducing revenue. During the depression a number of the tariff rates have been pushed up to a point at which they produce no revenue and merely prohibit legitimate trade. These rates require to be reconsidered in the light of the present exchange position. Industrial interests will no doubt press strongly for the maintenance of the highest possible protective tariff, but the advantages they obtain will be at the expense of the agricultural population. It is the duty of the Government to strike a fair balance between the interests of industry and those of agriculture, but I believe that in China the restoration of rural economy should have first consideration. In my opinion, therefore, a downward revision of the present tariff would be advantageous to China both in its financial and in its economic effects. The Maritime Customs is the basis of Chinese Government credit, and it is in the first interests of China both to maintain that service in all its traditional efficiency and to adjust the tariff so as to secure the maximum revenue.

The development of China will require the importation of capital goods, and this is probably the most promising field for British exports. Such exports would be greatly facilitated by a flow of credit to China, where capital is scarce, and the yield under proper management should be fully remunerative. In the past the United Kingdom has done much to develop the railway system of China, but unfortunately many of the loan obligations thus incurred have not been fully met. These defaults have seriously prejudiced the credit of China, and her efforts to secure finance for new development purposes have been correspondingly hampered. The national Government appear genuinely anxious to settle outstanding obligations, within the limits of their financial possibilities, and also to remedy the serious defects in the administration and management of the railways, with a view to enabling them to meet their charges. It must be borne in mind that the defaults are, in the main, a

APPENDIX A 233

heritage of years of civil strife and social disorganization. If a reasonable settlement could be reached in regard to these old debts, the way would be open for financing extensions to the present railway system, and thus opening vast stretches of country to foreign trade. No other form of enterprise could be more beneficial both to China and to the United Kingdom and every effort should be made to overcome the difficulties.

Apart from railway financing, which calls for long-term credit, the possibilities of arranging middle-term credits deserve exploration. Such credits would be of particular value for financing public utility schemes. I have been impressed by the energy and capacity with which the municipal authorities are developing local projects of this character, and I think the British manufacturers and exporters should consult the banks operating in China, as well as the Government Departments concerned, with a view to obtaining finance for soundly planned projects.

There are also many openings for the investment of private capital in properties or undertakings in China; but, if investors are to be attracted to such ventures, confidence must be re-established by abrogating any measures that have the effect of discriminating against foreign capital, and, as regards real estate, by securing that the legal rights of mortgages are fully protected. Foreign capital cannot be expected to assist China unless it is assured of fair treatment.

I fully agree with the observations of the American Economic Mission, viz., "A vast change is coming over China: a modernization that, as compared with ten or even five years ago, marks many centuries." I believe that this change will make China not a less but a more fruitful field for British enterprise—commercial, industrial and financial. Our principal interest here is to promote the peace, the prosperity and the trade of China, and in working for this, it seems to me we are working in the interests of all countries trading with China. The reconstruction of China is a vast task which will take years to accomplish, and there is room for all to assist her in this task. The present Chinese Government have, despite conditions of peculiar difficulty, made remarkable progress in the restoration of law and order, the resettlement of the devastated regions, and the development of communications. Their recent currency reform was, in my opinion, planned on sound lines, and it is in the interests of everyone that it should succeed.

In conclusion I should like to express, on behalf of my colleagues and myself to the Chinese Government and their officials and to the Chinese and foreign bankers and traders whom we have met, our warm thanks for the assistance and hospitality extended to us wherever we went.

APPENDIX B

BRITISH NOTE OF JANUARY 14, 1939[1]

I am instructed by His Majesty's principal Secretary of State for Foreign Affairs to inform Your Excellency of the uncertainty and grave anxiety wherein His Majesty's Government in the United Kingdom have been left by the study of the Japanese new policy in Far Eastern Affairs as set out in recent statements by the late Prime Minister and other Japanese statesmen.

I am to refer more particularly to Prince Konoye's statements of November 3 and December 22 and to the communication made by Your Excellency to foreign press correspondents on December 19.

This uncertainty has not been removed by the conversations on the subject which I have had with Your Excellency from time to time.

From these pronouncements and from other official information issued in Japan, His Majesty's Government infer that it is the intention of the Japanese Government to establish a tripartite combination or bloc composed of Japan, China and Manchuria, wherein the supreme authority shall be vested in Japan and subordinate roles would be allotted to China and Manchuria.

Insofar as China is concerned, it is understood that the Japanese Government is to exercise control, at least for some time, through the Asia Development Council in Tokyo which will be charged with the formulation and the execution of policy connected with political, economic, and cultural affairs in China.

Your Excellency's own communication to the press indicates that the tripartite combination is to form a single economic unit and that the economic activities of other Powers are to be subjected to restrictions dictated by requirements of national defence and economic security of the proposed bloc.

According to Prince Konoye, the hostilities in China are to continue until the present Chinese Government have been crushed or will consent to enter into the proposed combination on Japanese terms.

China, he said, would be required to conclude with Japan an anti-Comintern agreement and Japanese troops are to be stationed at specified points in Chinese territory for an indefinite period

[1] London *Times*, January 16, 1939, p. 11.

presumably to ensure that the Japanese conditions for a suspension of the hostilities are observed.

Moreover, His Excellency stated that the Inner Mongolia region must be designated as a special anti-Communist area. It is not clear what is meant by this, but in the absence of fuller information it can only be assumed that Inner Mongolia is to be subjected to even a greater degree of Japanese military control than the other parts of China.

His Majesty's Government are at a loss to understand how Prince Konoye's assurance that Japan seeks no territory and respects the sovereignty of China can be reconciled with the declared intention of the Japanese Government to compel the Chinese people by the force of arms to accept conditions involving the surrender of their political, economic, and cultural life to Japanese control, the indefinite maintenance in China of considerable Japanese garrisons, and the virtual detachment from China of the territory of Inner Mongolia.

For their part, His Majesty's Government desire to make it clear that they are not prepared to accept or to recognize the activities of the nature indicated which are brought about by force. They intend to adhere to the principles of the Nine-Power Treaty and cannot agree to a unilateral modification of its terms. They would point out that until the outbreak of the present hostilities, the beneficial effects which the treaty was expected to produce were steadily being realized.

The Chinese people were maintaining and developing for themselves an effective and stable government and the principle of equal opportunity for commerce and industry of all nations was bringing prosperity to China and her international trade including that with Japan. His Majesty's Government, therefore, cannot agree, as is suggested in Japan, that the treaty is obsolete or that its provisions no longer meet the situation, except insofar as the situation has been altered by Japan in contravention of its terms. While, however, His Majesty's Government maintain that a modification cannot be effected unilaterally and must be by negotiation between all signatories, they do not contend that treaties are eternal.

If, therefore, the Japanese Government have any constructive suggestions to make regarding the modification of any multilateral agreement relating to China, His Majesty's Government, for their part, will be ready to consider them. Meantime, His Majesty's Government reserve all their rights under the existing treaties.

I am further instructed to refer to that portion of Prince Konoye's statement of December 22 wherein he states that Japan is prepared to give consideration to the abolition of extraterritoriality and the revocation of foreign concessions and settlements in China. This inducement to China to accept Japanese demands would appear to entail but little sacrifice on the part of Japan, for if the Japanese Government succeed in their plan for the control of the country, they will have no further need for extraterritoriality or concessions. On the other hand, His Majesty's Government would recall that they undertook and nearly completed negotiations with the Chinese Government in 1931 for the abrogation of British extra-territorial rights. The negotiations were suspended by the Chinese Government in consequence of disturbed conditions following the seizure of Manchuria by the Japanese forces in that year, but His Majesty's Government have always been ready to resume negotiations at a suitable time and are prepared to discuss this and other similar questions with a fully independent Chinese Government when peace has been restored.

In the conclusion, I am to state that if, as is possible, His Majesty's Government have in any way misinterpreted the intentions of the Japanese Government they feel it is because of the ambiguity wherewith those intentions have so far been expressed and they would welcome a more precise and detailed exposition of the Japanese conditions for terminating the hostilities and of Japanese policy towards China.[2]

[2] London *Times,* January 16, 1939, p. 11.

APPENDIX C

ANNOUNCEMENT OF MARCH 8, 1939, ON THE CREATION OF AN EXCHANGE EQUALIZATION FUND FOR CHINA[1]

Mr. Pethick-Lawrence: (by Private Notice) asked the Chancellor of the Exchequer whether he had any statement to make as to proposals for assisting to maintain the stability of the sterling value of the Chinese dollar.

The Chancellor of the Exchequer, Sir John Simon: Yes, Sir. The stability of the Chinese dollar is a matter of great importance to this country in view of our financial and economic relations with China. The Chinese Government have achieved considerable success in their efforts to maintain the convertibility of Chinese currency for trade transactions, to limit its depreciation in exchange against sterling, and to keep the rate reasonably stable for many months. They have informed His Majesty's Government that they intend to continue their existing monetary policy and that, as part of the policy, they desire to establish a stabilization fund of £10,000,000 in addition to their own reserves. They have invited the two Chinese Government banks to subscribe a total of £5,000,000 to the fund and the two British banks, namely, the Hong Kong and Shanghai Bank and the Chartered Bank to subscribe the further £5,000,000 between them. The British banks have agreed to subscribe these amounts subject to receiving an undertaking from the Treasury to reimburse them for any loss that might be incurred when the fund is wound up. The arrangement would be that the fund would operate for twelve months, but it could be continued for further periods of six months by agreement; if the necessity arose, however, the fund could be wound up at an earlier time.

His Majesty's Government would welcome the setting up of this stabilization fund, the successful working of which would be of material assistance to British trade and enterprise in China, and the Treasury have agreed, subject to legislative approval being obtained, to give to these British banks the guarantee against loss for which they ask. A bill is being prepared and I hope to be able to present it early next week.

[1] *Parliamentary Debates,* House of Commons, March 8, 1939.

SELECTED BIBLIOGRAPHY

PRIMARY SOURCES

Australia, Department of External Affairs, *Current Notes on International Affairs*, Canberra.
Carnegie Endowment for International Peace, *Treaties and Agreements with and Concerning China, 1919-1929*, Washington, 1929.
China, Board of Trustees for the Administration of the Indemnity Funds Remitted by the British Government, *Reports*.
China Maritime Customs, *The Foreign Trade of China*, Shanghai.
—— *Monthly Returns of the Foreign Trade of China*, Shanghai.
Federation of British Industries, *Report of the Mission to the Far East, August-November 1934*.
Feetham, the Hon. Richard, C.M.G., *Report to the Shanghai Municipal Council*.
Great Britain, Board of Trade, *Statistical Abstracts for the British Empire*.
—— *Statistical Abstracts for the United Kingdom*.
Great Britain, Colonial Office, *Annual Report on the Social and Economic Progress of the People of Hong Kong*.
—— *The Economic Survey of the Colonial Empire (1935)*, Colonial No. 126.
Great Britain, Foreign Office, *China No. 2 (1926), Report of the Advisory Committee, together with other documents respecting the China indemnity*. Cmd. 2766.
—— *China No. 3 (1926), Report of the Commission on Extraterritoriality in China*. Cmd. 2774.
—— *China No. 3 (1927), Papers respecting the agreements relative to the British Concessions at Hankow and Kiukiang*. Cmd. 2869.
—— *China No. 4 (1927), Papers relating to the Nanking incident of March 24 and 25, 1927*. Cmd. 2953.
—— *China No. 1 (1928), Papers relating to the settlement of the Nanking incident of March 24, 1927*. Cmd. 3188.
—— *China No. 1 (1930), Chinese mandate of December 28, 1929, regarding extra-territorial rights in China, and correspondence between His Majesty's Government in the United Kingdom and the Chinese Government in connexion therewith*. Cmd. 3480.
—— *China No. 2 (1930), Convention between His Majesty's Gov-*

SELECTED BIBLIOGRAPHY

ernment and the President of the National Government of the Republic of China for the rendition of Weihaiwei, and agreement regarding certain facilities for His Majesty's Navy after rendition, Nanking, April 18, 1930. Cmd. 3590.

—— *China No. 3 (1930), Papers regarding the disposal of the British share of the Chinese indemnity of 1901, September 19-November 14, 1930. Cmd. 3715.*

—— *Treaty Series No. 44 (1930). Exchange of Notes between His Majesty's Government in the United Kingdom and the Chinese Government regarding the Rendition of the British Concession at Amoy, September 1930, Cmd. 3711.*

—— *China No. 1 (1932), Cessation of hostilities in Shanghai and neighborhood and withdrawal of Japanese forces. Resolution adopted by the Special Assembly of the League of Nations, Geneva, April 30, 1932, and Agreement concluded between the Chinese and Japanese representatives with the assistance of friendly powers, Shanghai, May 5, 1932. Cmd. 4077.*

—— *Miscellaneous No. 4 (1932), Reports to the League of Nations by the Committee of Representatives at Shanghai of Certain States Members of the League Council appointed to report on Events in Shanghai, February 6 and 12, 1932.*

—— *Treaty Series No. 5 (1935), Exchange of Notes between His Majesty's Government in the United Kingdom and the National Government of the Republic of China relating to Land Tenure and Taxation in the Former British Concession at Hankow and Kiukiang, Nanking, October 27, 1934. Cmd. 4836.*

—— *Treaty Series No. 15 (1935), Exchange of Notes between His Majesty's Government in the United Kingdom and the Government of India and the Chinese Government regarding the Establishment of a Commission to determine the Southern Section of the Boundary between Burma and Yunnan, Nanking, April 9, 1935. Cmd. 4884.*

—— *Treaty Series No. 28 (1938), Exchange of Notes between His Majesty's Government in the United Kingdom and the Chinese Government regarding Air Service Over China, Hankow, December 18, 1937. Cmd. 5712.*

Great Britain, House of Commons, *Parliamentary Debates.*
Great Britain, House of Lords, *Parliamentary Debates.*
Hong Kong, Economic Commission, *Report of the Commission appointed by His Excellency the governor of Hong Kong to enquire into the causes and effects of the present trade depression in Hong Kong and make recommendations for the amelioration of the existing position and for the improvement of the trade of the Colony. July 1934-February 1935.*

Hong Kong, Government Printers, *Blue Book for the Year.*
Hong Kong, Legislative Council, *Report of the Meetings of the Legislative Council.*
League of Nations, *Official Journal.*
—— *Official Journal, Special Supplement.*
Royal Institute of International Affairs, *Documents on International Affairs.*
Shanghai Municipal Council, *Annual Report and Budget.*
United States, Department of Commerce, Bureau of Foreign and Domestic Commerce, *Commerce Reports.*
—— *Far Eastern Financial Notes.*
—— *Monthly Trade Report—China.*
United States, Department of State, *Press Releases.*
United States Government Printing Office, *China: A Commercial and Industrial Handbook.*
—— *The Conference of Brussels, November 3-24, 1937.*
Wieger, P. Léon, *La Chine Moderne,* vols. 1-7.

Relevant Books

Allen, G. C., *Japanese Industry: Its Recent Development and Present Condition,* International Secretariat, Institute of Pacific Relations, 1940.
Bank of China, *Chinese Government Foreign Loan Obligations,* Shanghai, 1935.
Barnes, Joseph, editor, *Empire in the East,* Doubleday, Doran, New York, 1934.
Bau, Mingchien Joshua, *Foreign Navigation in Chinese Waters,* China Institute of Pacific Relations, Shanghai, 1931.
—— *Tariff Autonomy of China,* Institute of Pacific Relations, Kyoto, 1929.
Bisson, T. A., *American Policy in the Far East 1931-1940,* International Secretariat, Institute of Pacific Relations, 1940.
—— *Japan in China,* Macmillan, New York, 1938.
Causton, Eric Edward Nicholson, *Militarism and Foreign Policy in Japan,* Allen & Unwin, London, 1936.
Chapman, H. Owen, *The Chinese Revolution 1926-27,* Constable, London, 1928.
China Ministry of Industries, Committee for the Study of Silver Value and Commodity Prices, *Silver and Prices in China,* Commercial Press, Shanghai, 1935.
Clark, Grover, *Economic Rivalries in China,* Yale University Press, New Haven, 1932.
Coons, Arthur Gardiner, *The Foreign Public Debt of China,* University of Pennsylvania Press, Philadelphia, 1930.

SELECTED BIBLIOGRAPHY

Emeny, Brooks, *The Strategy of Raw Materials,* Macmillan, New York, 1934.
Field, Frederick V., editor, *Economic Handbook of the Pacific Area,* Allen & Unwin, London, 1934.
Green, O. M., *The Organization of News from the Far East,* Institute of Pacific Relations, 1933.
Griswold, A. Whitney, *The Far Eastern Policy of the United States,* Harcourt, Brace, New York, 1938.
Holcombe, Arthur N., *The Chinese Revolution,* Harvard University Press, Cambridge, 1930.
Hornbeck, Stanley K., *China To-day: Political,* World Peace Foundation, Boston, 1927.
Hsia, Ching-liu, *The Status of Shanghai,* Kelly & Walsh, Shanghai, 1929.
Hsu, Shuhsi, *Japan and Shanghai,* Kelly & Walsh, Shanghai, 1938.
Hubbard, G. E., *British Far Eastern Policy,* Information Papers No. 24, Royal Institute of International Affairs, London, 1939.
―― *Eastern Industrialization and Its Effect on the West,* Oxford University Press, London, 1935.
Institute of Pacific Relations, *Problems of the Pacific 1931,* edited by Bruno Lasker and W. L. Holland, Chicago, 1932.
―― *Problems of the Pacific 1933,* edited by Bruno Lasker and W. L. Holland, London, 1934.
―― *Problems of the Pacific 1936,* edited by W. L. Holland and Kate L. Mitchell, Chicago, 1936.
Ishimaru, Tota, *Japan Must Fight Britain,* Hurst & Blackett, London, 1936.
Johnstone, William Crane, *The Shanghai Problem,* Stanford University Press, Stanford, 1936.
Joseph, Philip, *Foreign Diplomacy in China 1894-1900,* Allen & Unwin, London, 1928.
Kane, Albert E., *China, the Powers, and the Washington Conference,* Commercial Press, Shanghai, 1937.
Keeton, G. W., *The Development of Extraterritoriality in China,* 2 vols., Longmans, Green, London, 1928.
La Fargue, T. E., *China And The World War,* Stanford University Press, Stanford University, California, 1937.
Kiernan, E. V., *British Diplomacy in China, 1880 to 1885,* The University Press, Cambridge, 1939.
Lieu, D. K., *The Growth and Industrialization of Shanghai,* China Institute of Pacific Relations, Shanghai, 1936.
MacNair, Harley Farnsworth, *China in Revolution,* University of Chicago Press, Chicago, 1931.

McCordock, R. Stanley, *British Far Eastern Policy 1894-1900*, Columbia University Press, New York, 1931.
Morse, Hosea Ballou, *The International Relations of the Chinese Empire*, 3 vols., Longmans, Green, London, 1910.
Pollard, Robert T., *China's Foreign Relations 1917-1931*, Macmillan, New York, 1933.
Pritchard, Earl H., *Anglo-Chinese Relations During the Seventeenth and Eighteenth Centuries*, University of Illinois, Urbana, 1930.
Remer, C. F., *A Study of Chinese Boycotts*, Johns Hopkins Press, Baltimore, 1933.
—— *Foreign Investments in China*, Macmillan, New York, 1933.
Royal Institute of International Affairs, *The British Empire*, Oxford University Press, London, 1937.
—— *China and Japan*, Information Department Papers, No. 21, Oxford University Press, New York, 1937.
—— *The Colonial Problem*, Oxford University Press, New York, 1937.
—— *Notes on Raw Materials in the Far East and Pacific Dependencies* (unpublished).
—— *Notes on the Textile Industry in Lancashire, India, China and Japan* (unpublished).
—— *Notes on the Economic Consequences of Recent Events in Manchuria* (unpublished).
Salter, Sir Arthur, *China and Silver*, Economic Forum, New York, 1934.
Sargent, A. J., *Anglo-Chinese Commerce and Diplomacy*, Oxford, 1907.
Shepherd, Jack, *Australia's Interests and Policies in the Far East*, International Secretariat, Institute of Pacific Relations, New York, 1940.
Soothill, William Edward, *China and England*, Oxford University Press, New York, 1928.
Stewart, John R., *Manchuria Since 1931*, Institute of Pacific Relations, New York, 1936.
Stimson, Henry L., *The Far Eastern Crisis*, Harper, New York, 1936.
Tai, En-sai, *Treaty Ports in China*, Columbia University, New York, 1918.
Tang Leang-Li, *The Inner History of the Chinese Revolution*, Dutton, New York, 1930.
Teichman, Sir Eric, *Affairs of China*, Methuen, London, 1938.
Wheeler, W. Reginald, *China and the World War*, Macmillan, New York, 1919.
Whyte, Sir Frederick, *China and the Foreign Powers*, Oxford University Press, London, 1927.

Willert, Sir Arthur, *Aspects of British Foreign Policy*, Oxford University Press, London, 1928.
Willoughby, Westel W., *Foreign Rights and Interests in China*, Johns Hopkins Press, Baltimore, 1927, 2 vols.
―――― *The Sino-Japanese Controversy and The League of Nations*, Johns Hopkins Press, Baltimore, 1935.
Woo, T. C., *The Kuomintang and the Future of the Chinese Revolution*, Allen & Unwin, London, 1928.
Wright, Philip G., *Trade and Trade Barriers in the Pacific*, Institute of Pacific Relations, Honolulu, 1935.
Wright, Quincy, *The Existing Legal Situation as It Relates to the Conflict in the Far East*, International Secretariat, Institute of Pacific Relations, 1940.
Wright, Stanley F., *China's Struggle for Tariff Autonomy 1843-1938*, Kelly & Walsh, Shanghai, 1938.
―――― *The Collection and Disposal of the Maritime and Native Customs Revenue Since the Revolution of 1911*, Shanghai, 1927.

Newspapers

China Press Weekly, Shanghai.
Daily Telegraph and Morning Post, London.
Hankow Herald, Hankow.
Hong Kong Weekly Press, Hong Kong.
Japan Advertiser, Tokyo.
Manchester Guardian, Manchester.
New York Herald-Tribune, New York.
New York Times, New York.
North-China Herald, Shanghai.
North China Star, Tientsin.
Shanghai Evening Post and Mercury, Shanghai.
Tientsin and Peking Times, Peking.
The Times, London.
Trans-Pacific, Tokyo.

Periodicals, Journals and Bulletins

Amerasia, New York.
American Journal of International Law, Washington, D. C.
American Political Science Review, Menasha, Wisconsin.
Annals of the American Academy of Political and Social Science, Philadelphia.
Asia, New York.
Asiatic Review, London.
Austral-Asiatic Bulletin, Melbourne.
British Chamber of Commerce Journal, Shanghai.

British Year Book of International Law, London.
Bulletin of International News, London.
Central Bank of China Bulletin.
China Airmail, Hongkong.
China at War, Chungking.
China Quarterly, Shanghai.
China To-day, New York.
China Weekly Chronicle, Peking.
China Weekly Review, Shanghai.
Chinese Economic and Statistical Review, Shanghai.
Chinese Economic Journal, Shanghai.
Chinese Social and Political Science Review, Peking.
Contemporary Japan, Tokyo.
Contemporary Opinions on Current Topics, Tokyo.
Crown Colonist, London.
Economica, London.
Economist, London.
Far Eastern Digest, Hongkong.
Far Eastern Survey, New York.
Finance and Commerce, Shanghai.
Foreign Affairs, New York.
Foreign Policy Association News Bulletin, New York.
Foreign Policy Association Reports, New York.
Fortnightly, London.
International Affairs, London.
International Conciliation, New York.
Japan Chronicle, Kobe.
Journal of the Royal Institute of International Affairs, London.
Memoranda, American Council, Institute of Pacific Relations, New York.
Monthly Circular, Mitsubishi Economic Research Bureau, Tokyo.
Oriental Affairs, Shanghai.
Oriental Economist, Tokyo.
Oriental Economist (Japanese edition), Tokyo.
Pacific Affairs, New York.
People's Tribune, Hongkong.
Political Quarterly, London.
Political Science Quarterly, New York.
Round Table, London.
The New Statesman and Nation, London.
Week, London.

YEAR BOOKS AND SURVEYS

China Year Book, Shanghai.
Chinese Year Book, Shanghai.

Japan-Manchukuo Year Book, Tokyo.
Japan Year Book, Tokyo.
Manchuria Economic Year Book (Japanese edition).
Moody's Governments and Municipals, New York.
Moody's Railroads, New York.
Survey of International Affair, London.

PERIODICAL ARTICLES OF SPECIAL INTEREST

American Council, Institute of Pacific Relations, "Recent Changes in the International Settlement in Shanghai," *Memoranda,* 1934, No. 8.

—— "Silver—Conflicting American and Chinese Interests," *Memoranda,* 1934, Nos. 21-2.

Anonymous, "Japan in China: the New Far Eastern Problem," *Round Table,* September 1935.

—— "Power Politics in the Pacific," *Round Table,* December 1934.

Anstice, E. H., "Shanghai: Its Problem and Its Future," *Asiatic Review,* July 1938.

"Asiaticus," "The Financial Cutting Edge in the Partition of China," *Pacific Affairs,* June 1936.

—— "The New Era in Chinese Railway Construction," *Pacific Affairs,* September 1937.

de Booy, H. Th., "The Naval Arm of Diplomacy in the Pacific," *Pacific Affairs,* March 1935.

Brebner, J. Bartlett, "Canada, the Anglo-Japanese Alliance and the Washington Conference," *Political Science Quarterly,* March 1935.

Chen, Han-seng, "Japanese Penetration in Southernmost China," *Far Eastern Survey,* November 4, 1936.

Chi, Ch'ao-ting, "China Monetary Reform in Perspective," *Far Eastern Survey,* August 18, 1937.

Chiang, Kai-shek, "China's War-Time Production Policy," *Central Bank of China Bulletin,* September 1939.

Dietrich, Ethel B., "British Commercial Policy at the Crossroads," *Far Eastern Survey,* March 23, 1938.

Eurasian, "The Aims of Japan," *Political Quarterly,* July-September 1934.

Green, O. M., "Great Britain and Japan's War in China," *Pacific Affairs,* June 1938.

Hanson, Haldore, "Smuggler, Soldier and Diplomat," *Pacific Affairs,* December 1936.

Hanwell, Norman D., "Shanghai's Worst Crisis," *Far Eastern Survey,* July 27, 1938.

Howard, Harry Paxton, "Anglo-Japanese Co-operation and Conflict," *China Quarterly,* Autumn 1939.

Hyde, Charles Cheney, "Legal Aspects of Japanese Pronouncements in Relation to China," *American Journal of International Law,* July 1934.
Johnstone, William C., "Status of Foreign Concessions and Settlements in the Treaty Ports of China," *American Political Science Review,* October 1937.
Kennedy, Capt. M. D., "The Future of Anglo-Japanese Relations," *Asiatic Review,* October 1938.
Kung, Ling-kai, "China's Economic Reconstruction and Foreign Investment," *China Quarterly,* Summer 1939.
Lin Yutang, "China Prepares to Resist," *Foreign Affairs,* April 1937.
Lockwood, William W., Jr., "Hongkong—Empire Bulwark or Hostage to Fortune?" *Far Eastern Survey,* February 2, 1938.
Lothian, Lord, "Crisis in the Pacific," *International Affairs,* March-April 1935.
McNair, Arnold D., "The Stimson Doctrine of Non-Recognition," *British Year Book of International Law,* 1933.
Mitchell, Kate L., "Revitalizing British Interests in China," *Far Eastern Survey,* June 23, 1937.
Peffer, Nathaniel, "Tientsin. Japan's New Challenge to the West," *Asia,* September 1939.
—— "Would Japan Shut the Open Door in China?" *Foreign Affairs,* October 1938.
Pennell, W. V., "The Anti-British Campaign in North China," *Oriental Affairs,* September 1939.
Pratt, Sir John, C.M.G., K.B.E., "China and Japan," *Fortnightly,* August 1939.
—— "The International Settlement and the French Concession at Shanghai," *British Year Book of International Law,* 1938.
Stewart, John R., "The War and Western Interests in North China," *Far Eastern Survey,* October 12, 1938.
Stewart, Robert R., "Great Britain's Foreign Loan Policy," *Economica,* February 1938.
Taylor, George E., "The Powers and the Unity of China," *Pacific Affairs,* December 1936.
Tiltman, H. Hessell, "Japan's Anti-British Drive," *Asia,* April 1938.
Tsou, P. W., "War-time Adjustment of China's Foreign Trade," *China Quarterly,* Summer 1939.
Wang, C. C., "The Pan-Asiatic Doctrine of Japan," *Foreign Affairs,* October 1934.
Wang, Ching-chun, "China Still Waits the End of Extraterritoriality," *Foreign Affairs,* July 1937.

Whyte, Sir Frederick, "The East: A Survey of the Post-War Years," *Foreign Affairs*, October 1932.
—— "The Far East in 1935," *International Affairs*, May-June 1935.
Woolsey, L. A., "Japanese in Kulangsu," *American Journal of International Law*, July 1939, pp. 526-30.
Wu, Leonard T. K., "China's Monetary Dilemma," *Far Eastern Survey*, December 4, 1935.
—— "China's Paradox—Prosperous Banks in National Crisis," *Far Eastern Survey*, March 27, 1935.

INDEX

Agreement for cessation of hostilities at Shanghai, 1932, 38-9
Allen, Professor G. C., 54
Amau Declaration of April 1934, 44-7
American
 Chamber of Commerce in Shanghai, 76
 Economic Mission, 68, 233
 Note of January 7, 1932, 23
 participation in Shanghai peace settlement, 1932, 38
 Silver Policy, 51-2
Amoy, 99, 195
Anglo-American co-operation, 29-42, 54-8, 103, 169-71, 176, 181-3
Anglo-German Loan of 1898, 6 footnote
Anglo-Japanese Agreement, 186, 193, 209
 Alliance, 11-2, 54, 227
 conversations, 90, 206-16
 co-operation, 54-8, 138
 Customs Agreement, 119, 184-6
 rapprochement, 88
 relations, 70, 78, 87, 152, 212
 Trade Treaty of 1911, 211-2
Anglo-Soviet negotiations of 1939, 193
Anti-British movement of 1925-7, 13-4
 of 1939, 206-7
Anti-Comintern Pact, 88, 193, 194 and footnote
Anti-Japanese activities in Shanghai in 1939, 108, 129
 feeling in China in 1932, 36, 70
appeasement policy, 92, 118
Arita, Foreign Minister, 88, 181, 183, 188, 207, 205-10, 211
 Japanese Ambassador to China, 79
 smuggling, 77
Asiatic Petroleum Company, 48

Baldwin, Stanley, 30 footnote
Banking Law, 81
Barnby, Lord
 Economic Mission, 89
Battle of Concessions, 11

Bernard, D. M. G.
 smuggling, 76
Bias Bay, 159, 160
blockade of the China Coast, 97-8, 205-6
Blue Shirt Organization, 49
Blum, Leon
 non-intervention policy, 64
bombing of civilians, 99-101
Boxer Indemnity funds, 60, 83, 86, 87
 disposition of, 15, 16 and footnote; 60, 61
 Rebellion, 11
boycott of Japanese goods, 44
British
 banking, 9
 Chamber of Commerce, 76, 133-4, 167, 209-10
 concessions, 15
 Courts, 5
 credits to China, 178, 179
 economic interests, 9
 Export Credits Guarantee Department, 82, 85-6, 177, 180
 financial aid to China, 61-3, 141-8, 151, 178-80; 180 footnote
 interests in China, 6, 151-2, 217-8
 investments in China, 7-9, 11, 81-2
 men-of-war, 5
 prestige in China, 43, 70, 121
 reaction to Lukouchiao, 93-5
 shipping, 7
 trade with China, 6-7
British American Tobacco Company, 8, 118, 119
Brussels Conference, 102-7
Butler, 90, 124, 125, 126, 128, 131, 147-8
 Anglo-American co-operation, 175
 Hongkew, 132
 letter to R. H. Morgan, 143-4
 occupation of Kulangsu, 196
 Tientsin blockade, 201
 Tokyo declaration, 170
 Ugaki overtures, 149
Butterfield and Swire, 7

249

Cadogan, Sir Alexander
  Yunnan-Burma border, 63
Caldecott, Sir Andrew, 81
Calder Marshall, R., 133-4
Canton, 4, 9, 15, 54, 157
  bombing of, 99
  Japanese occupation, 159-61
  river, 5
  trolley-bus system, 82
  waterworks, 82
Cecil, Viscount, 19-22
Central Bank of China
  exchange rate, 52 *and footnote*
  foreign exchange, 184
Central Reserve Bank, 81
Chahar, 49, 78
Chamberlain, Neville
  attitude on Far East, 167
  Craigie-Ugaki talks, 150-1, 153
  "makes my blood boil" declaration, 212
  Memorandum, 14
  non-intervention policy, 64
  Roosevelt's "quarantine the aggressor" speech, 102
  Tientsin blockade, 203, 209
Chang Chun, 79, 172
Chang Hsueh-liang, 18-9
Changkufeng, 155
Chapei, 28
Chartered Bank of India, Australia and China, 7, 189
Chen Loh, 188
Chiang Kai-shek, 50, 65, 70, 81, 140
China Association in Great Britain, 76
  in Shanghai, 209-10
China Currency Bill, 192
China's claim to Manchuria, 41
  Tariff Autonomy, 15
Chinese
  Customs Administration, 6, 72, 73, 78, 79, 97, 98, 107, 111, 118-21, 231
  Government Loans, 7-8
  Trading Commission, 193
  Maritime Customs, 69, 71, 112, 118, 184
  Salt Administration, 16 *and footnote*
  88th Division, 95
Clark Kerr, Sir Archibald, 142
Commission of Enquiry, 22, 42
Committee of Nineteen, 38, 40, 41
communiqué re Chinese Customs, 119-20

Communist movement in China, 26 *footnote*
Concessions, 4
Conservative Party, 42, 102
Consular Committee in Shanghai, 31
Convention of Peking, 10 *footnote*
cotton exports and imports, 221
Craigie-Arita Agreement, 205
  conversations, 206-10
Craigie, Sir Robert, 99, 181, 201, 204, 207, 211
Craigie-Ugaki talks, 150-6
Cranborne, Lord, 100, 101, 106, 108
Currency Ordinance, 67 *and footnote*
  reforms, 67-8, 229-30
  stabilization, 66, 189-93
Customs Agreement, 121-2, 125
  loans, 184-5, 190-1
  reductions of tariff, 122
  revenue, 78, 121, 126, 231

Davis, Norman
  Brussels Conference, 105, 106
Dollfuss, assassination of, 43

East Hopei Autonomous Council, 70, 73, 80, 122, 126
  Tax Office, 74
Economist
  Anglo-American co-operation, 56, 58
  F.B.I. Mission, 59-60
  oil monopolies, 49 *footnote*
Eden, Anthony, 33, 89, 90, 93, 94, 102, 103, 105, 111-3, 115
European War
  effect on British policy, 226
Ewo Cotton Mills, 8, 221
exchange control, 189
  equalization fund, 189-90, 237
  rates, 52, 53, 54, 82
export credits, 178
Export Credits Guarantee Department, 82, 85-6, 177, 180, 193
extraterritoriality, 3-5, 16-7, 55, 67

Far Eastern Advisory Committee, 100-2, 106
Federation of British Industries Mission to Japan and Manchukuo, 58-60
Finance and Commerce
  Anglo-Japanese Customs Agreement, 120
  British trade in South China, 225

INDEX 251

Finance and Commerce—(Continued)
Chamberlain's attitude toward the Far East, 167
comment on Mr. Hirota's statement, 139 *footnote*
fall of Nanking, 117
foreign-Japanese co-operation, 137
Japan and the International Settlement at Shanghai, 109-10
Japanese interference with British interests, 133
Japanese puppet governments, 134
Japan's policy, 173-5
Ladybird and *Panay* incidents, 116
League resolution, 143
Lukouchiao, 94, 95
Mr. Butler's letter to R. H. Morgan, 143-4
Mr. Kernan's letter to the *Times* of May 21, 1938, 143
open door policy, 135-6
Shanghai Municipal Council, 148 *footnote*
Sir John Simon's statement, 146
smuggling, 76
Forbes, W. Cameron
Economic Mission, 89
foreign loans to China, 62, 141, 185
military forces in Shanghai, 27-8
Foreign Office *communiqué* of January 8, 1932, 24-6
Four Power Consultative Pact, 12
Franco-Soviet Pact, 42
Fremantle, Sir Sydney
Anglo-American co-operation, 57

General Commission of 1932, 36-40
General Electric Company of China
Canton trolley-bus system, 82
German sale of railway materials to China, 61 *footnote*
gold standard
Great Britain, 51
United States, 51
Good-Will Mandate, 50 *and footnote*

Hainan
occupation of, 186-7
Railway, 81
Halifax, Viscount
Craigie-Ugaki talks, 150-1, 153
Tientsin blockade, 202, 203, 209
Hankow
British Concession, 63 *footnote*
capture of, 164-6

Hankow—*(Continued)*
Kuomintang Government, 14
smuggling, 74, 75
trade center, 223
Harbin, 39
Hidaka, Shinrokuro
letter to Municipal Council, 130
Hirota, 44, 46, 70, 95
Hirota's "Three principles," 70, 79
Hitler, Adolf, 43, 51
Hongkew, 107, 131
Hongkong, 5, 10, 53, 157-60
fortifications, 88
Economic Commission, 54
and Shanghai Banking Corporation, 8, 53, 189, 221
Shumchun incident, 212
silver standard, 53
trade with China, 224-5
Hoover, President, 31
Hopei Province, 78
Chahar Political Council, 70, 79
Kuomintang, 49
withdrawal of Chinese forces, 44
Ho-Umetsu Agreement of July 1935, 49, 50 *and footnote*
Hubbard, G. E.
Anglo-Japanese rapprochement, 89
Hull, Cordell, 169-70

India, 43
isolationism, 55, 103
Italy
Brussels Conference, 104 *and footnote*

Japan Society, 54
Japanese
attack on Shanghai, 1932, 28-40
1937, 95-6
Cabinet changes, 23 *footnote*
currency regulation, 189-90
demands, 79-80
domination in North China, 49, 78-80
Economic Mission, 89
Foreign Office, 45, 48, 77
invasion of South China, 157
Petroleum Industry Law, 49
recognition of Manchukuo, 39, 41
reply to Stimson Note, 27
trade with China, 7
victory parade in Shanghai, 110-1
withdrawal from the League, 42
Japan's trade wars, 88

252 INDEX

Jardine, Matheson and Company, 7, 112
Jehol, 44, 49
Joint International Truce Commission, 95

Kailan Mining Administration, 219
Kawagoe, 79
Kellogg-Briand Pact, 24
  Treaty for the Outlawry of War, 27
Kelly, Admiral, 31
Kent, meeting on board, 34
King George VI
  speech on Brussels Conference, 103
  speech on November 4, 1938, 166
Kirkpatrick, W. M., 85-6
Kiukiang British Concession, 63
Knatchbull-Hugessen, Sir Hughe, 96-7, 104 *footnote*
Konoye broadcast of November 9, 168
Koo, Wellington, 100, 142
Kowloon, 5
Kulangsu, 4, 195-8, 205
  five-point proposal, 195 *footnote*
Kuling Estate, 87
Kung, H. H., 81
Kuomintang, 13-4, 49, 70, 108
Kwantung Army, 73

Ladybird incident, 112-7
Lampson period, 14-6
Lampson, Sir Miles, 38
Land Regulations of 1869, 4-5, 129, 196 *footnote*
League of Nations, 19, 24, 36, 44
  Assembly Resolution of March 11, 1932, 41
  Council, 20-3, 26, 33, 63
  Covenant, 12, 18; 19 *footnote;* 28, 31, 37, 40, 41, 92
  General Commission, 36
  Lytton Report, 40
  non-recognition of Manchukuo, 42
Leased Territory, 5
Legal rights, 3
Leith-Ross, Sir Frederick, 68
Leith-Ross Mission, 63-78, 81, 85
  Statement, 229-34
Lindley, Sir Francis, 46, 57
Lin Yu-tang, 50
Locarno treaties, 64
London Naval Conference, 87
London Naval Treaty, 50

London *Times*
  Amau Declaration, 46, 47 *and footnote*
  Anglo-Japanese Customs Agreement, 120
  bombardment of Shanghai, 1937, 96
  dispatch of Japanese forces to Shanghai, 28-9
  export credits to China, 178-9
  fall of Canton, 160
  F.B.I. Mission, 58 *footnotes*
  General Matsui, 129
  Japanese reply to Stimson Note, 27
  Japanese statements re Amau Declaration, 45
Ladybird incident, 114
Leith-Ross Mission, 64-9
Lord Elibank's letter of April 23, 1938, 136
Lord Lytton's letter of July 5, 1938, 144
Lukouchiao, 93, 94
occupation of Hainan, 187 *footnote*
President Roosevelt's "quarantine the aggressor" speech, 102
Sir John Pratt's letter of November 10, 1938, 32
Sir John Pratt's letter of November 30, 1938, 24-5
smuggling, 77
Stimson Note, 25
Lord Lothian, 56-7
Lukouchiao, 92-5
Lytton, Lord, 144-5
Lytton Commission, 39, 41
  Report, 39-42

MacDonald, Ramsay, 18
Malcolm and Company
  Canton waterworks, 82
Manchukuo, 44, 48, 55
  Customs, 39
  Japanese recognition of, 39
  oil monopoly, 47-9
  salt revenues, 39
Manchuria
  economic development, 89
  Petroleum Company, 47-8
Manchurian Incident, 18
Marsden, Commander, 131
Matsudaira, Tsuneo, 27, 36
Matsui, General, 108, 111, 129
Matsuoka, 42
Maze, Sir Frederick, 78, 98, 184
mining companies, 9

INDEX

Ministry of Finance
  foreign exchange, 52
missionaries
  privileges of, 6
Mukden, 18-9

Nanking
  bombing of, 99
  fall of, 116
  Government, 49, 50, 122, 123
Nanlichuang, 73, 74
Nationalist Movement in China, 13-4
naval patrol rights, 5
Nazi-Soviet Pact, 214
Netherlands
  protest to oil monopolies, 47, 49
New York *Times*
  Brussels Conference, 103
1932 Agreement, 95 *and footnote*
Nine Power Treaty, 12, 24, 25, 27, 31, 32, 34, 41, 45, 46, 50
Noble, Sir Percy
  Yangtze shipping, 124
non-intervention, 92
non-recognition, 23, 32, 34, 47, 87
North-China Daily News
  smuggling, 75-6
North-China Herald
  Anglo-Japanese Agreement, 209-10
  Anglo-Japanese co-operation, 57, 138
  Anglo-Japanese Customs Agreement, 120
  Anti-Comintern Pact, 194
  British interests and Japanese policy in China, 117
  British loans for China, 141
  Brussels Conference, 104
  comment on fighting, 139-40
  currency stabilization, 190
  Customs tariff, 122-3
  fall of Canton, 160-1
  fall of Nanking, 116-7
  Japan and the International Settlement at Shanghai, 110
  Japanese position in China, 130-1
  Japan's policy, 174
  Ladybird and *Panay* incidents, 115-6
  Lukouchiao, 92, 93
  martial law in Hongkew, 131
  Nazi-Soviet Pact, 214-6
  occupation of Hainan, 187
  Stimson Note, 26
  third-party intervention, 99, 100, 162
  Tientsin conversations, 204

North-China Herald—(Continued)
  Ugaki overtures, 149, 153
  Wang Ching-wei, 58
  Yoshida's statement of April 19, 1938, 135

oil monopoly, 47-9
Okamoto, Suemasa
  Note to Mr. N. Hall of January 10, 1938, 124 *footnote*
open door policy, 11, 23, 24, 27, 33, 46, 47, 48, 56, 135-6

Pacific Affairs
  Leith-Ross Mission, 165
Pakhoi, 97
Panay Incident, 112-7
Paris Peace Pact, 21, 23, 27, 30-1, 37, 41
Paul-Boncour, 33, 40
peace negotiations, 1932, 36-40
peace overtures, 162
Pearl River, 159
Peiping, 44, 49
  Political Council, 49
Peking Provisional Government, 122
Permanent Court of International Justice, 22
Pratas Shoals, 97-8
Pratt, Sir John
  Letter to London *Times* of November 30, 1938, 24, 31
  Letter to London *Times* of November 10, 1938, 32
Provincial Courts, 5
Provisional Court Agreement, 43
Pu Yi, 39

railways, 8
  investments in, 60-1, 82, 83 *and footnote*; 84
  loans, 66 *footnote*; 69, 84-5, 179-80 *and footnote*
Reading, Lord, 20
Rengo News Agency
  Amau Declaration, 45
Revolution of 1911, 11
Rhineland
  remilitarized, 64
Roosevelt, President
  Economic Mission, 89
  "quarantine the aggressor" speech, 102

Round Table
  Anglo-American co-operation, 55, 56
  Anglo-Japanese Alliance, 55, 56
  Leith-Ross Mission, 64-7
  Washington Naval Treaty, 50

Salt Gabelle, 16
Settlements, 4
Shanghai, 4-5, 27, 53
  attack on, 28-40
  building, 53
  business reorganizations, 53
  coastwise trade, 222
  Conference of March 24, 38
  Consular Committee, 31
  defense forces, 99
  demilitarized zone, 80
  exports, 221-2
  foreign trade, 53, 222
  International Settlement, 4, 8, 107-8, 128-32, 187-8, 196-9
  Land Investment Company, 8
  Municipal Council, 4, 108, 128-32, 187-8
  neutrality of, 95 *footnote*
  outbreak of hostilities, 28-40
  Power Company, 107
  Press, 76, 109-11
  Provisional Court Agreement of 1930, 43 *footnote*
  public utilities, 9
  rehabilitation, 137
  shipping, 222
  smuggling, 75
  Stock Exchange, 53
  "War" of 1932, 39
  Waterworks Company, 107
Shantung, 12
Shigemitsu
  foreign loans to China, 62
shipping, foreign, 7
Shumchun incident, 212
silver, 51-4, 66 and *footnote*; 67, 211, 229
  Purchase Act, 51
Simon, Sir John, 22, 27, 30, 31, 32
  Amau Declaration, 45-6
  conference re Shanghai, 35
  General Commission, 36
  League of Nations Covenant, 37
  loans to China, 145-6
  Lytton Report, 40
  open door in Manchuria, 48-9
  recognition of Manchukuo, 39

Simon, Sir John—(*Continued*)
  Statement to House of Commons, February 22, 32
Sino-Japanese War, 11
smuggling, 71 and *footnote*; 72-8, 125
Soong, T. V., 81
South China
  British capital, 81
  economic development, 84
  invasion of, 157, 158, 159
  railway development, 84
Stanhope, Earl
  British loans to China, 63 and *footnote*
Stimson Doctrine, 23
  Note, 24-7
Stimson, Henry, 20 *footnote*; 23 and *footnote*; 31, 32, 34
Sung Cheh-yan, General, 78-9
Supreme Court, 5
Sze, Alfred, 19-20

Tada, General Hayao, 70
Tada Statement, 70
Tangku Truce, 44, 72, 80
tariff autonomy, 15
  question, 69
Taylor, George E.
  Leith-Ross Mission, 65
third power intervention, 213
  mediation, 160-1
Third Reich, 92
Thomas, J. H., 30
Tientsin, 4, 15, 44, 49, 112, 183, 214, 217-9
  blockade, 193, 195, 198-206, 209-11, 218
  British investments in, 218
  Japanese demands, 210 *footnote*
  smuggling, 74, 75, 77
Treaty of Nanking, 10 *footnote*; 15
  of Tientsin, 10 *footnote*
  of Versailles, 12
Treaty Ports, 3-4
Tsingtao, 97, 218

Ugaki, General Kazushige, 148-56
United Kingdom
  trade with China, 6
U.S.S.R.
  entry into League of Nations, 43
United States
  protest to oil monopoly, 47, 49

INDEX

vested rights, 3

Wang Ching-wei, 44, 58, 63, 70
Wang Chung-hui, 91
Washington Conference Treaties, 12, 15, 55, 92
    Naval Treaty, 50
Weihaiwei, 15
Wenchow blockade, 205-6
Whangpoo River, 126
    Conservancy Board, 127 and footnote
    dredging, 127-8
Whyte, Sir Frederick
    Anglo-American co-operation, 57
Willingdon Mission, 83
World Economic Conference, 41, 51
Wu, L. T. K., 66

Wuhan
    smuggling, 75
Yangtze River, 5, 44
    closed to commerce, 123-5, 171
    smuggling, 74
    traffic, 172-4
    valley, 50, 219
Yangtzepoo, 107, 131
Yen, W. W., 36, 42
Yoshida, Masaji, 90, 135
Yoshizawa, 20, 23 footnote
Yunnan-Burma Boundary Commission, 87 and footnote
    highway, 177-8
    railways, 179-80

Zimmern, Professor
    Anglo-American co-operation, 54